$\mathcal{E}$ NDC

This is a collection of insightful messages that will lead you to a deeper level of spirituality and closeness with Jesus Christ.

—*Jane Beck, Pennsylvania*

Every now and then someone comes along and offers a fresh perspective filled with personal life lessons. This writing and writer offer one of those opportunities. You will enjoy the bite-size chapters that allow reflection and meditation. Christy has done a good job of opening her heart and sharing her life lessons. So, enjoy.

—*William Lewis, Pastor of River of Life Church, Butler, Ohio*

Christy Christopher's devotions will touch your heart and awaken your spirit. It is evident that she embraces God as she cartwheels through joys and trudges through trials in life. Christy's writing is elegant, heartfelt and compelling—a gift from God that she is willing to share with you. Prepare to be enlightened.

—*Pam Mitchell, North Carolina*

Christy Christopher is first of all an intercessor. Talking to and hearing from God are a lifestyle for her. She and I have broken up fallow ground together in prayer so I know this firsthand about her. Now I find that she is also an excellent writer. God has given her that special ability to share effectively with others the things God has taught her, especially the principles learned from the challenging times. Her book has touched me deeply and I recommend it to any who will dare to believe that God is present with us here and now, whatever the circumstance.

—*Gloria Cotten, Author, Teacher, Conference Speaker, Antioch Ministries, North Carolina*

Christy's devotions are intimately insightful. She demonstrates a clear, profound, and deeply personal relationship with God. Her experience of God is obviously born of years of personal growth which is enriched and defined by daily walking with her Beloved, our Lord Jesus Christ. In these devotions, the reader is invited to join her in this abundant experience of Our Divine Lover.

—*Jim Barr, California*

This book is a real treasury of wealth that has been cultured inside Christy, like a pearl. As an artisan, she compels the reader to drink deeply of His presence, to know Him as He knows us, and to radiate and hold fast to His love. Christy exposes the truth of God's Word and man's need to be experientially transformed by the Lord through the Holy Spirit. I highly recommend her book to fellow 'pilgrims' looking for more of Him, like myself. Masterful.

—*Barbara Robinson, Cofounder of Prophetic Destiny International,*
International Teacher, Tennessee

The words in this devotional gently shout what He whispers to each of us: *"You are my favorite."* They breathe hope into my heart and strength for my spirit to receive His Being . . . so that I can become.

—*Cynthia Forry, Pennsylvania*

I wish that you could know Christy Christopher the way that I know her. She truly is a woman of the Word . . . a woman of passionate prayer . . . and a woman who hears God's voice. I have known her for nearly two decades, and in that time, I have seen a loving mother raise her family for Christ and His kingdom. I have also had a front row seat as Christy has served the Body of Christ with great joy and wisdom. Christy's book will touch deep places in your heart and will lead you into an intimacy with Christ for which you have been longing. If your heart's cry is to hear God's voice and to love Him more deeply, then this is the book for you.

—*Carol McLeod, Best-selling Author, Bible Teacher, Conference Speaker,*
Radio Host, Founder of Carol McLeod Ministries, Oklahoma

Truth spoken in a loud whisper—that is the response of my spirit. Reflections of the Father so beautifully penned—soft yet strong, reassuring yet challenging. With each reading, I find I want to both savor and share this daily convenience packed with richness for life. It's like fresh water and I want to tell people, "Lap it up." Truly, faith, hope and love will grow in the reader.

—*Pat Burleigh, Ohio*

So emotional when I think of what to say about this book. . . . God presented this gift to me during a time of deep sadness, despair and trials in my life. Christy's understanding and sharing of God's Word was life-changing for me and brought me closer to God in a way I never knew was possible. I get so excited when I meet someone who also needs the healing balm this devotional provides. Thank you, Christy.

—*Lois Cozart, Business Owner, Raleigh, North Carolina*

Are you asking God, "Why did this happen to me and my spouse?" Are you suffering the loss of someone dear or walking through the long-term illness of your spouse or beloved child? If so, then this is the right devotional book to read and keep at your bedside. Every page is filled with great wisdom and inspiration and encouragement to help get you through each day. Christy Christopher held my hand and led me back to Jesus through these pages as I stood beside my dearly loved husband through a long-term illness, separation, and finally widowhood. I learned that God is nearest to the brokenhearted and that He can and will take me through everything.

—*Dollie Glaser, Buffalo, New York*

UNTIL THE DAY
BREAKS
~ and ~
THE SHADOWS
FLEE

A devotional trilogy of faith, hope and love

Susanne,
Have Faith! Keep Hope!
Love Always!
Christ A. Chtgph
I COR. 13:13

UNTIL THE DAY
BREAKS
~ *and* ~
# THE SHADOWS
# FLEE

A devotional trilogy of faith, hope and love

CHRISTINE A. CHRISTOPHER

REDEMPTION
PRESS

Published by Redemption Press, PO Box 427, Enumclaw, WA 98022

Toll Free (844) 2REDEEM (273-3336)

Redemption Press is honored to present this title in partnership with the author. The views expressed or implied in this work are those of the author. Redemption Press provides our imprint seal representing design excellence, creative content, and high quality production.

ISBN 13: 978-1-68314-380-2 (Paperback)
978-1-68314-381-9 (ePub)
978-1-68314-382-6 (Mobi)

Library of Congress Catalog Card Number: 2017942592

These writings are dedicated to
my three children and their spouses:
Emily (and Jeff), Bethany (and Rodney) and Levi (and Rebecca)
God loves you intensely.

Know Him. Love Him.
You make me proud. You are parenting well and teaching my grand-children to love Jesus. What more could a Mimi ask for? I love you all so much.

I have no greater joy than this, to hear of my children walking in the truth. 3 John 1:4 (NASB)

Also to the daughter of my heart,
Cynthia Forry

Look what God has done. The gift of "you" in my heart is more precious than you will ever know. You are running your race with incredible grace and endurance. You will finish well.

$\mathcal{C}$ONTENTS

CONTENTS

LESSONS IN LOVE

CONTENTS

$\mathscr{P}$REFACE

$\mathscr{Before\ you\ ever\ read\ the}$ first page of this book, I want to talk to you. I want to make sure you've heard the Good News. You see, this book won't help you one bit or even apply if you first haven't taken care of this one thing. "What is the Good News?" you may ask. It's the Good News of the message of Jesus Christ, the Son of God (yet He *was* God) who came to this earth about 2000 years ago.

You and I are in need of a great rescue. It's one of the greatest rescue missions of all time. Without this rescue, we are all damned to an eternity separated from God. God cannot look at sin. You and I sin all the time. The only way God can look upon you and me is if we have accepted and applied to our life what Jesus Christ did on the cross. Contrary to popular thought, all roads *do not* lead to heaven *(John 3:16, 36; John 14:6; Acts 4:12; 1 Timothy 2:5-6; 1 John 5:11-12)*. The only way we can have a true, intimate walk with the God who created us is by the shed blood of Jesus covering us. He made payment for our sins with His blood *(Ephesians 1:7)*. Jesus Christ opened the way for you and me to come to God, to know Him and to receive all His benefits. When we accept this work of Jesus Christ, then and only then will we be accepted.

We will never be good enough to earn acceptance from God. The only work for the forgiveness of our sins that God will accept is the work that Jesus did for us on the cross. If you have never repented of your sins and asked God to forgive you and come into your life, do it now. I beg you. Do it now. Repent and change your way of thinking, be baptized with the Holy Spirit, and begin your new journey with God. Go ahead—ask God to come into your life now. Use your own words or pray something like this:

Dear Jesus, I am a sinner. I repent of my sins, and I accept Your payment for them. Wash over me now that I may be cleansed by the blood of Jesus. I now enter Your family. Instead of living for me, I will now live for You. Baptize me with Your Holy Spirit that I may receive the power to be Your witness. Teach me and lead me into all truth. Amen.

Repent, and each of you be baptized in the name of Jesus Christ for the forgiveness of your sins; and you will receive the gift of the Holy Spirit.
Acts 2:38 (NASB)

—*Christine Christopher*

$\mathcal{F}$OREWORD

Timothy, my son, I give you this instruction in keeping with the prophecies once made about you, so that by following them you may fight the good fight. 1 Timothy 1:18 (NIV)

In 1988, a man of God came to our church. His name was Lattie McDonough. The following is a prophetic word he spoke over me that night. This book is part of the fulfillment of that word God spoke over my life 29 years ago. When you know God has spoken something to you, fight the good fight with it. Don't give up, but walk in a way that you fulfill all the days ordained for you. Your days were written in His Book (Psalm 139:16).

The Prophecy

A bottomless pit. A bottomless reservoir of My Word is within you, says the Lord. Draw out! Draw out! Draw out! Be inspired! Let My Spirit move upon you. Get excited. Prophesy My Word. For I have put a mighty gift within you, says the Lord. And I will perfect the gift. I will perfect the delivery. And I will impart unto you the confidence that is necessary to move at My direction and speak My Word.

Yea, My daughter, I shall publish the words that you speak in many languages, says the Lord. I shall speak to the leaders of the churches and to the leaders of many countries by the word.

Publish it. I have called you to speak, says the Lord. I have called you to speak. And it is from the depth; you are now only touching surface revelation. But the waters are deep. Plumb My depths, My daughter, and you will find revelation so strong, and so moving, until you will be hardly able to stand after receiving My Word, says the Lord. The wisdom of your God is in the depths. Draw it out, says the Lord. I am just beginning with the gift.

Do not be concerned about what you are. For I have made you a voice. And that is all you need to know. Do not struggle with the gift. Do not allow your head to be turned when people say she is this or she is that. But I have said you are a voice to draw out of that that I have put within, and publish it to the world.

What avenues, My Lord, shall I find to publish? Be patient. I will show you, and I will open the doors of publication, for that which you speak. And I will send them in ways that you cannot imagine. And they will find a place in the hands of many across the waters. In unusual ways will they be published, says the Lord. I see copy machines just spitting your word out and just being taken everywhere.

The islands of the sea will publish your words, says the Lord. Yet are they yours?

Nay, but it is My Word that I have called you to speak.

$\mathcal{I}$NTRODUCTION

And now these three remain: faith, hope and love. But the greatest of these is love. 1 Corinthians 13:13 (NIV)

$\mathcal{T}$*his devotional trilogy—*$\mathcal{F}$*aith,* $\mathcal{H}$*ope and* Love—contains lessons learned and currently being learned from my personal journey with God. This book is not meant to be swallowed whole. It will serve you best if you sample a portion each day and meditate upon the truth of its content. It is my hope that as you make your way through these pages, God Himself will reach way down into your precious soul and increase your faith, renew your hope and empower you with His love once again.

The journey upon this earth will get rugged. It will suddenly turn steep. It will lead you into storms so ferocious that you think you might just die on the spot, but the One who engineers a pathway through the sea will also escort you through your fiery ordeal. Your heavenly Father will accompany you to the other side safely. He will offer you drink when your soul is parched. He will feed you bread from heaven when you are faint and can hardly take another step. God will encircle you with His loving embrace when your heart feels like it might break in two. One day, you will cross the finish line and enter into eternity with Him; but until the day breaks and the shadows flee, remember that He is the lover of your soul and the lifter of your head. Now, this very moment, three things remain: faith, hope and love. We need faith for the conviction of what's true. We need hope for a confident expectation for our future. And finally, what would our journey be here on earth without frequent love feasts with God and one another as we travel along?

While we base our theology on God's Word, our experiences with God make it all come alive. May these writings excite your heart into new life and hope. May you experience the winds of His gentle presence, soothing and calming your dear heart as you read through these pages.

ℒESSONS IN FAITH

Now faith is being sure of what we hope for and certain of what we do not see. Hebrews 11:1 (NIV)

"Faith is the art of holding on to things in spite of your changing moods and circumstances."
—C.S. Lewis

$\mathcal{U}$NTIL THE DAY BREAKS AND THE SHADOWS FLEE

My lover is mine and I am his . . . until the day breaks and the shadows flee. Song of Solomon 2:16-17 (NIV)

"He, who is all your joy, is near to you—in this moment. He could not   be closer if He were holding you, pressing you to Himself, your two faces touching. It is the embrace of the Spirit, as the Beloved draws you to Himself."

— Julian of Norwich (1342–1413)

Oh, great pilgrim of God (yes, you are great in the eyes of the eternal One), the journey is rugged and steep and, at moments, treacherous. You are not a single traveler. The host of heaven encircle you. Saints who have gone before you are in the grandstands of heaven cheering you onward and upward. God Himself is inside you. Jesus has prepared the road ahead of you. The great Comforter, the Holy Spirit, is empowering you to walk, climb and run. Lift up your head and let this soak into the recesses of your heart. It's truth. It's life. It's food for your soul. No one else can comfort you the way your heavenly Father can. Don't look anywhere else, because it won't satisfy. Your spouse, your parents, your best friend—not one person on this earth will bring the comfort that will sustain and nourish your soul as will the One who formed you in your mother's womb.

Go ahead and try if you must, but all will fall short and cause you to dismay. All will leave you empty-handed. All will disappoint, but your God will not. He could never be any closer than He is now. Your feelings will come and go as the ebb and flow of the ocean tide, but His presence will not. He could not be any closer.

Dear saint, take comfort in His nearness today. Hold on to the truth that He is yours and you are His until the day breaks and the shadows flee. Raw faith is necessary so that He can lead you through the dark and unsure pathways. There is comfort to be found if you accept His warm embrace. It's what He wants, and it's what you truly need.

WHAT? NO MORE SHINING SPLENDOR?

Who is among you who [reverently] fears the Lord, who obeys the voice of His Servant, yet who walks in darkness and deep trouble and has no shining splendor [in his heart]? Let him rely on, trust in, and be confident in the name of the Lord, and let him lean upon and be supported by his God. Isaiah 50:10 (AMP)

It is possible to love the Lord with all your heart, fear Him and walk in His ways, yet suddenly find yourself catapulted into deep trouble and darkness. Our feeble hearts have difficulty comprehending trouble and darkness. Our carnal soul (mind, will and emotions) may be throwing a temper tantrum all the while our spirit (the place of His presence) is thriving in peace and stability. Why? We have chosen to remain confident in the name of the Lord and be supported by Him.

We do our best to hear God's voice and obey Him, but sometimes an unexpected storm comes crashing in on the shores of our heart and simply knocks the breath right out of us. In an instant, the cloud of disorientation hovers above. The sun may be shining one moment, only to be shrouded the next. It can be scary and aggravating. In those moments, we can sometimes feel a great frustration toward God. We may be tempted to ask questions like "Where did You go? Why are You letting this get out of control? What happened? What are You doing?" and "What did I do wrong?"

If you read the Psalms, you will find many moments when the psalmist came upon deep trouble, and the "shining splendor" that was very much a part of his life suddenly vanished. There are many emotions—positive and negative—exemplified in the Psalms. God inspired the inclusion of these Psalms for a reason. They show that He is very able to handle any place in which we find ourselves—be it in joy, sadness, fear, anger, impatience or thanksgiving—the list goes on and on.

We will all experience moments of walking in darkness. It's not fun. It is difficult, but God seems to feel that it is beneficial for us at times. Otherwise, we may not see our actual condition. As we see our true need for God's power and strength, we will be better equipped to face the enemy of our soul.

One of the objectives of our adversary is to undermine our confidence in the name of the Lord. The name of the Lord is one of the most powerful weapons we can use. One day, every knee will bow and every tongue will confess that Jesus Christ is Lord *(Romans 14:11)*. Sometimes, when I am surrounded by deep darkness, my only reprieve is to utter the name of my Lord: *Jesus*. I believe the spiritual realm understands very clearly what to do when I utter His name in a moment of stumbling despair. Angels are dispatched to minister and help at the sound of one of His children calling out in the darkness. Demons have to flee when one of His own speaks His sweet, precious name.

Trust in the reputation of the God of the Holy Scriptures. Be convinced in His ability to come to your rescue. Have real and honest conversations with Him. When you are transparent with Him, He can minister to you in the center of your heart. Honesty is foundational in any healthy relationship. Remove your mask. Don't always try to look good when there are matters below the surface that need attention. It's okay not to know the way. It's okay to experience times of confusion. It's okay to feel what you feel; just don't make camp there. Get up and go to Him. Let your heart find faith. Discover the hope that is yours in Him. Your head will be lifted as you lean upon His name. His fame and His glory precede Him. One day, when the shadows flee and the dawn breaks forth, you will emerge from this place more deeply satisfied and in love with Him.

$\mathcal{I}$S YOUR FAITH DEAD OR ALIVE?

. . . but the people who know their God will display strength and take action. Daniel 11:32b (NASB)

Knowing God and knowing about God are two separate places. This verse in Daniel is speaking of what happens when a person has a real relationship with God. Two things will be evident: they will show strength and they will be a person of action. *Strength,* in the Hebrew language, means to prevail, to harden, to be courageous, firm, resolute, secure, encouraged, bold or to withstand.

Take action, in Hebrew, implies doing, fashioning, accomplishing, making, producing, dealing with, acting with effect, attending to, putting in order, celebrating, acquiring (property), appointing or bringing about.

There's a clear difference between knowing the God you serve and knowing *about* the God you serve. Daniel lays out a distinct picture for us here. When you really know the God that you announce you love, your life will not resemble the life of a person who only knows about God. When we get into difficult places, it will expose how much we trust and lean upon our God. It will reveal the strength—or lack of—we have found in knowing Him, and what actions we are willing to take will be evident.

Your response in a time of tribulation will expose how far you've actually come in your relationship with God. When all is well, there is really no need to display strength or do great exploits for God. It's when all hell is breaking loose around you that you will stand or fall according to your walk with God.

To know and love the Lord your God will be evidenced by a courageous spirit. There will be such a hardening against the tactics of the enemy and there will be resolution in your heart. Like David, you will find the encouragement and the ability to strengthen yourself in the Lord (*1 Samuel 30:6*). There will be nothing timid about you when the need arises to speak or take a stand. Any onslaught you encounter you will withstand, all because the Holy Spirit of the living God is being allowed to act and breathe through your whole being.

To know and love the Lord your God will also be evidenced by action. Benchwarming is not listed as one of the gifts of the Spirit. There are no sidelines in God's kingdom. All are called to be active participants. If you really know the God who you say you love, then the hallmark of your life with Him will be action. God Himself said in James 2:17 that faith without works is dead. When you really know your God, you will have moments when the Spirit of God is prodding you to make something happen and produce something in the kingdom. A life properly aligned in a relationship with God will be influential. When you act, it will be with effect. Your life will bear real, eternal fruit.

Each time we encounter a place of great personal challenge, it is a call from heaven to become even more intimately acquainted with God. Be quick to enter behind the veil with Him and get what you need to keep traveling forward with no unnecessary detours or delays. None of us is perfect but a work in progress. We all have our growing edges; but as we grow and mature, each trial should bring us closer in appearance to the God we love. This God Himself displays great strength and takes action in the affairs of mankind every single day.

SUFFER TO LEARN, LEARN TO SUFFER

Although He was a Son, He learned obedience from the things which He suffered. Hebrews 5:8 (NASB)

S*uffering involves pain and great* distress. It can incorporate injury and loss. Suffering includes anything distressful.

Jesus Christ did not have the upper hand while He was on earth. He traveled down a birth canal and had to grow and mature just like every other human being. He had to learn obedience. I would suppose that He fell down as a child and scraped his knees. He probably had his feelings hurt from time to time. Although we are not told what happened, his earthly father Joseph is not mentioned in the scriptures in his teen or ministry years. He may have had to grieve His father's death. We aren't told specifically every time He suffered, but it must have been similar to what we face as we grow and mature. He learned to obey and submit to His heavenly Father through distress, pain, disadvantage, loss and all kinds of unpleasant situations. He suffered and obeyed until the day He died.

One of the purposes of suffering is for you to learn obedience. Just settle that in your mind and heart right now. Suffering, loss, disadvantage and unpleasantness will intrude upon you all the days of your life. These elements have been allowed by God to remain as part of the package deal of salvation. Suffering is not the enemy; rather, it should be thought of as a companion. Suffering will teach you many lessons if you choose to embrace it.

We don't learn obedience when everything is going our way. We learn obedience when our circumstances are contrary. If Jesus learned obedience this way (and He did), then you can be sure that this is your path as well.

It's God's desire that we obey because we love Him. Very often we turn it around and obey in hopes that God will accept and love *us*.

Charles Finney once said that we must break up the fallow ground of our heart and agree with God against our self. Self just doesn't want to give up in this way. Self wants what it wants when it wants it. Self avoids suffering, making it a great enemy of obedience.

If God has said that suffering is for our learning, then we must learn how to suffer. Suffering is a potential seedbed for new sprouts of faith to arise in our hearts.

$\mathcal{I}$'LL TAKE ANOTHER DRINK

Now on the final and most important day of the Feast, Jesus stood, and
He cried in a loud voice, if any man is thirsty,
let him come to Me and drink! John 7:37 (AMP)

When my cat is thirsty, she goes to one of two sinks and sits there waiting for someone to turn on the faucet. She has a regular water dish by her food, but she prefers the fresh, running water from the faucet. One morning when I saw her in the sink, John 7:37 came to my mind:

> *On the last and greatest day of the festival, Jesus stood and said in a loud voice: Let anyone who is thirsty come to me and drink.* (NIV)

When you need a drink of water, nothing else will satisfy. Let's flip this thought over to the spiritual realm. Jesus was speaking of water for our souls.

The word *drink* in the Greek is *pinō*. It means to receive into the soul what serves to refresh, strengthen and nourish it unto life eternal.

Jesus offers you sips of His water all day long. If you refuse His drink, you will become parched and dry in your spirit.

John 7 continues in verses 38 and 39:

> *He who believes in Me, as the Scripture said, "From his innermost being will flow rivers of living water." But this He spoke of the Spirit, whom those who believed in Him were to receive; for the Spirit was not yet given, because Jesus was not yet glorified* (NIV).

There is an activity of the Holy Spirit that is separate from our initial salvation experience—the daily drink of the refreshing that only comes from His presence.

You will not only be refreshed and strengthened but you will become a refreshing current of living water to all who come your way. The goods will be in your hand. Life and encouragement will flow like a fountain. There will be perfect satisfaction and fulfillment simply in being near the One who continually offers a drink of His living water. You will experience firsthand the secrets of drinking from the Fountain that shall never run dry.

If you are dry, what are you waiting for? Get up to the holy sink of heaven and sit tight 'til He turns on the faucet.

THE REWARD IS WORTH THE RACE

Find Me as your shelter. Search Me out. Seek Me in the place of trouble and difficulty. There are gems and jewels for you to find as you dig deep. There are hidden strategies just waiting to be downloaded into you as you mine for the gold that belongs to you.

There are new springs for your spiritual roots as you dig deeper with Me. It must be more than outward appearance and looking fine. I am most concerned with the part of you that's hidden from others but not hidden from Me.

My glory is all around you. My covering is over you. My Spirit fills you. You have everything you need in Me. You have no lack in the Spirit. Be careful to stand in the place provided for you in My presence. Life can be compared to a minefield. Life requires you to hear My voice and obey in order to avoid stepping where you should not. There are traps and tricks and devices of the enemy prepared for you; but as you listen to Me and follow My lead, what has been formed against you will not succeed.

Take My hand. Let's walk along the shores of life in step together. Take My hand and I will lead and guide you. Take My hand and I will show you places your mind could never imagine. Take My hand. I will dispatch angels at your side to minister to you.

Sometimes, I will offend your mind in order to grow your heart. Sometimes, you will find yourself in places of darkness and questioning, but take heart. I am growing you as you choose to look My way and see what I will do next. I am raising you into the child that I have planned and prepared for you to be. As your mind is offended in your circumstance, your heart gains strength. As you continue on in Me, you will see what I am doing, and it will be okay. It will be more than okay. It will be gloriously okay.

Trust Me when the road disappears from your feet. Trust Me when the light turns to darkness. Trust Me when I ask you to do something impossible. Take that leap of faith and you will find yourself in the secure wrap of My arms.

You are in training, a type of spiritual boot camp. The word for you is: ENDURE. The word for you is: PERSEVERE. It's the one who finishes who will attain the prize. It's the one who keeps on keeping on who will have the reward. Keep doing right. Keep acting right. I see your love for Me and our union is strong.

Keep giving and loving those around you. This is the test. This is what I am watching. This is what I will be rewarding. Don't give your reward away, for the reward will be worth the race. The beauty and glory that forms in the struggle will be worth it all.

$\mathcal{K}$EEP YOUR CHIN UP

My eyes are upon you, and My hand is guiding you. I am a God of detail. I am a God who orchestrates situations. I am a God who not only orchestrates surroundings but also allows certain events to occur in your life.

Your situations contain details that I have placed there for your safety and protection. Configurations that you deem unnecessary, I call needed and valid for the growth and formation of your life in Me. Situations that act as barriers that won't go away no matter what you do can be of Me. I may have placed them there. Sometimes I just need to get your attention. There are moments that the very wall that you keep knocking yourself against is really and truly Me.

I am committed to your growth and well-being. I am even more committed than you. It's to your benefit that you trust Me at every corner and crossroad. The pressure can form you if you permit it. Your attention is not to be on what you can see and feel but on what you can't see and feel. This is called the life of faith, and it's impossible to please Me without it. It's impossible to thrive in the Spirit without it.

Faith requires vision using your inner eye. The physical eye is needed to get around physically, but the spiritual eye is needed to get around in the spiritual realm. Faith requires knowledge of the Truth, for if you have put truth in your heart, My Spirit can remind you in moments of pain or frustration. Faith will come as you read and meditate upon My Word. To live the true life of a Christian is to live a life that is opposite from the world. Until you understand this principle, you will continue to strive and struggle in your journey.

Do not take example from the world. For when you apply worldly principles to the spiritual life, there will be much stumbling and tripping when trying to understand My ways. When you apply worldly understanding to My ways, nothing will make sense. My ways require My Spirit within you to interpret what I am doing and teach you. My ways are not your ways. That's what it means to walk with Me. It's a realization that your ways will take you nowhere. My ways will take you to places in the Spirit which I have prepared for you.

My Holy Spirit within you is key to connecting My ways with your understanding. Why have I said, "Be filled with My Spirit"? Your understanding will grow as you stay in tune with My Spirit. Therefore, seek My Spirit and search Me out on all occasions so that you may see and know more clearly what I am doing.

Lastly, I am the God of all comfort. "All comfort" means whenever you need to be comforted, there will be a supply just for you. I see your weary days. I am acquainted with your pain. I walk with you in it. I experience it with you, but I also offer you the provision of comfort and refreshment. Come to Me as often as needed, and I will give specific attention to your strengthening. Be encouraged this day. I know the battle is fierce at moments. One day, you will reap the reward of continuing today and not giving up.

POSSESSED WITH HOLY VISION

Call to Me and I will answer you and show you great and mighty things, fenced in and hidden, which you do not know (do not distinguish and recognize, have knowledge of and understand). Jeremiah 33:3 (AMP)

"Call to Me . . ." The verb *to call* in the Hebrew means to utter a loud sound. I define this as getting down to business with God. When you really mean business with God, He will answer you. It may not be in your time or in your way, but it will certainly be in His time and in His way, and that's what you really need anyway. He is the one from whom you need the real answer. You don't need anyone else's opinion of your situation. You need God to respond to your cry. Granted, He may use another's vocal chords to answer you; but when He answers you, you will know it by the Spirit. It will bear witness with your spirit if you are yielded to Him.

However, sometimes, part of the information is simply hidden from us. There are things in life that are downright perplexing. God will not reveal all things to everyone. God wants to be sought out. He is glad to reveal, but He won't reveal to just anyone. There are criteria for those who will find answers in God. When you don't know something, how often do you run to the bookstore to pick up a book on the subject? How often do you run to the phone to call your friend or pastor? Now these resources in and of themselves aren't wrong. What's wrong is the order in which you do them. Your first action when in need of answers is to call out to God, seeking first His kingdom, seeking first His answers, seeking first His opinion of your predicament. He may then lead you to a book or a person, or He may speak to you while you are reading His Word. The key is to receive guidance for the next step out of our initial time of calling out to Him. If you get no direction, then wait. Timing is everything in God's kingdom.

Now, if we do life God's way, let's talk about what's going to happen. He will answer you, or He will give you peace until an answer comes (*Philippians 4:7*). He will show you the treasures of His heart.

I heard someone remark, "I am a seer because I am a looker." Don't just pray and then flippantly announce, *"Que sera, sera"* (what will be, will be). No, no, no. Picture this: You mix up a cake. You put it in the oven, wait and then start checking to see if it's finished. Likewise, put your entreaty into the oven of God's Throne Room of Grace, wait awhile, then start looking and checking to see if the answer has come yet.

God has declared that He's going to show you great things—things too big for you to comprehend on your own. As you look to Him, the

Holy Spirit within you will help you discern the answers. Vision will come, and what was covered will be revealed. You will become possessed of sight and a privileged guest of unveiling truth.

This word, *mighty*, has an interesting meaning in the Hebrew. It indicates things fenced off, inaccessible or enclosed, cut off, mysteries, secrets and things withheld. Could it be that God saves certain revelations for those who are really seeking Him out? It doesn't mean He desires to hide from us out of frugality. It means that He saves certain riches for those who draw closest to Him. Remember the verse that declares Him as a rewarder of those who diligently seek Him? *(Hebrews 11:6)*. Point made.

Call to Him. He will answer. What you haven't yet perceived may be unveiled suddenly, right before your eyes, but in His time and in His way. Formerly hidden realities will come into the light. An *"aha"* moment in the Spirit, so to speak, will suddenly march into your heart.

I hope that you will be on the front row of anticipation as you wait for the curtain to rise and see firsthand God's plan for you. May His thoughts invade your soul and give you firm footing for your next step.

$\mathcal{E}$MOTIONAL QUICKSAND

God is our refuge and strength, a very present help in trouble.
Psalm 46:1 (NKJV)

The words "very present" jump off the page to me. Very present is the Lord. He is not absent. He is here, now, with me. He isn't going anywhere. Maybe I feel Him or maybe I don't, but feeling is irrelevant. *I don't have to feel Him to understand that He is close.*

In a world so bent on feeling, you have heard, "If it feels good, do it." We who know Jesus Christ personally are not limited to feelings. Feelings make good servants but poor masters. We are not, or we shouldn't be, controlled and ruled by our emotions.

Feelings should never dictate how we serve God. Our obedience should be solely sourced in the Word of God. If I don't "feel God's presence," it makes no difference.

God gave us emotions, so they are not in and of themselves evil or sinful. Emotions are a vehicle. Emotions can be a warning to us that we are about to enter the land of sin. Emotions, when serving the Spirit of God, can bring pleasure and joy. Emotions can be the very vehicle that drives us straight to the throne of grace in our time of need.

Be careful how you interpret your emotions today. Are they an outflow of your union with Jesus or, acting as quicksand, are they pulling you into a downward spiral away from God and the people you love?

Learn to examine your emotional life regularly. Put your emotions up against the Word of God and see how they line up. Allow the Holy Spirit to be in the driver's seat of your emotional vehicle. You will then experience emotions the way God intended.

A NAIL-BITER 'TIL THE VERY END

The Lord is slow to anger and great in power and will by no means clear the guilty. The Lord has His way in the whirlwind and in the storm, and the clouds are the dust of His feet. Nahum 1:3 (AMP)

The more I live, the more I am absolutely convinced that God is in control. He is sovereign. He is almighty. He is not to be challenged. He is Lord. He is Savior. He's my Almighty God.

One August afternoon, a storm was brewing and a tornado came through my neighborhood. I wasn't home at the time. I had just left the house and within an hour, it hit. It didn't touch down at our house, but two properties over it struck my parents' barns. It resembled a war zone. Debris was everywhere. Their yard was littered with barn roof metal and wooden shingles. Split trees and fallen limbs were strewn across the yard. Despite the damage to their property, my parents were safe.

Nahum 1:3 tells us that God has His way in the whirlwind. God had His way that day. Sometimes, people do get injured or lose their lives. I am very grateful God spared my family. What an object lesson for life. We live our lives, day in and day out, just going about our business. Then all of a sudden—BOOM. An event occurs that is traumatic, tragic or life altering. We are instantly jolted into realizing what's most important in life—our life with God and our life with people.

God permits difficulties in the lives of the inhabitants of earth. Do you think He sometimes allows catastrophic events so that we may engage in a proper check with reality? Possibly—there will always remain an element of mystery with God. When difficult situations arise, there are no quick or easy answers. We can, however, extract the precious out of the seemingly worthless.

It's critical to maintain a mindset that God is in control, and He will have His way; and if you've given your life to Him—no matter what happens, life or death—you are safe in His loving care, and you will be with Him always.

The first part of the verse we are looking at in Nahum 1:3 speaks of the guilty not being cleared. There are moments when tragedy comes on both the good and the evil. We must not jump to conclusions or raise suspicions of God's final judgments before it is time. Life on earth is going to be a nail- biter until the very end.

God is great in power. The clouds are the dust of His feet. Wow, my Father in heaven is a big God. My Gentle Shepherd is also the Lion of the Tribe of Judah. He is all you need Him to be, and more.

One day, He will pull the curtain on this thing we call life on earth, and time will be no more. Some will be welcomed into heaven's gates *(Matthew 25:34)*, and others will be thrown into hell's flames *(Matthew 25:41)*. It's enough to make you fear and tremble if you give it honest thought.

I hope that the fear of the Lord has been stirred in you today. I pray that you are secure in Him. I pray that you are ready to meet Him if you die today. May you see His way in the whirlwind of your life.

YOUR LIFE: GOD'S MESSAGE TO THE WORLD

And God said, Let there be light: and there was light.
Genesis 1:3 (KJV)

The word light in the Hebrew is *'ore.* This word means more than just physical light that comes from the sun or moon. Remember, He hadn't created the sun or moon yet. The sun and moon were created on day 4 *(Genesis 1:16-19).*

'Ore means light of day, light of heavenly luminaries, lightening, light of life, light of prosperity, light of instruction, Jehovah as Israel's light and a few more that I won't list here.

I find this very intriguing. At the very beginning of Genesis when God is in creation mode, He is thinking, "Okay, before We even get started with this, let's turn on the lights." He started with darkness. Not only was this physical darkness, but there was no reflection of Himself since man hadn't been created yet. There was no life, no prosperity, no instructions about anything and no light for Israel. There was nothing here.

You see, before there was light, there was a whole lot of nothing. Genesis 1:2 (KJV) tells us:

> And the earth was without form, and void; and darkness was upon the face of the deep. And the Spirit of God moved upon the face of the waters.

Let's look at this a bit closer. The word *darkness* means obscurity or secret place. It reminds me of Psalm 18:11:

> He made darkness His secret hiding place; as His pavilion (His canopy) round about Him were dark waters and thick clouds of the skies (AMP).

Did you know that you can find God in the secret place of darkness also? Just because you can't see, you're not prospering, you don't understand or you feel lifeless doesn't mean God is far away. Quite the contrary, my friend. God abides in your darkness. Now, back to Genesis . . .

When He spoke into the dark void to create light, more than physical light came into being. What also appeared was the possibility of life, prosperity and instruction. These lights came into the atmosphere of the earth along with physical light.

We can correctly conclude that God is all about light. Since we are created in His image *(Genesis 1:27)*, light is a very important thing for us. When we can't see, we want to find the light switch or pull up the blinds. We have been created for sight and have been given the capacity to learn and prosper. God provided all of this when He uttered, "Let there be light."

God knew who He was about to create—that would be us. But before He would bring us into existence, He wanted to make sure we had everything we would need to see and be prosperous and have the ability to learn. Notice, however, that He didn't totally remove the darkness. We have day, and we have night. The same is true in life. We experience times when circumstances are clear and prosperous and times when we can't see in front of our faces.

Now, back to the light . . . let's jump into the New Testament:

You are the light of the world. A city set on a hill cannot be hidden; nor does anyone light a lamp and put it under a basket, but on the lampstand, and it gives light to all who are in the house. Let your light shine before men in such a way that they may see your good works, and glorify your Father who is in heaven. Matthew 5:14-16 (NASB)

In light (no pun intended) of our quick study in Genesis, this word that God calls *us* is very interesting. The word *light* here in the Greek means this: a heavenly light such as surrounds angels when they appear on earth; anything emitting light; a star, a lamp or torch; of truth and its knowledge, together with the spiritual purity associated with it; that which is exposed to the view of all; openly; publicly; the power of understanding, especially moral and spiritual truth.

Okay . . . I'm really exhilarated here. I don't know if you're getting this or not, but God is communicating to us:

Since I'm inside you now, you are the power of understanding moral and spiritual truth in this world. You are a star in the backdrop of darkness. You are one who emits light. You are to be exposed and on public display. You are a torch of truth and its knowledge. You are a reflection of purity. The sinful world is void and empty of My instruction, My life and My prosperity.

God announces, "I will speak into the world with *your life!*"

Is that awesome or what? Wow. I'm just amazed at the plan of God. He has really thought this out and made His choice to use us. We are the representation of Him on earth. It's humbling. It's a fearful thing, but it's the plan from the foundation of the earth. God is light. God lives in you. Thus, you are the light of the world.

I sat in the audience one evening listening to a man of God, Clayton Collins (author of *Breaking the Power of Darkness*). He shared how when the Holy Spirit comes in you, your life becomes the witness that Jesus is alive. Your words will be spirit and life to others and will speak to something on the inside of them and they will know it is true.

Friend, you are a light situated in the backdrop of darkness. You are seated with Him in heavenly places right now. You have everything you need to go make history with God.

A ROAD BUILDER THROUGH THE SEA

Your road led through the sea, your pathway through the mighty waters; a pathway no one knew was there! Psalm 77:19 (NLT)

God has a track record of leading His people into unfamiliar territory. He will lead us down paths that look impossible. He makes new roads for us on which to travel. We think we know best; but if we are gutsy enough to follow God's lead, we will see some incredible scenery as well as places totally unknown to us.

Think of it—a God who's famous for building roads through the sea. Mighty waters can signify to us immense hardships or enormous impossibilities.

When the children of Israel came to the Red Sea, it looked like an impossible situation. They simply saw what was in front of their faces. On the other hand, God saw how He was going to build a road right through it. This is why we need faith. This is why we need to trust God. He sees more than we do. He's in the front seat, and we're in the back seat. Our vision is limited. God's isn't. Faith gives us God's vision. That's why we need it.

What are you facing today? Listen very carefully to God. I think I hear Him telling you something . . .yes, I do.

Hey. I see a road right through the middle of your sea: a path no one knew was there except Me. Trust Me, Child, and follow Me. I'll take you right through on the path I have built just for your feet.

$\mathcal{E}$MPOWERED TO BE CALM

Blessed (happy, fortunate, to be envied) is the man whom You discipline and instruct, O Lord, and teach out of Your law that You may give him power to keep himself calm in the days of adversity, until the [inevitable] pit of corruption is dug for the wicked. Psalm 94:12-13 (AMP)

There is power from God available for the purpose of keeping yourself calm when hard times come. He will teach you and train you in such a way that when trouble comes (and it will), you will operate in peace and sweet assurance.

Sometimes, it feels like all hell is breaking loose around your feet. Sometimes, there isn't instant deliverance. Sometimes, it takes time before situations calm down around you. A child of God who has enrolled in the "School of the Holy Spirit" will be ready and equal to whatever comes his way. You can tell a lot about your spiritual maturity by how you respond in a tough situation.

The Word of God teaches us to remain calm. If we know how to tap into the vast resource of power that God has reserved for those who have remained under His tutelage, then we will walk in peace. His instructions must be absorbed into the very fiber of our being. The power to stay calm in times of adversity will be a natural by-product of walking with Him. You will be light and like a city on a hill to which others will be drawn *(Matthew 5:14)*.

One day, dawn will break and the shadows will flee. Your adversary, the devil, will be thrown into the eternal fire prepared just for him and his angels *(Revelation 20:10)*. Until then, you are empowered to be calm in the crisis.

CREATION PREACHES

I love God's creation. Every time I spend time outdoors, I am refreshed in some way. I am renewed in my faith. I am encouraged if I have been down. Funny how fresh air is good for the soul.

There's the spectacular sea, the majestic mountains, the vast woodlands, the blooming flowers, the fowl of the air, an afternoon thunderstorm, the whispering wind, the sky dressed in white fluffy clouds, the stars in the backdrop of a black night . . . and so much more. God made it all for His pleasure *(Revelation 4:11)*, but I benefit also simply by living here. I can learn volumes about Him just by being an observer of all that He has created around me.

Why do you think God went to so much effort (probably no effort for Him, though) to create such a massive world with such intricate detail? I believe one reason might be so we could experience Him. It is a way that He could help us understand first, that He is, and second, that He is a big God. Creation speaks its own language. The language of the universe explains without words that there is a being much bigger than you and me.

But the basic reality of God is plain enough. Open your eyes and there it is! By taking a long and thoughtful look at what God has created, people have always been able to see what their eyes as such can't see: eternal power, for instance, and the mystery of his divine being. So, nobody has a good excuse. Romans 1:19-20 (MSG)

I used to wonder about anyone born who had never heard the name of Jesus Christ. How would they ever get into heaven if they hadn't even heard the salvation message? Then I came across these verses in Romans. I believe with all my heart that God gives each human being the same opportunity to accept or reject Him. Creation really does preach. Creation actually does proclaim the majesty of God, so much so that one is without excuse when it comes to accepting or rejecting God.

There's too much majestic beauty in creation to ignore God's existence. If you are struggling in life right now for any reason, go outside and take a walk; or go somewhere and experience a touch from God through His creation. As you do this in faith, God will meet you. You will find refreshment in your soul that wasn't previously there. No, your problems might not go away, but you will find power to keep walking. You will find a sustaining strength to keep you going. Hope may just find its way back into your heart.

Go on. Step out that door. Take a deep breath. Breathe in the fresh air, and breathe in the fresh presence of God.

$\mathcal{H}$IDDEN TREASURE

It is the glory of God to conceal a matter, but the glory of kings is to search out a matter. Proverbs 25:2 (NASB)

God delights in concealing things; scientists delight in discovering things. Proverbs 25:2 (MSG)

The Hebrew word for glory is *kabowd,* meaning honor, heaviness, splendor, dignity, reputation, reverence.

The Hebrew word for *conceal* is *cathar,* meaning to hide.

The Hebrew word for the phrase *to search out* is *chaqar,* meaning to search through, explore.

A notable attribute of God is obscurity. Sometimes He is not quick to be found. Have you ever noticed that? A true seeker will find Him. There may be a small season of delay, but the serious seeker will find God.

I will give you the treasures of darkness and hidden wealth of secret places, so that you may know that it is I, the Lord, the God of Israel, who calls you by your name. Isaiah 45:3 (NASB)

On your journey, God wants your undivided attention as you seek Him. How serious are you? He is not mean or heartless. It's a love affair, a game of hide-and-seek, if you will. There's nothing more powerful than His love for you. He uses certain ways to root you in His absolute steadfast love. Proverbs 25:2 talks about one of His attributes—concealing a matter. One of the objectives of God's heart is for man to become an expert in searching Him out. God wants you to get good at exploring Him. He wants to expose His love, His treasures and His wealth to you.

Some of His ways will remain hidden because we won't take the time, effort and energy to look. It's almost like the Lord is whispering, "Hey, I have secret treasures in dark places, and they're for you. Come on, it's fun. Let's run in our glory and do this together. I will conceal things, and I want you to uncover the surprises and treasures. You will be rich. You will be wealthy. You will enjoy this journey if you put your mind to it. Come on. It will be fun."

Your adversary wants you to get bogged down and disheartened with details you can't understand. God wants you to get busy and search Him out.

This will cost you. It will cost you time. You may need to lay something down in order to pick up your spiritual flashlight and go into that deep, dark place you can't understand. It will mean that you need to zero in on what you are really after in this life. Will it be the pleasures of this world, or will it be Him? Go ahead. Start your treasure hunt.

It's your glory to discover Him.

The End of Time

. . . even to the time of the end: many shall run to and fro, and knowledge shall be increased.
Daniel 12:4b (KJV)

Alexander Graham Bell made the first transcontinental telephone call in January of 1915 (www.wikipedia.org). Since then, knowledge and travel have exploded in worldwide growth. Two scenarios will be occurring until the end of time. First, people will be running back and forth and going here and there. Second, knowledge shall be increased. Just think of the last 100 years. Travel and knowledge have become the hallmark of life as we know it. One can't keep up with the latest and greatest way to travel or the cutting edge of technology in the world of science or computers. If I buy a computer today, in one year or less one with greater capability will supersede it. The speed at which modern-day living is being improved upon is phenomenal.

. . . many shall run to and fro . . .

The original language denotes moving around quickly. Isn't that the case? It seems we are always looking for a better or quicker way to arrive at our destination. It reads: ". . . *and knowledge shall be increased.*" The meaning implies multiplication. One just needs to look over his shoulder 100 years to see this.

What does this mean to us? Think about it. God told Daniel way back in 606 B.C. that these events would happen. We are in that day. What day? "*The time of the end . . ..*"

Wow. This is what God has foretold. We need to sober up in the Spirit.

Do you know what else will cover the earth?

. . . for the earth shall be full of the knowledge of the LORD, as the waters cover the sea. Isaiah 11:9b (KJV)

Before God closes the curtain on life as we know it, there won't be a place in the whole earth that is without the knowledge of the Lord. He will have His way on earth. The advertisement of His fame will be everywhere.

We will either board the boat and start rowing or miss the boat altogether. The events are happening even as we speak. Think of a great *tsunami*. It comes whether we believe it will or not. It's inevitable and cannot be stopped. So, it will be at the end of the age: the day of the Lord comes.

CONSIDER WELL THE PATH OF YOUR FEET

When you walk through the fire you will not be scorched, nor will the flame burn you. Isaiah 43:2b (NASB)

Do we attract undue demonic attention to ourselves when we decide to wallow and complain in our personal fiery trial? Do we have a spiritual "kick me" sign on our backs when we stop trusting God and start feeling sorry for ourselves? When we go through the fires of life and decide that we will just stop and make camp by our unbelief and complaints rather than continue walking, are we a spiritual magnet for more harassment from the devil?

Life is difficult enough, but we can compound our problems by wallowing in our miseries and hardship. How often do we turn what may have been a short, difficult season into a greater season of trouble simply because we had a rotten attitude? Sure, you may have just been sideswiped, but God calculates how you respond to the difficulty into the mix. The Israelites turned an 11-day journey in the wilderness into a 40-year trip. Their unbelief and complaining attitude angered God (*Psalm 106:32*). Consequently, God did not allow that generation into the Promised Land. They wandered around in desert places and *greatly* prolonged their misery.

Friends, when we are in a hot spot, the best thing we can do is keep our eyes fixed on Jesus and allow Him to take us through as quickly as possible. Sometimes, it does take a bit of time, but understand that you can prolong your difficulty by your attitude. *God is not as interested in how long you are in misery as He is of building your character.*

Look at Proverbs 4:25-27 (AMP):

Let your eyes look right on [with fixed purpose], and let your gaze be straight before you. Consider well the path of your feet, and let all your ways be established and ordered aright. Turn not aside to the right hand or to the left; remove your foot from evil.

Now let's go over to Philippians 3:13 (MSG):

By no means do I count myself an expert in all of this, but I've got my eye on the goal, where God is beckoning us onward—to Jesus. I'm off and running, and I'm not turning back.

If you find yourself in the fiery furnace of life right now, set your gaze straight before you. I pray that you would run to Jesus and not turn back. If necessary, remove your foot from evil. I hope and pray that you would be made stronger in God as a result of this hellish season.

$\mathcal{T}$HE FOUR SADDEST WORDS IN THE BIBLE

*For thus saith the Lord GOD, the Holy One of Israel; In returning and
rest shall ye be saved; in quietness and in confidence shall
be your strength: and ye would not. Isaiah 30:15 (KJV)*

And ye would not.

I believe the four saddest words in the Scriptures are found right here
in Isaiah. God is daily extending rest, salvation, peace, confidence and
strength to us. He's stating, in essence, "Here, take what you need, return

to Me; I'll help you get through this." But so often, we won't. We need it so badly. In the pool of our stubbornness, we insist we know better.

What is God trying to communicate to us here? The two main components are salvation and strength. The Hebrew word for *saved* is *yasha`*, meaning liberty, deliverance from, to be spacious, opulent (which means wealthy, rich, affluent, richly supplied). The Hebrew word for *strength* is *gĕbuwrah,* meaning mighty acts, might, valor, bravery.

So . . . what do we need to do to be delivered and to be strong? We must RETURN and REST.

The Hebrew word for *return* is *shuwbah,* meaning conversion. *Webster's 1998 American Family Dictionary* defines conversion as a change from indifference, disbelief, or antagonism, to acceptance, faith or enthusiastic support.

Conversion does not stop at the gates of salvation. I daily need to be converted about one thing or another. Every time I doubt, I need a fresh conversion of trusting Jesus with my life.

How many times in my day could it be said of me, "And ye would not"? How many times do I choose weakness over the strength offered me? How many times do I refuse to be converted once again to faith and trust?

I must return and rest, and my deliverance will ultimately come. When I return to Him and find rest, my turbulent soul will settle again in quietness and confidence. I will find myself in a position of strength before God.

Instead of *"and ye would not,"* I hope you *will* today.

$\mathscr{T}$HE TEST

$\mathscr{I}$ $believe$ one of the greatest tests of my faith is in times when life is peppered with relentless disappointment. It's in moments like this that I will either sink down in discouragement and depression, or gather my hope in the One who has the game plan. The words that come out of my mouth will be the ambassador of my heart. My body language, tone and verbal communication is the telltale evidence of the condition of my heart.

I believe God purposely gives me Holy Spirit exams, in order that I see the condition of my soul and the maturity of my faith. Often, I feel I am at a certain level of faith when a sudden and unexpected storm rises upon the current of my soul and I am swept out to sea in a flurry of emotions. Immediately it is obvious where fresh growth is needed. I am raw and bare and in need of the covering and care of my heavenly Father.

Our Father is faithful to provide us with clear evidence of our progress or lack thereof. None of us are exempt. Every one of us has a "growing edge" as a friend used to say. What is easy for one, is mountain-scaling difficulty for another. Each has a mandate from heaven, a call and a unique destiny all lined up by the Holy One. Each test will be heart tailored according to our strengths, weaknesses, fears and concerns.

So, back to the question ... What if ... it's not going my way?

Corrie ten Boom said, "When a train goes through a tunnel and it gets dark, you don't throw away the ticket and jump off. You sit still and trust the Engineer."

"*It is* good that *a man* should both hope and quietly wait for the salvation of the LORD." Lamentations 3:26

If the enemy can get us to *constantly* talk about everything that is going wrong and lose our hope in God, then he has successfully caused us to fail the test. It's a grit of the wills: God's will invading my will or my will repelling God's will.

Disappointment is real. It is ugly. It is painful and can be like a relentless wave upon the shores of my heart. A full-blown embrace of disappointment will carry me off into the land of narcissism every time. That land is a place of excessive self-love at the cost of total disregard for any other. For the child of God, these sorts of waters should shout, "Danger". In God's kingdom, if you disregard the "no swimming" sign in the waters of narcissism, you might as well count on a life of depression, darkness and fishes of fear constantly nipping at your toes. You will drown my friend. You simply won't make it.

A self-centered thought life is in constant war with a God-centered thought life.

What is ... God-centered thinking/actions when it's not going your way? (*things I can control when life feels out of control*)

Being quiet instead of sinning by damaging someone with your words ("Watch your words and hold your tongue; you'll save yourself a lot of grief." Proverbs 21:23 MSG)

Talking to God about what hurts and disappoints ("Cast your burden upon the LORD and He will sustain you; He will never allow the righteous to be shaken." Psalm 55:22 NASB)

Getting counsel from a trusted mentor who will speak God-truth to you ("For by wise guidance you can wage your war, and in abundance of counselors there is victory." Proverbs 24:6 ESV)

Speak to hope and tell it to turn around and reenter your heart (You will be secure, because there is hope" Job 11:18 NIV).

Slam the door on depression and discouragement ("David was greatly distressed ... but found strength in the LORD His God." 1 Samuel 30:6 NIV)

Repent from self-centered thinking and let God-centered thinking come in—you will be refreshed. ("Repent, then, and turn to God, so that your sins may be wiped out, that times of refreshing may come from the Lord." Acts 3:19 NIV)

Write, draw, listen to calming music, go for a walk in God's creation. The cathartic effect it will have on you will help blow out the cobwebs and give you a new lens with which to view life and all that is happening to you. ("Be transformed by the renewing of your mind, so that you may prove what the will of God is," Romans 12:2 NASB)

Even as I sit at this desk, musing on these things, I am looking out the window watching a gentle snow sprinkle the winter earth, bringing a blanket of white to my storm-tossed soul. Could it be that I am saved once again from myself? I think so.

$\mathscr{I}$ HAVE CHOSEN YOU

$\mathscr{T}here\ is\ a\ divine\ formation$ occurring in your heart right now, in this season, in this time. You may feel as though you might just crumble. You may be thinking, "Lord, I can't handle it anymore."

The Lord opens His arms to you today and says,

My Child, be patient with My ways. Persevere with Me. My plan takes time. Come here and become undisturbed in My presence. The struggle is there to form and shape you into My image. The enemy is there to bring bitterness to your soul; but I declare to you today: lift up your eyes and receive My healing oil upon your heart. Let it be as a covering against those lies that want to penetrate your soul to cause you to doubt your faith, to question Me and to call into question My purposes. This thing is from Me. This thing will make you or break you depending upon your attitude in this season. I am forming a kingdom in this earth that will not be destroyed. Bring resolve into your heart today. Declare your course. I have chosen you for such a time as this. I have selected you to be one that will not be destroyed. I have walked with you in the past, and I am walking with you now.

I am coming again for My Bride. Oh, how I love you. Don't resist the process, for you will not be disappointed in your God. Be patient with your Creator. Remove expectations off of your brother or sister. Release people to be people. Release Me to be God. Surely, I will not disappoint you. Surely, I am the only One who will by no means desert you, will not in the least forsake you and will absolutely never leave you without support. Sometimes, you forget this. Realign your focus. I am coming again for a spotless Bride. I am forming you and fashioning you for that day when my Father will announce: Go get your Bride.

$\mathcal{M}$AYBE WHAT YOU NEED IS SOME GOOD OLD-FASHIONED REPENTANCE

$\mathcal{S}$*ometimes on our journey, we* feel as if the streams of refreshing have dried up, and we have no idea why. Jeremiah felt this exact way in Jeremiah 15:18 when he said, *"Will you indeed be to me a deceitful brook, like waters that fail and are uncertain?" (AMP)*

Jeremiah had served God and walked in His will. He had come to a season in which he felt God had left, and the brook had dried up, so to speak.

Therefore, repent and return, so that your sins may be wiped away, in order that times of refreshing may come from the presence of the Lord. Acts 3:19 (NASB)

Sometimes, God will answer us with one simple word: Repent. This is what He told Jeremiah in the next verse. The NIV puts it this way: *If you repent, I will restore you.*

God is a God of simplicity. He has a way of narrowing it down for us.

This six-letter word can change the course of our lives. According to the original Greek word, to *repent* means to change one's mind for the better.

Friends, to repent simply involves changing your mind. When you change your beliefs, then your behavior will follow suit. We tend to focus on the behavior, when the root of our behavior is simply our faulty belief system. What lies have you embraced as truth? Ask the Holy Spirit what the root belief system is where you are indulging in sinful behavior.

In other words, ask God to search your heart and see if there is any faulty belief system in you. Often, we have developed an attitude of sin which has acted as a dam, stopping the flow of refreshing and strength that belongs to us in God. God does not desire for you to be a pauper in the Kingdom. He has riches in the Spirit to lavish upon you. You have no reason to be sequestered from His provisions of power, strength and refreshing. God makes it known: if you repent, I will restore you. If you turn from your distrust, doubt and unbelief, I will bring refreshing back into your life; and you will then be useful to Me again.

Return to loving obedience. Change your way of thinking. Your sins will become whitewashed as if they never happened. Resuscitation will envelop your dry and weary heart. A time of refreshing will invade your soul.

This cooling and refreshing will come from God's presence and invade your presence. It's a promise that you can take to the bank.

God does answer Jeremiah in verse 19:

Therefore, this says the LORD to Jeremiah, "If you repent and give up this mistaken attitude of despair and self-pity, then I will restore you to a state of inner peace so that you may stand before Me as My obedient representative; and if you separate the precious from the worthless examining yourself and cleansing your heart from unwarranted doubt concerning My faithfulness, you will become My spokesman" (AMP).

An Appeal

Father, I repent. I give You permission to reveal any faulty belief system that is producing the fruit of sin in my life. Convict me of any belief or thought that opposes your heart for me. I am dry and withering in my soul. Cleanse me, I ask. I need Your cool refreshing to come and restore me. I turn now from the belief system that has entangled me. Come to me now—I long for Your refreshing streams of living water. I receive the life in abundance that belongs to me. I desire to be Your witness. Amen.

MY HAND IS FROZEN TO MY SWORD

. . . but he stood his ground and struck down the Philistines 'til his hand grew tired and froze to the sword. The LORD brought about a great victory that day. The troops returned to Eleazar, but only to strip the dead. 2 Samuel 23:10 (NIV)

This verse is speaking of Eleazar, one of David's mighty men. Notice that it was the Lord who brought about the great victory, but the deliverance of the Lord may include our working, diligent hand. To become weary and tired is sometimes part of the process as the Lord works on our behalf.

Where do we get the idea that we never need to work and labor because deliverance comes from the hand of the Lord? Every so often there's an "instant miracle," and we are sideswiped by a touch from God. Most of the time, He chooses to co-labor with us in it. When does your child learn the most: if you do everything for him or if you include him in coming to the end of a process?

In God's order, there is always something to do. We can even become tired and weary of just standing quietly, waiting on the Lord. Let us not become weary of doing right, even though we may get tired and exhausted in the midst of the battle.

Eleazar's hand grew tired and froze to the sword. Wow, let's take this thought somewhere. For us, what is our sword? Ephesians 6:17 explains that our sword (our weapon of defense and offense) is the Word of God.

If you're going to grow tired, then grow tired with the Word of God frozen in your hand.

There are many reasons for fatigue. There is a good tired and a bad tired. The bad tired is when you are tired because of sin and disobedience. The good tired is when you are tired because of speaking the Word and defeating the devil in your battles.

Folks, we are in a constant battle. Believe it or not, it's a fact. If you are a Christian, please be reminded today that you will win the war. You may lose a few battles here and there, but you will win the war. Jesus paid for your victory on the cross. He made an open display of your enemy when He rose from the grave. For now, however, you will continually be engaged in battles as you claim your spot in the kingdom and earn your heavenly rewards. Let the Word of God freeze to your hand. Let it become a part of your very being, hidden in your heart, and you will see great victory in God.

YOUR LIFE IS A VICTORY PARADE

Attention, Israel! This very day you are crossing the Jordan to enter the land and dispossess nations that are much bigger and stronger than you are. You're going to find huge cities with sky-high fortress walls and gigantic people, descendants of the Anakites—you've heard all about them; you've heard the saying, "No one can stand up to an Anakite."
Deuteronomy 9:1 (MSG)

God sometimes leads us right into the path of an enemy much stronger and more powerful than us. Our God, the One who loves us with unending love, the One whose tender mercies are available to us new each morning, the One who saved our soul from hell, the One who promises, "I will never leave you nor forsake you," this same God will at moments lead us right into the camp of our enemy, whom He knows is too great for us.

Wow. Why? Because He knows we will win when we take Him with us. Because He knows that if the battle wasn't bigger than ourselves, we would gloat over the victory and think we accomplished it alone. Because He knows our faith needs a channel to form and grow into pure gold. Because He knows that we are blinded to the condition of our heart, and it sometimes takes a confrontation with our Goliath to help us see our true spiritual state. (The story of Goliath is found in 1 Samuel 17.)

Do you know what? When we follow His lead, it's a guaranteed victory.

In the Messiah, in Christ, God leads us from place to place in one perpetual victory parade. Through us, he brings knowledge of Christ. Everywhere we go, people breathe in the exquisite fragrance. Because of Christ, we give off a sweet scent rising to God, which is recognized by those on the way of salvation—an aroma redolent with life. 2 Corinthians 2:14-15 (MSG)

Living your life on earth as a Christian should resemble a victory parade. As you pass by the onlookers, there should be an exquisite fragrance—the aroma of Jesus Christ Himself.

In Deuteronomy 9:1, God is basically saying: *Come on, Israel. I want you to cross over Jordan and seize this large, overpowering enemy that you totally fear. Go into these sky-high cities with giant citizens and bring them to ruin. Totally destroy them. OK?*

What God said to them next is critical:

Today know this: God, your God, is crossing the river ahead of you—he's a consuming fire. He will destroy the nations; he will put them under your power. You will dispossess them and very quickly wipe them out, just as God promised you would. Deuteronomy 9:3 (MSG)

Friend, who or what is a "sky-high city" enemy to you? What living soul or situation appears in giant form and causes you to shudder in fright every time you think about it? What person or scenario torments your mind every single day? What have you empowered that grips and paralyzes you with fear beyond measure?

Hear His whisper:

Cross over your Jordan today and start walking. Understand that I am going on ahead of you. I will defeat your enemy to the point that by the time you arrive on the scene, you will barely have to blow upon him and he will tumble over. I will do this for you, I promise. Start walking by faith right now, and head on over to the enemy's camp to face him. I only lead you in triumph over your enemy. You cross over, and I will put him under your feet.

Go on and just do it. See God's hand stretched out to you right now. He is inviting you to put on the armor He's given you and cross over to the new land—a place you have never been before, but a place promised to you from God Himself. He's already been over there. It's time to come out of your comfort zone of fear. (Yes, if it's been a part of you for so long, it is now your comfort zone.)

It's time to taste the land flowing with milk and honey. You were born for better than what you are experiencing in this moment. You've been walking around in the desert too long now, haven't you?

Who or what is your Anakite today? Face him. Defeat him.

$\mathcal{B}$ECOMING A GOD PLEASER

*If you need wisdom, ask our generous God, and he will give it to you.
He will not rebuke you for asking. But when you ask him, be sure that
your faith is in God alone. Do not waver, for a person with divided
loyalty is as unsettled as a wave of the sea that is blown and tossed by
the wind. Such people should not expect to receive anything from the
Lord. James 1:5-7 (NLT)*

$\mathcal{A}$ couple of other translations convey that last sentence this way:

For that man ought not to expect that he will receive anything from the Lord. (NASB)

Don't think you're going to get anything from the Master that way, adrift at sea, keeping all your options open. (MSG)

A person who wavers back and forth in what he believes would be classified as an unstable person in the kingdom of God. One way to please the Lord is to continually walk in faith.

It's impossible to please God apart from faith. Why? Because anyone who wants to approach God must believe both that he exists, and that he cares enough to respond to those who seek him. Hebrews 11:6 (MSG)

So often we involve the Lord as a last resort. Sometimes, we lay our request before God, but in our mind, we think, "Well, if God doesn't do it this way or that, I have another plan to bail myself out."

James is speaking here of when we have a need for wisdom. True wisdom from God is worth standing firmly upon 'til the day you die. God sets the precedence for when we come to Him. What pleases Him is when one of His children comes to Him boldly, yet humbly, with full and absolute confidence that he will get an answer from Him. In that child's mind, there is no other source or any other possible way of an answer except from his heavenly Father.

There are two ingredients that must accompany our dialogue with the Lord. First, we must believe that God exists. But that's not enough—even demons do this *(James 2:19)*. Second, we must believe that He rewards those who diligently seek Him *(Hebrews 11:6)*.

Faith is work. But in God's kingdom, you are compensated for this. There is great reward for the soul who travels earth in an unrelenting, faith-filled pursuit of God.

This is at the top of God's priority list for us. Your faith walk will determine what you get from God. You can't please God without it. You won't get anything from God if your faith is contaminated with a wavering heart. James 1:7 confirms this.

Jehovah (the self-existent One) is an all-or-nothing God. He is a hot or cold God. You are either one of His sheep or one of the goats to be cast off on that final day *(Matthew 25)*. *Yeshua* (Savior) is not impressed with our mediocre, lukewarm, dim mindset of what He can do. As a matter of fact, it makes Him sick to His stomach to find a child of His who is lukewarm *(Revelation 3:15-16)*.

Granted, this is a pretty high standard that God has set before us in His Word, and none of us are perfect in our faith. We are continually growing and learning. But it's good that God has put the standard before us. At least we are clear on what pleases Him. Let there be no doubt or wavering about that.

Let's turn to a story in Mark 9. I encourage you to read the whole chapter, but there's one key conversation that the father of a demon-possessed son had with Jesus that day. Verse 24 declares, *"Immediately the boy's father cried out and said, 'I do believe; help my unbelief.'" (NASB)*

I do believe, help my unbelief. What an honest confession. What an avenue of approaching God that could promote growth and maturity in us. This is where most of us find ourselves in the story line of our lives.

Here is where we find our "growing edge." We believe, but we are not consistent in our belief—thus the need for God to help us. We have a great need for God's aid. He will help us if we ask.

God will not beat our lowly little head when we fall short; rather, He will lift us up and come to our aid. Jesus gave the father of this boy a miracle. The father was certain that Jesus had the power and could perform the miracle. He also knew his heart had room to grow in his faith. There are moments when we simply need the mercy of God in our condition. Then there are other moments when we should be able to believe without wavering. We are old enough in God to know better.

It all boils down to the condition of our heart. Is it soft before God or hard and rebellious in nature? Our heart is what grabs the attention of our heavenly Father as He responds to us *(1 Samuel 16:7)*.

A true life of faith is a life that is lived on purpose. It's a life that is bent on trusting God. It's a life that is deliberate and not tossed back and forth as a cradle in a strong wind. Let this be our goal. Let this be our condition when we cross our finish line.

A Petition

Father, I do believe, but I know I need to grow in my faith. I give You permission to continue to give me circumstances to believe You without wavering. Grow me up, I pray. Help my faithlessness. Convict me when I should know better. Convict me when I am straying and wavering. Thank You for Your aid and power to grow my faith even more today. In Jesus' name, amen.

$\mathcal{V}$OICE OUT OF THE WIND

Father, engulf me in Your wind. Hide me under Your breath. Center me in the air currents of Your Holy Spirit. Harmonize me with Your wind words. Let our life of love together bear fruit in the earth that will be rock solid for eternity. Thank You for this opportunity to know You and make You known. Be glorified in the voice out of Your wind ... amen.

The wind blows where it wishes and you hear the sound of it, but do not know where it comes from or where it's going; so is everyone who is born of the Spirit. John 3:8 NASB

There is something about the wind that reflects spiritual mystery along the journey. Wind is invisible to the natural eye. Its effects are not. On a cold windy day, the wind chill factor makes it feel much colder than it is. A gentle breeze can bring refreshing on a hot, scorching day. Wind can erode and cause environmental problems. The speed of wind can destroy via hurricanes and tornadoes. The capture of wind can create electricity and empower. It takes wind to fan the flames of a smoldering fire.

In Genesis 8 God brought a wind that caused the flood waters to go down for Noah and the inhabitants of the ark. Wind was a very important factor in God's dealings with the Egyptians and His children. In Genesis 41, it was an east wind that brought a seven-year drought to Egypt. In Exodus 10 it was that east wind again that brought the plague of locusts upon the Egyptians followed by a west wind that took them away and out to sea. It was the Lord's wind once more in Exodus 10 that opened up the Red Sea so His children could cross on dry ground. In Exodus 15 it tells us that they crossed, and Pharaoh's army pursued, only to be greeted by the wind of God that shut the sea up and drowned them all. Numbers 11 tells us how God's wind brought the quail to His people to satisfy their hunger. Second Samuel 22 is a very wonderful chapter, but tucked in there at verse 11 it says, "And He rode on a cherub and flew; And He appeared on the wings of the wind." Wind ... that has wings? God has escaped my box of logic. In Psalms 104, God walks upon the wings of the wind. In Psalm 135 He brings forth the wind from His treasuries.

The Hebrew word for treasuries is the word *'owtsar* meaning storehouse, magazine of weapons (fig. of God's armory). So, the wind is a weapon in God's hand. The stormy wind is simply fulfilling His orders in Psalm 148. In Ecclesiastes 1, it tells of the circuit of God that the wind is to follow. God, at times, may ask us to call for His wind to bring breath and life to another according to Ezekiel 37.

In the Gospels, Jesus used the stormy wind upon the sea several times to teach His disciples the importance of faith and trust when the winds of trial came upon them with great surprise and fury.

In Acts 2 the mighty rushing wind of God came upon those in the upper room that day to usher in the promise of the sweet Holy Spirit. Their lives were turned upside down with the power to witness and testify of the newly risen Lord Jesus.

Through these scriptural examples, we have clarified that wind, comes straight from God. If I am born of His Spirit, then His wind will be a frequent companion in my life. His wind, when allowed, will carry me places I would have never ventured on my own. The wind of God, through me, will destroy hell and usher in His glory.

His voice speaks out of His wind and I must ... hear it.

His voice speaks out of His wind and I must ... speak it.

His voice speaks out of His wind and I must ... write about it.

His voice speaks out of His wind and I must ... live it.

Through the breath of my Beloved, I will be challenged, nourished, refreshed, disciplined, protected, fought for and cloaked in His glory. The wind gust of glory will at times come swooping down on me infusing my heart with sheer joy and ecstasy that only heaven can produce. The wind of God at times will come straight from His mouth to mine and, in an instant, resuscitate my breathless soul to life again. The airflow coming from the epicenter of His affections towards me swirls around my wounded heart causing miraculous healing and wholeness that years in the counselor's office could never imitate.

A FORM OF GODLINESS WON'T CUT IT

And he shall speak great words against the most High, and shall wear
out the saints of the most High.
Daniel 7:25 (KJV)

As a child of God, one of the objectives of your enemy is to wear
you out. The original word for *wear out* in this passage is an Aramaic

word, *bĕla*. It means to harass constantly, to wear away and to afflict, to trouble.

Satan thinks he can wear you out the way a garment becomes worn. With great and constant harassment, he thinks you will fade away and fall off like an overused garment. The sad part is that he will be successful with some of us. His top priority is to speak against God and what God has said and to render you powerless.

If you walk in your own strength, this will happen to you. Walking with Christ is not a form of religion. Truly traveling with the Most High is a journey of power.

> *"BUT UNDERSTAND this, that in the last days will come (set in) perilous times of great stress and trouble [hard to deal with and hard to bear]." 2 Timothy 3:1 (AMP)*

Saints, because it is getting closer and closer to the end, we have been promised that life on earth will become more difficult. It's one of the promises of God's Word that we would just as soon pass over. God is telling us:

> *"My Child, you have need of My power to make it clear to the end. Don't try and do this alone."*

> *Don't be naive. There are difficult times ahead. As the end approaches, people are going to be self-absorbed, money-hungry, self-promoting, stuck-up, profane, contemptuous of parents, crude, coarse, dog-eat-dog, unbending, slanderers, impulsively wild, savage, cynical, treacherous, ruthless, bloated windbags, addicted to lust, and allergic to God. 2 Timothy 3:1-4 (MSG)*

Have you run into any of these types recently? The next verse tells us:

Having a form of godliness, but denying the power thereof: from such turn away. 2 Timothy 3:5 (KJV)

There will be people all around in these last days who claim a form of godliness but lack true Holy Spirit power in their lives. This word *power* in the Greek is the word *dunamis*. It's the word from which we derive our modern word *dynamite*. It means strength, ability, power for performing miracles, moral power and excellence of soul and power consisting in or resting upon armies, forces, and hosts.

Feeling a bit worn-out these days? Time for a Holy Spirit infusion of DYNAMITE. There's no need to stay in the interrogation chair and continue to take all the harassment of your adversary. Is he condemning you? Are you hearing these sorts of voices?

- You're not good enough.
- You've gone too far—God can never reach you.
- You have sinned too great a sin to ever find God.
- God does not love you.
- Did God really say . . .?
- If God loves you, then why is He allowing all this suffering in your life?
- Your depression is too dark—there's no hope for you.
- Nobody loves you. You are unlovable.
- God is ashamed of you.

Well, my dear friend, if you have been washed in the blood of Jesus Christ, get out of Satan's interrogation chair. Your Father in heaven has prepared a table before you in the presence of your enemy. It's a table He has prepared just for you and Himself. It's a table filled with the riches of His glory. It's a banquet table spread uniquely for you.

Get up. Take your tired, weary feet and go over now to His table. The interrogation is over. The price has been paid for you to sit with the King. He wishes your company today. He desires to lavish His love upon you. He will turn your weary heart into a warrior's heart. He will turn your mourning into dancing. He will speak lover's words to you in the secret place. You will arise from His table in strength and power to do His great exploits.

The trap of weariness has been exposed.

$\mathcal{D}$ODGING DIFFICULTY PRODUCES WEAKNESS

$\mathcal{I}$'m working things out. $\mathcal{I}$t's time to trust and not doubt. It's time to remove your focus off of what you see. There is a hidden work of My Holy Spirit that will come forth in a timely matter. Matters of heaven and earth are at stake. Souls hang in the balance. Souls are My heartbeat. Time is quickly being swallowed up by eternity. A great birthing is occurring in the earth. It's the birthing of all that I have promised for I have promised much, and I will be true to all of My Word.

You are My instrument in the earth. What touches you has already touched Me. What comes to you has already come to Me. What affects you has already affected Me. So, when it comes to you, remember that it came to Me first and has passed onto you accompanied by My power to go through it—not around it but through it. Too many take the easy way, thus robbing themselves of the strength that builds as one goes through a time of testing. Those who dodge difficulty will remain weak in the Spirit.

Sorrow may desire to have you. Fear may want your attention; but I have orchestrated your days through the blood of Jesus Christ so that in the end, the victory in My camp is sure. Look not to the current status of your life and conclude that this is the end. Look not to what your eyes see in the natural and calculate without Me. For this is a great danger and will take you places that will only create a spiritual injury to you.

Look at your surroundings, and then put Me in the equation. Look at your overwhelming flood, then see your Lifeguard, the Guardian of your life, standing in the middle.

Here is where you will be clothed with the garment of hope. Here is where I can dress you for the battle. Here is where your path to victory will begin.

I am not calling you to ignore what you see and feel. I am calling you to put Me in the middle of what you see and feel. This is how you will gain the victory in your emotions. This is how you will overcome when the fire and flood seek to destroy you. This is how transformation will occur in your emotions and eyesight.

Put the God of your life in the middle. Put Me there so that when you look at your dreadful circumstances, you see Me seated upon My throne. See Me at work on your behalf. See Me at work to advance My kingdom in the earth. For your vision is a good indicator of your destination.

What you see and how you react is key, my dear one. Do you see yourself equipped? Do you see yourself strong in the Lord? I have given you the power to ponder and imagine. Use it to further the kingdom of God in your own soul. Use your mind to think good thoughts. You are in the middle of the war on this earth. This is your Captain speaking to you. I offer you the strategies of heaven. I offer you the pathway to victory. You may lose a battle or a skirmish here or there; but take heart, dear one, I have already won the war. You are on the right side of the battle.

$\mathcal{B}$ECOMING INACCESSIBLE TO YOUR FOE

*The fear of man will prove to be a snare, but whoever trusts in the
LORD is kept safe.*
Proverbs 56:11 (NIV)

$\mathcal{W}hat\ is\ the\ status\ of$ your life at the moment: fear of man or trust
in the Lord? Are you ensnared, or are you safe?

What is a snare? In the Hebrew, a *snare* denotes an iron ring put
through the nostrils of a beast. That's a pretty vivid picture. A snare is a
trap, and trickery is part of what makes up a snare.

What is trust? The Hebrew word for *trust* here is *batach*. It means to be secure, to fear nothing for oneself—and this is my personal favorite—to throw oneself or one's cares on another.

When I become anxious, I am to hurl those concerns into the hand of God. Can you picture yourself taking your cares like a baseball and tossing them as hard and fast as you can to the one with the catcher's mitt?

When I fail to trust, I will become a slave to my fears. It's as simple as that. To trust the Lord means that I will inherit a promise of safety. In the Hebrew, the word *safety* is the word *sagab*, meaning to be inaccessibly high.

Wow . . . think of that. When I am truly in a place of trust, I am put in a high place of inaccessibility. Talk about security systems.

. . . and raised us up with Him, and seated us with Him in the heavenly places in Christ Jesus. Ephesians 2:6 (NASB)

In Christ Jesus, we have been elevated to high places with Him. We have been placed in an inaccessible spot. The trouble is that we sometimes choose to get off our chair and go down into the places where danger and snares become more of our reality.

In choosing to trust the Lord, I will become inaccessible and out of the reach and grasp of my adversary who wishes to put his iron ring through my nostrils and lead me around like one of his enslaved animals. I will be seated with Christ in a high place of shelter and safety.

Saint, it's the secret place that is off-limits to our enemy. It's the place of trust, and it's the place of security. When you enter His shelter, there's no storm that can touch you. When you throw your cares upon your Master, He envelops you like an armored garment; no harm can come to you. All hell may be breaking loose around your feet, but your heart is secure, and you are safe with Him.

Your heart and flesh may fail, but God will be your stronghold. There's a part of you that becomes unreachable to the hand of the enemy.

Fear is the trap. Trust is the way out.

$\mathcal{F}$OR GOODNESS' SAKE

[What, what would have become of me] had I not believed that I
would see the Lord's goodness in the land of the living!
Psalm 27:13 (AMP)

When I deny my God-given gift to believe, I will faint. When
I don't choose faith as the storm brews, I will become unstable. There
are voices that want my ear. There are emotions that want to dominate.
There are lies that compete for the truth in my heart.

Choosing to be certain in a God who brings goodness is at the heart
of every true pilgrim of God. This choice has to be made over and over
again, day in and day out, as I face challenge after challenge.

However, even in my wavering, I can be certain of a God who comes swooping down upon me to rescue me from my doubt and misunderstanding of His way. This is part of His goodness. For His goodness' sake, He will rescue me. Sometimes, I just need to be rescued. Sometimes, I just need Him to come and get me.

I do believe; help my unbelief. Mark 9:24 (NASB)

He helps my unbelief—over and over and over again. I have faith, but I always have room to grow. Because of this, the testing and trial will come; and the opportunity to increase in my faith will be a constant choice on my journey with God.

Looking back on your walk with God, is this your testimony? Can you utter, "What would have become of me had I not believed that I would see the goodness of the Lord?"

There will be soul-searching moments in the life of every saint. Sight will fail. Emotions will be turbulent. Hearing will become difficult. The dark will consume.

The Word of God charges us to believe always in the goodness of the Lord as we journey upon this earth. Men will fail you. Loneliness may become your companion. Relentless sorrow may beat against the chambers of your heart. Friends may betray you. Saint, become *certain* of the goodness of the Lord. Become *firm* in your footing. Speak to the Lover of Your Soul just as Job did:

Though He slay me yet will I trust in Him . . . Job 13:15 (KJV)

This is where the rubber meets the road. This is the place of true spiritual maturity and muscle. Here is the meat of the kingdom of God.

FAITH—believing what I can't see now but know I will see then. This is what brings pleasure to Him (Hebrews 11:6).

In all of this, you get to decide what will become of you. You get to accept the gift of faith or not. You have the power to choose life. You have the ability to believe in the goodness of the Lord in the land of the living. You have the breath to simply cry out, "Lord, I need rescued."

A Supplication

Father, I believe You. I know there are times when my actions speak otherwise. So, I ask, won't You help my unbelief? Take me to the place where I choose to believe all the time that I will see Your goodness in the earth. Take me to the place of believing without having to see. Give me Your vision. Help my unbelief. Come and rescue me from me. Amen.

ᏇHEN IT DOESN'T MAKE ANY SENSE

We must go through many hardships to enter the kingdom of God.
Acts 14:22 (NIV)

Not everything makes sense this side of heaven, does it? The story of our life may include painful chapters that will need to be concluded over in eternity for the happy ending. Profound grief might suddenly grip our soul so tightly that only in our death shall we find complete liberation from it. There can be moments when we can't seem to gather all the puzzle pieces to complete the picture here on earth.

A very close friend of mine told me that she just stopped asking the "why" question. I suppose that would be a good place to rest in certain situations. Otherwise, one might be continually tormented in his mind. Once we have examined our hearts in a hard situation and are clean before God, we must not spend much time asking "why," but rather maybe "how." How will I walk with You, Lord, through this? Please show me each step of the way. Lead me, O Great Shepherd of my life.

I asked the mother of a child with Williams syndrome—whom they said would never live past six months but is now in his thirties—how she dealt with the "why" question when he was born. How did she move past that to the wonderful way she is now with her son? She said she sat down with her mother one day after her son was born and asked her, "Why me—why not someone else?" Her very wise mother said to her, "I don't ever want you to ask that question again. You were chosen for this task, so you can do it. Your sister with four healthy children was not chosen. She couldn't have handled it, but you can." That was the turning point for this mother. I listened for 30 minutes to the ups and downs of those thirty-some years. She loves her son deeply and cares for him like no other person could. I sat there in awe of the Lord who has led her through the "how" of life's trials.

If everything did make perfect sense, would we even have the need for faith? Would we ever have reason to trust God if everything always went our way? Could it be that life's perplexities are one way God is trying to get us to know Him and understand Him better? Would we even seek Him out if we had no needs? I'm not sure we really would.

There are so many sides to God. Could it be that the diverse trials we encounter are really a divine invitation to know another facet of Him? It's possible.

ℒET'S TEAR THE DAM APART . . . GOD

He opened the rock, and water gushed out; it ran in the dry places like a river. Psalm 105:41 (AMP)

My river will flow wherever you allow. Is there a dam in your soul that is stopping the flow? Let Me clear the way. Let's remove the debris—maybe some stones of regret?— possibly some limbs of barred up pain?—perhaps some clay formed by the wounding of your soul? What about a little mud and dirt from sin, all hindering the good flow of My living water?

Living, refreshing, breathing, saturating crystal waters straight from My heavenly throne—for everywhere it's allowed, there's life and healing.

My people are choosing stagnancy. My people are choosing muddy waters to live by. My people choose waters that are contaminated. My people are building and maintaining the dams that separate My supply from them. What I offer is not being accepted. What I have freely provided is not being used but going to waste.

Come, you who are weary and bent over with the trials of this life. Let's remove the hindrances. Let's take the dam apart to bring a fresh release of My flow. My heart grieves at how My people walk in darkness. My heart is sorrowful as I see how My people are trying to serve Me out of their own strength. Many are so bowed down and can hardly move to make the next step. This is not My plan, nor My design. I did not choose this for you.

I am the God of intimacy, yet My people fear intimacy and do not come close. As I called in the Garden of Eden, "Adam, where are you?" I ask again today, in this late hour, "ADAM, WHERE ARE YOU?"

Even creation is groaning with birth pangs to see you come forth as My shining children in the earth. All of creation is groaning in birth pangs for the manifestation of My kingdom on earth, eagerly awaiting, expecting and hoping for soon relief. Can you hear the groans? It's in the tremors, the quakes, the whirlwinds, the flooding and cyclones. Creation groans.

Come, My people. Come up here and sit with Me where I am, and I will show you great possibilities which you did not know. Be transformed in your patterns of meditation. Think as I think. Be as I am. Rule as I do. Don't settle. You don't belong here anyway. Your home is with Me in eternity.

$\mathcal{W}$HEN IT'S TIME TO GO HOME

Precious in the sight of the LORD is the death of his saints.
Psalms 116:15 (KJV)

People die all over the world every day, all day long. But when a child of God passes on, it's no light matter before God.

The word *precious* in the Hebrew is the word *yakar*. It means highly valued, prized, rare, weighty, costly, glorious and influential.

This word *precious* is the same word that is used to describe the "precious" stones upon the crown that was placed on David's head in 2

Samuel 12:30. In 1 Kings 5:17, it's the same Hebrew word that describes the "costly stones" that were used to lay the foundation of the temple. It's the same word for "excellent" that is used in Psalms 36:7 to describe the Lord's loving kindness. Isaiah 28:16 speaks of the "precious" cornerstone, which is Jesus Christ. It is also the same word used in Psalms 116:17. It's a word that God has reserved to use for very particular matters. These are matters very close to the heart of God.

"Saint" is a word we don't use very much today, but I purposely chose the King James Version to bring this word out into the light a little more clearly. *Saint* in the Hebrew denotes faithful, kind, godly, holy one. There are those who have been canonized by the Catholic Church, but I believe the Word of God shows it to be even more encompassing. Any one of us who are following God through Jesus Christ, any who continue in faithfulness, would be considered a "saint" before God.

When one of God's faithful ones—ever before the sight of God—dies, it is a weighty matter. It is important to understand that it was God's choice and timing for that one to go to be with Him. Our earthly minds will not always comprehend the reasons why it was time for our loved one to go on, but before God in heaven, it was time (Ecclesiastes 3:1-2).

I believe God uses death to influence as well. He will use any means possible to draw others into His loving kindness and salvation. It will cost, which is why it's precious. There will be an amount to pay—sometimes it's a life.

When someone we love or even just know dies, there is a rippling effect that occurs all around. People think of that person and remember how he lived his life and what was most important to him. There is an influence upon those left behind. In these sorts of times, you might find people getting their lives right with God. I believe this can be a major reason God may take some of His saints home.

God has called each and every one of us to be His witnesses in this earth. Sometimes, only in death can we become a greater witness for

Him. Our lives had a certain influence while we were living, but there comes a time when God decides, "Now I will take you to glory with Me, and your witness in the earth will multiply like it never could while you were living."

When Jesus was on the earth, He was just one person. He said He had to go to the Father. When He did go to the Father and the Holy Spirit came, just look at the spiritual explosion that occurred as the church was born.

A grain of wheat must fall onto the ground and die in order to bring forth more fruit *(John 12:24)*. This is what death can accomplish. When someone you love and hold closely dies, he multiplies in your heart. It's precious, it's valuable and it's a weighty thing. It's a gloriously costly matter to you.

A holy moment loomed that day I stood in the room and looked on the floor where my friend died in her home because of a house fire. We said, "This was the place where Erlynn met God face-to-face." It was holy, sacred ground. It was weighty, costly and precious at the same time. Even though we prefer not to think about it, death will visit each one of us one day unless Jesus returns.

When it's your time, what kind of a rippling effect do you want to have on those left behind who are grieving your departure? You have control of that now. How will your witness in the earth be multiplied by your home going?

God says it will be precious to Him.

$\mathcal{B}$ITTERNESS OR BEAUTY

See to it that no one comes short of the grace of God; that no root
of bitterness springing up causes trouble, and by it may be defiled;
Hebrews 12:15 (NASB)

One evening as I was pulling weeds from my flower garden, I came
across this weed with a serious root system. Right away, the Holy Spirit
reminded me of this verse in Hebrews. A root of bitterness will spring
up causing trouble with a capitol "T" every single time. No exception—
period. In life, every one of us have plenty of choices from which we can
pick to be bitter—a failed marriage, betrayal, disappointments, sudden

death of a loved one, friends who become distant, misunderstandings, being used by someone, hypocrites in the church, physical, mental or sexual abuse—and I'm sure you could add some others. We must resist the temptation to be a resentful and bitter person.

A nice, green, healthy weed of bitterness starts as a seed. The seed can come in the form of a lie. For example, "They meant to harm you," or "You are not worth loving" or "No one wants you" and on and on. Then we add to it by nursing and rehearsing it over and over again. Nursing and rehearsing an offense is like the sun and the rain. That's all a seed needs to germinate and start growing roots. One day, that root of bitterness breaks forth in the soil of your heart, and you have a full-blown weed that will produce nothing but trouble for you and for those around you.

When a weed of bitterness is left to grow and come to full maturity, it will most likely go to seed. You know what that means? When left unattended, it will produce more weeds and eventually take over the garden of your heart. Not only that, but it will begin to defile others around you.

Your heart is a garden before the Lord. There are beautiful flowers growing, but there is a constant need for the Gardener to pull up any weeds that begin to appear. This is one reason we have the Holy Spirit living inside us. If you are listening, you can be sure He will convict you when you need it. Bitterness comes when we won't forgive. Forgiveness pulls bitterness out by the root.

You were meant to reflect beauty in the garden of your heart. So long as we have to contend with our flesh and the devil, we have need of the Master Gardener to visit us and kill the root of the weeds. Allow Him to pull up the weeds in your heart. Make room for all the beauty He has planted.

$\mathcal{S}$ PIRITUAL POSTURE

For He inflicts pain, and gives relief;
He wounds, and His hands also heal.
Job 5:18 (NASB)

A while back, I began an eight-month corrective treatment plan with my chiropractor. The initial x-rays showed curvature in directions there shouldn't be. My back was continually aching and my posture was a bit slumped. I am now in my sixth month of treatment and feeling the wonderful results of repeated trips to the office for an adjustment. My back pain has disappeared and my posture feels great. As I walk, there is a new ease in walking straight and tall. My spine has reluctantly, but finally, given in to its new place of correctness. At the end of each treatment, my favorite part is laying on the hydrotherapy table as warm, pulsating water moves up and down my body. It's the soothing end, for the sudden jolt and jerk I just received at the hands of my chiropractor.

Recently as I lay on the hydrotherapy bed, the Holy Spirit began to talk to me about this physical process I was going through and how there is a mirrored spiritual application. I see now, that at times, He calls me into seasons of His divine corrective treatment.

My spiritual carriage is in need of constant attention. My Christian stance is top priority to my Father. Are others being drawn in because of my walk? Or, is my spiritual gait reflecting pain that won't be healed, showing curves and twists that expose the need for holy adjustment? Is there anyone watching that desires the posture I am walking with? Am I exemplifying true spiritual transformation?

If you are troubled on all sides, facing pain and loneliness like never before, being tested and challenged like it was the end of the world, be careful you haven't just entered into a season of corrective treatment with the One who is the Author and Finisher of your faith.

Stop and ponder something. You may be thinking you are fighting your adversary when, in all honesty, you may be rebelling against the One who is saying it's time for a season of corrective treatment. Your thoughts and focus are twisted and curved in places that do not satisfy heaven. Your ability to stand straight and tall in the Spirit has been compromised and you are in need of His loving hands to take hold of you in places that will feel like a swift jerk and jolt to your spiritual senses.

As a true child of God, you will not ever be exempt from regular, heavenly re-alignment. As the image of Christ is slowly, but steadily, being formed in you, there will be an ever-increasing interruption to your poor spiritual posture. He will put His hands upon your weary and tired, crooked consecrated back and bring what may seem like a momentary painful jolt backward, yet when you find yourself upon His table of rest afterwards, a new freedom to live and move will invade your life. You will stand straighter and taller than ever before.

God's whisper ...

Child, you and I are traveling now upon ground that is new to you. All the adjustments I have given to you thus far have given you the ability to walk where we are now. Yet there are still spiritual thoughts and attitudes, forms and reactions, that need altered in your life. I know you can feel the need for My hand of alignment. Lie down now upon My table and relax in My adjusting care. Even though My hand may inflict pain, it is necessary to bring you into new health and recovery. I only wound to repair. Your adversary only wounds to destroy. Breathe in My breath. Relax in what I need to do. Understand My heart. Allow My hands to touch you where it hurts. Yes, you may feel a jolt and jerk, yet only for a moment and then the corrective path begins.

Come to My table often. Come into My care and you will see how I will cause you to stand straight and tall. It will be less tiring for you and you will be amazed at the ease in which your newfound alignment will cause you to travel. Where you were bent over, there will be a fresh tightness in your backbone to more effectively discern the adversary of your soul and your vision will be clearer as your head will be lifted up and the view will open up in greater width and expanse.

You will become more attune to My touch and soon the treatment will be complete and the season accomplished.

Yet, will it be finished? No, only ready for the next season of growth and transformation. When we are finished, My glory will be seen through and through and the sight of you will be stunning, full of grace and glory, ready to be My Bride.

CORRECT CALCULATIONS

When you are stretched beyond what you think your limit is, do you think I have stepped off the throne for a minute? The truth is, I want you to become stretched beyond what you think you can do. I want you to step out of your zone of comfort and self-reliance. How else will you find Me? How else will you learn to depend on Me? Fires and floods are the two ways I can get your attention when you are taking a personal detour away from My plans for you. I can almost always count on you quickly turning to Me in the midst of trouble. Sometimes, you would never come unless there was another episode of hardship.

If you can do it, you don't see your need for Me. So why are you surprised when the journey becomes wearisome? You can certainly count on moments when everything is out of your control. For when this happens, it's your first clue that you have been enrolled in your next course of the School of the Holy Spirit.

When you gave your life to Me, you also gave Me permission to grow and change you. This will not happen unless you learn how to rely upon Me for everything. I will allow some events to happen that seem chaotic, painful or out of your control. Difficulty can really be My grace extended to you in *disguise. No, you won't always see it that way, but the end result is maturity and knowing Me more intimately.*

The way in which you measure the difficult trials you go through must include the thought that I am taking you to the next level of Christ likeness. If you exclude this mindset, you will be drawn into places of doubt concerning My hand upon you. And this couldn't be further from the truth. My hand is continually upon you to encourage and guide you. My thoughts towards you are only for your good. The plans that I laid out for you when I created you are only plans that will bring you into righteousness, peace and joy in the Holy Spirit.

It's well worth your time to think in the manner that I have taught you. It's a valuable lesson to learn to not fight Me in the process of Christ likeness.

Your job is to surrender and yield. My job is to transform you into My likeness. And I'm going to get the job done, for I have promised that I will finish what I have begun in you.

Take heart, My beloved. I am proud of you. I know it's been a long journey so far, but trust Me. You're doing fine and it's going to be beautiful. Remember Who lives in you and walks beside you at all times. Remember the kind of love that is always shining upon you. Remember Who died for you. When was the last time someone died for you, anyway? Let Me bring comfort to you when you are full of sorrow and sadness. Let Me soothe your soul when anxiety wants to overtake you. Would you please allow Me to hold you when you are shaking with fear? Tough times will continue to encroach upon you, but the sooner you learn how to find Me when they come, the quicker you will begin passing the tests I put before you.

Learn to think from the end; for when all is finished, you and I win. Stop calculating without Me; for when you calculate with Me in the problem, the solution will always be in our favor.

$\mathcal{A}$ HEART SET ON PILGRIMAGE

Blessed are those whose strength is in you, who have set their hearts on pilgrimage. Psalm 84:5 (NIV)

And Jacob said to Pharaoh, "The years of my pilgrimage are a hundred and thirty. My years have been few and difficult, and they do not equal the years of the pilgrimage of my fathers."
Genesis 47:9 (NIV)

$\mathcal{G}$*od has not chosen to* exempt us from pain and trial. As we mature in Him, those same places of difficulty can begin to pale in comparison to the treasury of His friendship. Scripture calls us pilgrims. Pilgrims are on their way to a place. The new land we are traveling towards is heaven. In heaven, there will be no more tears, sorrow, death or pain *(Revelation 21:4)*. Just the thought of it brings a wave of joy over my tired soul.

The Scriptures tell us, *"Blessed are those whose strength is in You . . ."* *(Psalm 84:5)*. In this passage, the Hebrew word for *blessed* means "happy." I will be happy when I am in His strength. "The joy of the Lord *is* my strength." *(Nehemiah 8:10.)* Verse seven of Psalm 84 tells of how I will go from "strength to strength."

Therefore, we could maintain that when I am unhappy I am not existing in His strength. The other reason I might be unhappy is that my heart has not been set on pilgrimage. What could this mean? It could mean that I do not think that my present circumstance will ever end. It could mean that I feel stuck.

My friend, this, too, will pass. You are His pilgrim, and one day the scenery will change, and you will no longer be in this place. Set your heart on pilgrimage. Set your heart in the traveling mode. See the heavenly hills that await your arrival.

Pilgrims get tired. Their feet get sore. They get thirsty and hungry. Sometimes, pioneers walk in desert places for a long time. Other moments, the climb becomes so steep that the traveler wonders if he can even take the next step. A true pilgrim of God has the understanding that he will arrive safely to his destination. Why? Because he will find joy in the strength of His God, and his heart is set on pilgrimage. He knows that part of the cost is to continue when tempted to turn around. He realizes there's no looking back. He has a real understanding of the great cloud of witnesses cheering him on. Angels come alongside and minister to him from time to time *(Hebrews 1:14)*. A true pilgrim will go from strength to strength. One whose heart is set on pilgrimage is not perfect but has a perfect heart towards the Lover of his soul and will follow Him all the days of his mission on earth.

$\mathcal{R}$IDE MY WAVE

I tell you, now is the time of God's favor, now is the day of salvation.
2 Corinthians 6:2 (NIV)

It's a day of action. *It's a time to toss hesitation when I put something in front of you to do. I desire that you would not second-guess My words to you. Rather, step out. You hear My voice more than you realize. I am speaking and you are hearing. Step out and fling your fear. Adventure and surprises await you.*

I will use you as one with a surfboard waiting for the wave. For I will send you waves. You will see a wave and hear the call to get on your surfboard and ride that wave. My wave may feel intimidating in your natural mind, yet in your spirit you will have a witness that this is such a moment that new territory must be taken and it's time to stand up and go with it.

It's a time of acceleration and it's a time where I will multiply what you do. As the little boy offered his lunch, I took it and fed thousands. For there is an urgency for the gospel to get out and there is an urgency that people know of My love. You are my avenue of choice. You are my representation in the earth. You are who I have.

I could accomplish My purposes without you, but I don't want to. So, get on your surfboard and begin watching for the waves that I will bring you. It's time to be lifted up on my waves that I may take you into new places of influence and expansion. It's My joy and delight to bring you the wave and watch you stand up on your board and see where I will take you and how we will make history in the earth together. I will stretch and grow your faith in ways that will thrill your soul as you go forth into the new that I have for you.

STABILITY IN THY TIMES

And there shall be stability in thy times, abundance of salvation,
wisdom, and knowledge: the fear of Jehovah is thy treasure.
Isaiah 33:6 (AMP)

If there is ever a time and need for stability, it's now. There is no stability in this world system. There is no stability in our governments. There are no shining examples of stability in our school systems. The only place actual stability can be known on this earth is in the life of a true child of God.

A faithful person is going to stick out like a sore thumb in this ambiguous world. True fidelity can be achieved by becoming a student of the most stable person in the universe—God Almighty Himself.

The best part is that He lives in us. When my emotions are getting the best of me, I must train myself to open up His gift of stability. I must tap into the great wisdom and knowledge of the Ancient One who is as close as my next breath. I must fear Him and honor Him more than my sinful flesh and emotions.

The reason I can be stable is because I have learned to walk in the fear of the Lord. I have trained myself to remind my soul to be still, and know that He is God (see Psalm 4:10). I am stable because I function according to the wisdom of the Spirit, for the wisdom of His Spirit is foolishness to the wisdom of this world. The natural mind cannot conceive the matters of the Holy Spirit of God.

Do what brings stability. Meet with God regularly. Drape His Word around your soul often. Listen to His whispers of love and guidance. Stability will be a given as you fear the Lord and honor Him with your time.

Stop making an idol out of your fears, frustrations and disappointments. Become stabilized in Him. Let your cluttered mind return to peace and stability.

Hear His whispers now:

Child, I am your stability. Enter in. Let Me fill you and touch you and help you. I will calm your stormy heart. I will make your strength equal to your challenge. I will show you off. I will use you to help others find their stability in Me, but right now let Me envelop you and surround you. Today, let's see how you can find new footing to continue on your journey. Taste and see the stability I have for you for your time.

THE KING'S DAUGHTER

Who can find a virtuous woman? For her price is far above rubies.
Proverbs 31:10 (NKJV)

The word virtuous in the Hebrew might surprise you by its meaning. It means strength, might (especially warlike), efficiency, wealth, army, force, man of valor, host, substance, to show oneself strong, to display valor, leader of the army, the strength of a tree (spoken poetically of its fruits), leader of the army in the day of warfare (that is the day of sending the rod of Messiah's strength out of Zion when He rules in the midst of His enemies and strikes through kings in the day of His wrath).

This doesn't quite measure up to some of the preconceived ideas of a meek and quiet person, does it? This doesn't quite line up with someone who is a doormat for everyone to walk on. This isn't talking about someone who never rocks the boat.

A virtuous woman is a crown to her husband . . .
Proverbs 12:4 (KJV)

When you are who God made you to be as a woman, you resemble a crown upon the head of a king. You are a mark of victory. You are a symbol of regal dignity for your husband. Your head and leader is covered in strength, wealth and victory. A symbol of regal power sits upon his head when you are who God made you to be.

The Proverbs 31 woman is no wimp. She is a leader when hard times come. She is the first to tangle with the enemy when he approaches. When weakness would overtake her, she finds her strength in the Almighty One. She is as immovable as an oak, standing strong in the midst of adverse winds, always displaying fruit for others to partake. She is not afraid of war. She has the strength of a man of valor.

Woman of God, don't settle. Rise up today and take your place in the kingdom of God. Stop being wimpy and mushy. Stop cowering when it gets difficult. Be the one who will lead. Stop being a follower and stop waiting for someone else to do it. Now is your time. Today is the day of your rising. Shake the dust off yourself and arise into a new day with your King.

The Lord gives the command; the women who proclaim the good tidings
are a great host. Psalm 68:11(NASB)

*N*O ONE ELSE CAN MAKE YOUR SOUND

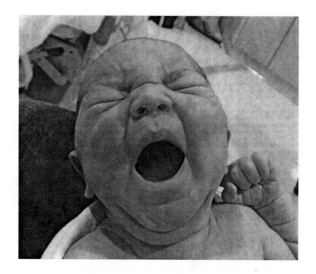

Let me tell you about two kinds of Christians. There are those who allow God to speak through their life and those who don't.

Consider this. Think of each of us as a trumpet in the Lord's mouth.

We go through trials and hardships that cause a polishing and can bring out the shine in us. Every so often, God takes us out of His case, examines us and makes sure we are assembled, cleaned and oiled. He asks us, "May I play you now?"

We are glad when the Lord picks us up and oils us so that we feel loved and valued, but we are sometimes content to stay in the safety zone of the case and just look good. The problem is that we never allow the Lord to raise us up to His mouth so He can blow through us, or we seldom give Him permission to strum on our strings that the world may hear His song through us. We cower when He turns to use us for what we were created to do. At times, we refuse His breath to blow through us, sounding an undeniable clarion call of His message to the world.

God created each one of us with a certain sound. He created us to be held in His hand and played. Very often, we are content to stay in the case. We are content to be shined and polished and even picked up every so often to be examined by Him, yet we refuse to be used for our full purpose. We disobey because we choose silence.

Listen to the voice of the One who crafted you:

My beloved, it's time to go beyond what you've known in Me and begin to let Me blow through you and use you to create a sound of My love in the earth. You were created to make My music. It's music from heaven. You have great potential to make a sound in the earth that is as unique as your personality, yet reflects My heart. No one else can make your sound.

What if all of God's people would allow Him to play His melody through them? What an orchestration of heavenly sound would fill the earth.

What kind of an instrument are you? One who is content to be used for show-and-tell purposes only? One whose only desire is to look good? Or are you one who is exclaiming, "Lord, play me, use me, blow through me and change the world through me. Make your music through me, I pray." Think of it. You are the instrument—He is the breath for you to make a sound. He is the One who will play your strings with beauty and loving kindness. He is the One who has the power to pick you up or set you down.

Just remember—no one else can make your sound.

THAT'S MY GOD

"God, the one and only—I'll wait as long as he says. Everything I hope
for comes from him, so why not?
He's solid rock under my feet, breathing room for my soul, an impreg-
nable castle: I'm set for life."
Psalm 62:5-6 (MSG)

Resting in my Savior is the only real answer for me. The deeper the rest, the less of a grip anything else can have on me. It's actually a very freeing place. God *is* in control. So, we can wait as long as He takes, right? YES. He's the Rock under my feet. He's the breathing room for my soul.

My confidence level will show in my trust of Him. As we grow, so do our storms and troubles. We must find faith to match the fury of whatever God allows our adversary to fling at us. If I am God's, I have nothing to fear. Earth can't have a hold on me. Satan cannot clench me. My flesh can't dominate me. Only if I give these things authority can they rule me. Whatever controls me has power over me. If God, then God. If my flesh, then my flesh.

Practice resting. I'm talking about a real composure of ease. The next time you are in a squeeze, make a conscious effort to go into that place with God. You know—the place where you park your fears and anxieties. You will be warmly greeted with His hand of fellowship. Where He is, fear can't be. Where He lives, evil can't practice.

One frigid Ohio morning, I had the privilege of taking a test on the way to work. I was given an opportunity to see if I could practice entering into His rest. I had a twenty-minute drive to work. My car was on empty the whole way there. First, I wanted to fear. "What if I run out of gas? It's only one degree out." I pictured myself walking on the side of the road, not properly dressed.

Then I decided that my only hope of making sure I reached my destination was to turn to God, the One in charge of my life's affairs. He gave me a gift. It was a mental picture of me at the pump, putting gasoline in my car. That meant I was going to make it. If He showed

me I would make it, then it must be true. I began to think on the picture He gave me and not focus on the picture of fear that wanted my attention very badly. I was then escorted into a place of rest, where my soul could breathe freely, and my faith took root. That's my God.

Guess what? I safely and uneventfully arrived at the gas station. Just as God showed me, I lived out the vision He gave me of pumping gas into my car.

When you are in a bind, look for what God is doing, align yourself with it and you will not be disappointed. Truly I am set for life.

THE REVOLVING DOOR

One day, I had an impression that I believe is from the Lord. I share it with you now:

THE PICTURE

I saw a picture of a revolving door with people stuck in it, going around and around. The revolving door led into a great corporate headquarters-type building. It was a tall, skyscraper structure, one of great expense and luxury. The problem was that very few were going into the building. Others were either continually going around in the revolving door or just watching from the outside of the door.

WHAT I HEARD

Many of My people are stuck in the revolving door going 'round and 'round. They have assumed that this is everything it means to serve Me. People in the revolving door going 'round and 'round are people who have become stagnant and fruitless in My kingdom.

Many times, I have come to you in your revolving door life and ministered to you. I have always come to you when you have cried out. Today, it's your turn to come to Me where I am—just beyond the revolving doors.

I summon you to step out where you haven't been. I am just beyond the revolving door. Come to Me this time. Step out of your stagnation. Step out of your defeat and into the new place that I have for you. There are many new dimensions in the Holy Spirit for you to discover. Some of My people are convinced that life in the revolving door is all there is on this earth. This couldn't be farther from the truth. There are new places in the Spirit to discover and explore. You have only scratched the surface of the threshold of what I have for you. There are dimensions in the Holy Spirit yet untapped by most of My children.

There are levels and floors for you to arise into as you step out of your revolving door. There are new views and sights for you to see that you would never imagine on your own.

Think of the scientists. Think how they study and observe and push through to new discoveries in the universe. I am continually allowing them to find new depths in the universe. They are discovering whole galaxies that no one ever knew existed.

I have planned for it to be the same, when it comes to the operation of My Spirit. There are whole spiritual galaxies yet to be discovered in My kingdom. Become a scientist in the Holy Spirit. Study, look, listen, probe, push, pursue . . . step out of your revolving door. Come to where I am this time. Yes, I will always come to you when you call out for Me, but in this moment, I am calling out for you to come to Me. Step out of the comfort zone. Step out into the unknown, yet not unknown by Me. Experience the new in Me.

There's so much more.

Time is running out. Time, that is, as you know it. The increasing challenge of living in this world requires stepping out of your revolving door. The degree of brightness in your witness in the earth will be hinging upon your choice to step into the new. The bolder your step into obedience, the brighter the light will shine through you so those who are coming into salvation can be led and see the path.

You should look more and more different from the world with each passing day.

Don't become entrapped in only the entrance of what I have for you. The entrance is only the place to come through into more. The revolving door is only a door into greater dimensions of what I have for you. Come now to Me and leave the stagnation of the revolving door.

Step out.

Listen.

Look.

Obey.

And the threshold will take you on over to new territory in My Holy Spirit. There are fresh abilities to overcome. There is new strength for the journey and a deeper closeness in My presence. Greater spiritual vision and insight await you, just beyond the revolving door.

Come on over to Me now. I await your arrival.

$\mathscr{P}$ENCILS, PEOPLE AND POINTS

$\mathscr{P}$*encils come in many different* sizes, shapes and colors. They are used in teaching elementary children how to write. They are put to use on test day. They are employed for art. They are tools on construction sites to mark measurements.

Indulge me here, and let's compare people to pencils. Different kinds of people have different points and purposes to their lives. The mark we leave on this world will depend upon a couple of factors. Were we sharpened when we became dull? Did we allow God to pick us up and use us in His master plan to teach, measure, create beauty or erase errors? Did we use our erasers? In other words, did we forgive others' mistakes and shortcomings? That's what forgiveness is—erasing the mistake so that it can no longer be seen.

What is your point, and is your point sharp so it can be legible when in use? Is your life legible, and is there a point to it? Good question, Lord. No pencil would be of any use without a point. Think of a Christian who has never been sharpened once. You can't even write with a pencil that has never been sharpened.

Are you available 24/7 (24 hours a day, 7 days a week) for God to pick you up, put you in His hand and communicate the message of His heart to the world through your "pencil"? When you make a mistake, or someone else makes a mistake, are you quick to use your eraser? When your point becomes dull, do you let Him sharpen you? Sharpening means that you might feel some pain and grinding, and there might be some loss of what you are in order to make room for the fresh and new. Don't you appreciate a fresh, newly-sharpened pencil? Likewise, there's nothing equal to a person who has been freshly made new by God in the great Heavenly Sharpener and available for His use.

WINTER SOLSTICE OF THE HEART

In 2010, the lunar eclipse coincided with the winter solstice for the first time in nearly 400 years. It was a day when we saw the light of the sun the least, coupled with a night when even the brightness of the moon was shortened. Let another six months pass, and we will enjoy once again the longest day of the year when summer solstice greets us once again.

The four seasons swing in and out. There is an ebb and flow with light and dark. We can always count on a rise and fall in temperatures. Therefore, we would do well to walk carefully and understand that there are days and seasons for all things. There are difficult days, less difficult days and even easy days.

The winter solstice could be compared to our most difficult days when the sunshine of God and all the evident blessings have shortened, and darkness seems to carry the trump card. Jesus had one of those days a time or two—a time when evil seemed to rule and the light of God seemed eclipsed. I can imagine that the night before He was crucified may have been one of those moments for Him.

Even when we see less of our natural sun, its presence is with us just the same. Even when our moon is eclipsed, its existence is sealed and intact. View from earth is temporarily hindered, yet the sun and the moon continue their existence right on, even when we can't see them. What *seems* real is really not real.

Saint, God is in you and around you no matter what you see or feel. His presence remains even in your lack of ability to perceive it. His presence remains in sunlight or at night. No matter the season or solstice of your life, there is no less or more of Him to be found than is right now. His existence is not determined upon your ability to feel Him. His being is not contingent upon your good or bad actions. He is the faithful and true. He is the everlasting God. He is the One who put the sun and the moon in their places. If creation preaches *(Romans 1:20)*, then take a lesson from the sun and the moon. God put them there for our warmth and light, yet we can go a step further in understanding God's presence. He is with us, no matter the weather or season in our life. His existence is constant despite the changing atmosphere of circumstances constantly swirling all around us.

Why be surprised when the light of His presence becomes eclipsed by other things? It will happen to us all. Every pilgrim upon His pathway will suddenly and most assuredly awaken to a day when the light has been shortened. Yet His mercy and grace greet us with a kiss each morning, arming us with all we need to travel in the dark.

Our companion, the Holy Spirit, has been sent to us for our comfort and to lead us into all truth *(John 16:13)*. Our understanding will fail us in the dark. Our very own emotions will trick us and alter our belief system in God if we permit them to do so. Our divine Guide is an all-weather Friend who will never forsake us, or leave us without support.

Has winter arrived in your heart? Has a chill come that shakes you to the bone? Are the negative wind chills blasting your being, making it next to impossible to function because of your frostbitten heart?

Take heart, dear one. Jesus invites you into His shelter. A warm fire has been prepared just for you and Him. He wishes to talk to you. He is waiting for your fellowship. The Holy One of Israel has instructions for you to not only survive but thrive in this winter solstice of your life. You are not alone in the chill. There are others in their winter season. It's a time to rest and regroup. It's a time to contemplate and meditate upon the Lover of Your Soul. Don't deny Him. He stands knocking at the door of your heart. Unburden your soul and answer the door. Ask Him to come in. He will hold you and love you and destroy the chill that wants to take you down.

> *"Two are better than one; because they have a good reward for their labor.*
> *For if they fall, the one will lift up his fellow: but woe to him that is alone when he falleth; for he hath not another to help him up."*
> *Ecclesiastes 4:9-10 (KJV)*

Jesus and you will have a good reward together. Open up your chilly heart, and soon winter will pass. If you close your heart to help from the Master, your winter season might become extended; and you may not survive it.

Winter comes to all of us, but remember it's only for a season. Spring is on its way. Winter will have to give birth to new life, colors and sounds.

ℰNGAGE IN PROPER FEAR

Unhealthy fear paralyzes. Fear of the unknown is what stops *you in your tracks from experiencing the next level of relationship with Me. There is a great fear factor in My people today. There is a fear of deeper realms of the Holy Spirit. There is a fear of "missing it." There is a fear of stepping out and becoming embarrassed. There is a fear of hearing the wrong voice.*

There is a fear of rejection. There is a fear of man. There is a fear of doing something odd or different from the status quo.

This is wrong fear—the fear that brings great shackles. This is the sort of fear that the adversary implants in you. The fear of the Lord has been replaced with the fear of man.

Healthy fear sets the captive free. Man has become elevated above the Lord in places of service and surrender. Surrender to self and others have come in where they have no place. Because of this, the work of the kingdom of God has suffered. Progress in your life has come to a subtle slowdown.

I am going to restore the fear of the Lord in My house. I am going to reteach what it means to be fearless. I am going to lead you and show you the healthier way in your journey with Me. For without the fear of the Lord in your life, you will become stagnant and neutral.

What is the fear of the Lord? The fear of the Lord is only the beginning of wisdom and understanding. When you understand your rightful place and My rightful place in your life, you will run with Me. You will walk and not faint. You will be infused with supernatural ability to be and act as a child of the King.

For too long, you have been bent down in your life, settling for crumbs when you could have had a feast in the Holy Spirit. The devil wishes for you to fear the things of My Holy Spirit. He knows that once you get a taste of the good wine, you will continue to crave and desire more of it. Surrender your mind, will and emotions to the Holy Spirit now. Surrender your vocal chords, feet and hands.

It will be an adventure that earthly-minded people never experience. Your natural mind will fight tooth and nail the things of the Spirit, but you must master it. Your mind must be mastered. Your will must be broken in My presence. Your personal will is the one thing that is your greatest hindrance.

When you believe a lie, then your will is formed accordingly. When you believe a truth, your will is also formed accordingly. Be careful what you believe, for it will form your future days with Me.

In My loving kindness, I am coming for you. I am coming to your rescue in the area of what you fear. For what you fear is nothing to fear at all, but what you don't fear is really the fear you need.

The fear of the Lord is to revere Me as the one and true Person of the universe who loves you alone for all that I have created you to be. The fear of the Lord will bring instant priority to your life. It will cause what really matters to surface and face you. Without the fear of the Lord operating in your life, dear one, you are destined to your own demise. Without it, you will remain in the ditch you now lie in. The fear of the Lord will take you places and grow you up in wisdom, stature, growth and maturity.

Come now, and give yourself to My presence and understanding. Engage in the proper fear. Put away the fear of man. Stop giving in to yourself. Lay down your fear of greater experiences in the Holy Spirit. It's what you truly need in this hour of trial and testing.

$\mathcal{B}$UT AS A RESULT. . .

We were crushed and overwhelmed beyond our ability to endure, and
we thought we would never live through it.
In fact, we expected to die.
But as a result,
we stopped relying on ourselves and learned to rely only on God, who
raises the dead.
2 Corinthians 1:8-9 (NLT)

There are moments of crushing upon the journey when you will
feel that you have gone beyond your ability to endure. There will come
times when your heart won't stop bleeding, and you begin to wonder

if you will survive this hellish season. The time seems to linger longer and longer, and you begin to wonder if it really *is* a season, or will it just make camp and stay forever upon your doorstep.

The Apostle Paul related very well to this place and lived to tell about it. He not only got through it but extracted the precious from the worthless. He said that, as a result, he stopped relying on himself and began relying upon God in ways he hadn't before. For if God can raise the dead, then He ought to be trusted with each and every trial, pain and difficulty. Paul literally thought at moments he was going to die. The sentence of death was in his thoughts, and he was thinking, "This is it. It's my time to go." But it was not. There was yet a work of trust that needed to be built into the walls of Paul's heart.

God knew it would take this great kind of a difficulty to break the hardness of Paul's heart. God could see the other side; therefore, He rescued Paul by permitting things that would be beyond his ability to endure. You can look at it two ways: God is mean, or God is loving. The truth is that God is loving, and we are the ones who are mean and hard-hearted by nature. This wisdom is understood only by the Holy Spirit. This way of thinking is foolishness to the worldly mindset. Without the Holy Spirit to teach us, this way of thinking is really upside down. No, God is not the author of evil.

Who knows how much we are truly protected from? Only eternity will reveal it.

Why are we not saved from crushing, overwhelming crisis moments? God loves us too much to leave us in our self-absorbed depravity. God knows the hardness and stubbornness of our hearts too much to leave us there. Come into agreement with God against your dark self. Leave self and cling to God in the fires of life.

When I rely upon myself and my own resources, I am only inviting more misery and hopelessness into my life. God will allow me to be crushed. God will permit certain difficulties to touch my "untouched" heart. He knows the folly of a self-relying soul. Therefore, because of His immense love for us, He gives assent for the rising rivers to attend our way. The Hand of Providence waves permission for the crushing to come down until we are broken in spirit. One who is broken is positioned for the hand of the Master to rebuild what has been resistant to His loving care. A broken spirit is something God will not ignore *(Psalm 51:17)*.

Not all pain will bring injury to us. Pain, allowed by our Creator, can assist us upon our journey with Him. It can propel us to the place (when we are finally willing) of intimacy and trust with the only true Lover of Our Soul. Tell your soul to trust Him today. Did you know you can talk to your soul that way?

> *Bless the LORD, O my soul: and all that is within me, bless his holy name. Psalm 103:1 (KJV)*

David told his soul to bless the Lord. Certainly, I can tell my soul, "Trust the Lord, and all that is within me trust His holy name." What will be the result of your crushing? What will be the result of your overwhelming state of mind?

You get to tell the ending of your story on this earth:

"However, as a result of all these things that happened to me . . ." (You fill in the rest.)

$\mathcal{T}$HE CRUCIBLE OF PRAISE

Let another praise you, and not your own mouth;
someone else, and not your own lips.
The crucible for silver and the furnace for gold,
but man is tested by the praise he receives.
Proverbs 27:2, 21 (NIV)

$\mathcal{P}$*raise is the act of* expressing approval, admiration or commendation. The Word of God is giving us a warning here in Proverbs. Do you feel the need to commend yourself to others? Don't. We are to keep quiet about ourselves. If something good needs to be said about us, let others be the ones to approve us. Picture someone picking up a flashlight and trying to shine it upon himself. This would be a pretty strange sight. However, if someone else were to pick up a flashlight and shine it on you, it wouldn't look as awkward or strange.

That's how praise works. Don't praise yourself. If you are deserving of some admiration, allow it to come from another's lips. If you feel the need to promote yourself in a boastful way, then there may be a need for some serious soul-searching. It always comes down to a matter of the heart with God. For God does, indeed, look at our hearts and our motives. Praise by others towards us is allowed by God, but be careful—it's a test. Praise is compared to a crucible. A crucible is a container in which substances are heated up to very high temperatures. It's an instrument of severe testing. Praise from others is an instrument of severe testing in us.

There are several ways that we will be approved by God. One way is here in the furnace of praise. You might not immediately think of praise as a test, but it really is. What do we do with praise when it comes our way? Do we put it on a stack of previous praises and become haughty and prideful? If this is the case, then we are surely failing our heavenly test.

Do you ever give someone a compliment, and he just passes it off? It feels as though your words were meaningless and fell to the floor when they came out of your mouth. We need to learn how to receive the praise of men. When someone compliments you, or praises you for something you have done, simply say, "Thank you." If you need to continue to appropriately pass the praise on to God, then do so. "Thank you. I am very grateful for what God has given me that I can share with others," would be a good way to respond. Then, inside, where does it go in your heart? As an inward prayer, give glory to Whom glory is due.

Do compliments feed your pride or keep you humble? When you know in your "knower" that no good thing is in you (in and of yourself), then humility will be at your side. We are to think no more highly or lowly of ourselves than what God has said about us.

When we are praised by men, then cower and feel undeserved, this is also a form of pride. To think any differently than what God thinks of you is a selfish, prideful attitude whether it's more highly or lowly than what He thinks of you. Each extreme is thinking more or less of yourself than you ought.

I can do all things through Christ who strengthens me.
Philippians 4:13 (NKJV)

Now listen to what Jesus Himself said:

By myself I can do nothing . . .. John 5:30a (NIV)

If Jesus said He could do nothing in and of Himself, then you can bet your boots that we are in the same spot. There is nothing good that comes from us that didn't first originate with the good God who lives within us.

"So, my very dear friends, don't get thrown off course. Every desirable and beneficial gift comes out of heaven." James 1:17 (MSG)

Keep yourself in godly perimeters. When you step out of His boundaries, then you step out of reward and favor from God. With God, we can do anything; without Him, we can do nothing. What is the conclusion? When you are praised, praise Him. When you are spoken well of, whisper to your soul, "God is the source of anything good that comes from me." Stay humble and pass the test.

WHY IS MY PAIN PERPETUAL?

Your words were found, and I ate them; and Your words were to me a joy and the rejoicing of my heart, for I am called by Your name, O Lord God of hosts.

I sat not in the assembly of those who make merry, nor did I rejoice; I sat alone because Your [powerful] hand was upon me, for You had filled me with indignation.

Why is my pain perpetual and my wound incurable, refusing to be healed? Will you, indeed, be to me like a deceitful brook, like waters that fail and are uncertain?

> *Therefore, thus says the Lord [to Jeremiah]: If you return [and give up this mistaken tone of distrust and despair], then I will give you again a settled place of quiet and safety, and you will be My minister; and if you separate the precious from the vile [cleansing your own heart from unworthy and unwarranted suspicions concerning God's faithfulness], you shall be My mouthpiece. [But do not yield to them.] Let them return to you—not you to [the people]. Jeremiah 15:16-19 (AMP)*

The Hebrew word for *pain* is *kĕ'eb,* which means pain (mental and physical), sorrow. The Hebrew word for *perpetual* is *netsach,* which means eminence, strength, victory, enduring, everlasting.

Jeremiah was honest with God about his place. He couldn't understand why. Why won't this pain go away? Why does the strength of it overpower me and secure victory over my mind and body? Pain keeps coming, and there is no end in sight. In all reality, sometimes we are bombarded with events that just keep toppling us over in sadness and sorrow. Sometimes, it's all we can do to come up for a breath of air.

Eventually, we come nose to nose with God. We turn to Him; and since He is in control, we find ourselves wondering where He was when all hell broke loose in our lives.

Jeremiah was remembering former days of finding God's words and eating them. Jeremiah remembered a former day of joy and rejoicing in his heart. He couldn't understand how he landed in this place of wounding and pain. He felt stuck. His heart felt terminal and incurable.

The prophet of God turns to God in frustration. He wonders if God has left him in his misery. Disappointment swarmed all around his heart. He even wondered if God had lied to him. Jeremiah was in a pit. The God who had sustained him seemed far away and distant.

After Jeremiah laid out his soul before God, the Lord had an answer. The Lord's first words to his suffering servant are, "If you return . . ."

Jeremiah had turned in the wrong direction and had walked away from God in his thinking. Wrong thinking will escort you down a path that will distance you from God in your mind and thoughts. There's only one solution—return. Return to where you were when you got off track.

It's simple. Return to God, and He will return to you.

Draw near to God and He will draw near to you.
Cleanse your hands, you sinners;
and purify your hearts, you double-minded.
James 4:8 (NASB)

God will not be a part of our pity parties. He has no use for them. When we attend our pity party, we enter into a zone that puts us right on the radar of our adversary. God knows it, and He condemns it. Distrust and despair are kindred spirits that come with a vengeance when we have placed the pain and wounding of our hearts upon the throne. God will not share His throne with anyone or anything.

God told Jeremiah to give up his mistaken tone of distrust and despair. He was saying, in essence, "Come on, Jeremiah, you know better than this. Come back to Me, and enter into the place of quiet and safety once again. I can't use you as My mouthpiece when you are in this place."

We must *separate* ourselves from the dirty, vile thinking of unbelief. We must look to the precious truth of who God is and embrace it with holy fear, no matter what we're feeling in our bodies or emotions. The Holy Spirit must rule in our lives if we are to remain in sweet fellowship and be useful to our God.

He loves us too much to allow us to find a place of peace and quiet while we are in a place of unbelief and distrust. We can't have it both ways. Peace and quiet are the fruits of intimacy with Him. Torment and confusion are the fruits of listening to our own untrusting emotions and pain.

Ignoring your pain and suffering is not the solution. Wallowing in your pain and suffering is not the cure, either. Rather, returning to Him in your pain and suffering is the right choice for advancing forward and experiencing His healing oil all over your tired, bleeding heart.

Return and find healing. Return and find rest. Return and find peace. His welcome banner awaits you.

THE WARFARE OF STILLNESS

Stillness: motionless, stationary, undisturbed, silent, calm.

. . . Stand still, and I will hear what the Lord will command . . ..
Numbers 9:8 (KJV)

The Hebrew word for this word *still* is the word *amad*. It means take one's stand, remain, endure, be in a standing attitude, delay, persist, to station.

Why is it so difficult to station myself quietly? When things are out of my control, I will always be tempted to do this or that in order to gain control. Just when I need to take my stand will come the greatest temptation to take action.

Hey, Lord!—[waving arms]—I'm over here, can't you see me? Are you doing anything? S.O.S. Lord!—[waving arms again].

There is power in being quiet. There is warfare in stillness. There is authority in remaining in Him. Demons must bow to me when I am enduring in Christ. When I need to hear His orders, my directions are to become stationary. I am to stand at attention so I can hear. I am to remain until I get my next assignment. I am to do what I was last commanded to do until I hear otherwise.

Delaying activity on my part opens up my ability to hear more clearly.

Am I waiting for the outcome of something? Ruth 3:18 (KJV) has a word of advice for me:

Then said she, sit still, my daughter, until thou know how the matter will fall . . .

In 1 Samuel 9:27 (KJV) here it is again:

. . . but stand thou still a while, that I may shew thee the word of God . . .

When I am in a motionless position, I am really positioning myself for the showers of the Holy Spirit upon me in that place. When I quiet myself, comfort from My Father can enter into my bruised and bleeding heart. I am in great need to remain in Him. I need to persist in speaking to my soul that God is in control. Don't allow your soul to throw a temper tantrum similar to a two-year-old in the aisle of a grocery store. Say to your soul often, "Be still and know that He is God" (see Psalm 46:10).

Saint, this is the way through—there are no shortcuts to growing up. There are no mountain hoppers in God. There are just mountain climbers. On your journey, there will be moments when you have lost your way. These are times to stop. He may tell you to take a couple steps backwards because you've stepped off the path. He may say to rest awhile and regain your strength. He may say, "Keep walking. There's a place for you to rest just around the corner."

The important thing is to hear His voice, and to hear His voice requires an uninterrupted place of quietness.

$\mathcal{L}$OOK WHO'S CHEERING YOU ON

Do you see what this means—all these pioneers who blazed the way, all these veterans cheering us on? It means we'd better get on with it. Strip down, start running—and never quit! No extra spiritual fat, no parasitic sins. Keep your eyes on Jesus, who both began and finished this race we're in. Study how he did it. Because he never lost sight of where he was headed—that exhilarating finish in and with God—he could put up with anything along the way: Cross, shame, whatever. And now he's there, in the place of honor, right alongside God. When you find, yourselves flagging in your faith, go over that story again, item by

item, that long litany of hostility he plowed through. That will shoot
adrenaline into your souls! Hebrews 12:1-3 (MSG)

Don't ever entertain the thought that you are alone in your walk
with Jesus. Did you know that there is a large heavenly host watching
you and cheering you on? It's those saints who faced their giants and
prevailed. They might have lost their lives on earth, but they didn't skip
a beat when it came to living to their fullest potential here. God is the
one who said when they were to take their last breath on earth and their
first breath in eternity.

We have David, the giant slayer. Then there's Deborah, a judge of
Israel. Think about Joseph, whose life of extreme emotional and physical
pain propelled him to second in command of Egypt because he stayed
the course with his God. What about Daniel, a young man whose fear
of God far surpassed the fear of man or beast? Consider Stephen, who
in his final breaths during his stoning, interceded for his persecutors that
God would forgive them. Paul, the apostle, landed himself in prison
many times, beaten and persecuted for his unswerving faith. The line-up
goes on. Study it out for yourself. Hebrews 12 is the hall of fame for
showcasing many who walked in faith.

This is just the tip of the iceberg when it comes to the heavenly cloud
of witnesses surrounding you today. Think of your life, for a moment,
as a playing field with grandstands all around. You are in the fight for
your life. You are wrestling with your soul. You are battling powers and
principalities that you cannot see with your natural eyes. You may be
tired today. You may be ready to just give up. You may be bent over in
emotional pain. Confusion may be circling your mind like a swarm of
bees on the attack.

Take heart, dear saint of God. There is a huge cloud of witnesses
surrounding you today. Listen for their cheer. Quiet, now—do you hear
it? Tell your soul to be still. I hear it. They are calling your name. They

say, "We did it, and you can too. We found our God to be faithful to His every word to us, and you will find the same thing."

You are not alone in your tribulation. You have the Holy Spirit inside you. You have the ministering angels specifically assigned to you now. Last, but not least, there is a whole throng in heaven watching, waiting and cheering you on.

Take heart, my friend. Be comforted by the company around you. They know what it means to endure great perplexity. Those who are now with God in heavenly places enjoying their rewards salute you. You are bound with them. You are connected and fastened to them in the Holy Spirit. Read their stories. Be involved in the pain and hardship they endured while on earth. Allow their stories to inspire you. It's all written down for your example. All who faced death for their faith are watching you and cheering you on.

God has not left you powerless or without example. You have everything you need today *for* today. You will have everything you need tomorrow *for* tomorrow. Now get up and strengthen yourself in the Lord. God will not visit your pity party. He is, however, happy to throw your provision party. There are wonderful provisions for you today. Keep running the race, my friend. Run like the wind. Run because you are a winner.

The real party is yet ahead of you. Heaven will be such a holy celebration of sweet victory—the eternal party of the ages. Our greatest celebrations on earth will pale in light of what's ahead for the saint who endures to the end.

STUDY/DISCUSSION QUESTIONS ON "LESSONS IN FAITH"

1. As a believer, why do we sometimes give our emotions more authority over us than necessary?

2. How can a "dark night of the soul" season (suffering in any way) be helpful to the child of God? Find a Bible verse to back up your answer.

3. Read John 7:37. What does going to Jesus and getting a drink from Him look like for you?

4. Think of a time when you saw or knew something in the spirit (Holy Spirit revealed) before it was ever seen in the natural realm. How was this helpful to you in your relationship with the Lord? List a Bible story or a verse that backs up this spiritual truth.

5. Why do you think God is so intrigued with light? Remember He said "let there be light" several days before He even created the sun and the moon. Share a meaningful verse about the light of God.

6. Read Psalm 18:11. Ask the Holy Spirit what insights He may have for you and share them.

7. Think of a time in your life when God didn't remove a situation that was difficult. It was a time when He asked you to go straight through it. How did you grow and benefit from that season? Were there any special verses that became stepping stones to help you get through it?

8. What is a good way to measure your true maturity in God?

LESSONS IN HOPE

May your unfailing love rest upon us, O LORD, even as we put our hope in you. Psalm 33:22 (NIV)

"Hope sees the invisible, feels the intangible and achieves the impossible."
-Helen Keller

PRACTICING BEGGARY

Thus says the Lord: Stand by the roads and look; and ask for the eternal paths, where the good, old way is; then walk in it, and you will find rest for your souls. Jeremiah 6:16 (AMP)

Sometimes, I just need to stop. I need to tarry. I need to cease my mindless activities in order to look. I need to look and see where I have lost confidence and hope. I need to question my habits. Where is the course of my life? I need to stop and do some pondering and serious thinking. Am I on the right road, or did I take a wrong turn somewhere?

In the Hebrew, the word *look* is the word *ra'ah*. Part of its meaning is "to look at each other, to face." It seems the Lord could be saying, "Child, look at Me. Turn around and face Me." If you have children, have you ever told them to look at you when you were talking to them? Point made.

And "ask."

This word *ask* actually means "practice beggary." Muse on that for a minute. I must practice begging God for the right way. I must look for the "old" path. It's the path that has no beginning or end. I need to search out the eternal path so I can have true life. Saint, there is a road perfectly formed for you. It's the course for your life.

When you find the path, and begin walking in it, the promise straight from the mouth of God for you is this:

"You will find rest for your souls."

A true condition of rest will come upon you. It will feel light upon your shoulders. It will invade your mind and soothe your emotions. It's laid out here in the Word of God for us. He speaks to us today, but the sad part is the rest of the verse. The people to whom He spoke in Jeremiah's day did not respond very well to the Word of the Lord. Here is the rest of verse 16:

"But they said, we will not walk in it!"

Stop and stand by your road today. Search out the ancient path. I pray that when you find it, you will walk in it. The holy rest of God Almighty is on its way to saturate your mind and heart.

Renewed hope and direction bring forth a restful ease in our hearts, for in the rest we find Him. There is ease in His presence. There is no striving and struggling when we walk the ancient pathway with Him, just restful fellowship and satisfaction saturated in hope for tomorrow.

THE WORM WILL FLY

For the one who loves Jesus Christ with all his heart, this is the true picture of what God is doing in his life. One day, we will emerge with a new body of splendor. We will come forth as the butterfly, no longer bearing resemblance of a lowly worm. In that day, the worm will fly. We will shed this earthly shell and enter into glory where there will be no more sin and no more suffering. Beloved, you have all the reason to entertain thoughts of hope.

> *But we all, with unveiled face, beholding as in a mirror the glory of the Lord, are being transformed into the same image from glory to glory, just as from the Lord, the Spirit. 2 Corinthians 3:18 (NASB)*

The worm spins the cocoon. This can be compared to our state before salvation. Before we are saved, we are the worms. We are lowly, and we crawl on the ground; but when we enter into the work of the cross through the salvation of our souls, we begin a process of staggering transformation. It's a process of sanctification. It's the holy activity of working out this newfound salvation from God. What will emerge will not resemble the worm at all.

> *. . . in a moment, in the twinkling of an eye, at the last trumpet; for the trumpet will sound, and the dead will be raised imperishable, and we will be changed. 1 Corinthians 15:52 (NASB)*

Until then, we are always under the watchful eye of our heavenly Father. He is seeing to it that we are in a continual process of transformation, readying us for the day when we will be the very picture of  Him. The butterfly begins as a mere worm. Then comes the transfiguring process. The lowly is changed into the majestic. Similarly, we enter salvation just as we are, but God cleanses us and applies the righteousness of Jesus to us. We then enter into our metamorphose season. I'm so glad God sees the final state of our condition. He knows the squeezing and pressure we must have in order to accomplish this great transforming—mostly hidden—work. For it is not yet known by us what we will be. We see only the difficulties and struggles. If God would shorten the time of the cocoon, we would die before we were fully developed.

Friend, I don't know what you are facing today. Maybe you are in one of the biggest trials of your life. Maybe you have entered a dark night of the soul season. Possibly you are in a wintertime. All your green leaves have fallen off, and there is a great dormancy of ministry and fruitfulness. Are you in great sorrow or grief? No matter what state you are in, if you belong to Him, *it is not in vain.*

You are in the chrysalis of this earthly life. There are deep, hidden transformations happening to you right now. There will be no recognizable parts of your old nature when God is finished with you. He is after beauty, grace and liberation. This can come only out of times of restriction, darkness and yielding to the cross of Jesus Christ.

Don't quit. Rest in His plan. Stand firm, and don't fight the process; for the glory of your latter state will not even compare to the former *(Haggai 2:9).* The worm will one day fly with great beauty, liberation and splendor.

*Y*OUR SURVIVAL KIT

. . . rejoicing in hope, persevering in tribulation, devoted to prayer,
Romans 12:12 (NASB)

REJOICING IN HOPE

Hope is needed to get through something difficult.

Paul tells us to rejoice in the bright side of hope. Rejoice at the onset of the smell of trouble. Keep your hope. Don't lose sight of it. You need hope. Let it be your companion, always. Hope is not wishful thinking. When one is in Christ, hope is the lifeline. Hope is the lifeboat to help us stay afloat.

Hope deferred makes the heart sick. Proverbs 13:12 (NIV)

When our hearts are sick, life's sorrows and tribulations will seem ten times worse. Keep your heart well. Keep hope. Why keep hope? Because when it's all said and done, we win.

PERSEVERING IN TRIBULATION

In the original language, *perseverance* means to bear bravely and calmly ill treatments.

God will give you the power to be brave in tribulation. God will give you the ability to be calm in the storm. When God tells us something to "be," then in Him we are able. In Him we can do it. To persevere means to stay the course and see the thing through to the end.

Saint, there is a finish line, and there is a prize for those who finish. There remains, then, the need for hope and perseverance. Ill treatment is part of this earthly life. God has not chosen to make you exempt. So, go on through your season of difficulty with the finish line in mind. Go on, now. Don't give up, but keep walking and running. Crawl, if you must, but keep on just the same.

DEVOTED TO PRAYER

There is a need in you and me to be in communion with God all day long. A normal Christian life means continual conversation with God. Prayer is simply a two-way dialog with God. Let's not make it something it's not. One doesn't need to find a "prayer closet" just to talk with God. (However, taking special time just to be with Him is important.) You have a perfect "prayer closet" within the confines of your own heart. Talk to him in the marketplace as you are going about your way. He's with you always. He's beside you all the time. Take time to remember your constant friend and companion. Beware of busying yourself to the point of forgetting He's there.

What a package deal for us. What a kit for survival— hope, perseverance and prayer.

Friend, stir up the hope that is yours in Jesus Christ. Persevere in your present time of difficulty. I ask the Father that He would show you the importance of communing with Him all day long. May you be devoted to prayer.

$\mathscr{H}$EAVENLY
ESCALATORS

From the end of the earth will I cry to You, when my heart is over-
whelmed and fainting; lead me to the rock that is higher than I [yes, a
rock that is too high for me]. Psalms 61:2 (AMP)

$\mathscr{S}$*ometimes, we find ourselves in* spots where we feel we are at the
extremity of our endurance. We are at the far border of what we can do,

express, think or feel. The place is extreme—maybe as far away from sanity as you have ever felt. You are on the outskirts of what should be normal. Your position is on the outside looking in. Your understanding is nowhere to be found. Logic has run away while emotions are running all over you. Your thinking fails you. However you want to describe it, you are overwhelmed and fainting in heart.

In those moments, it is critical to cry out to God. The psalmist is our perfect example of what to do. He says, "*I will*" go to God.

Now, my friend, is the time to engage your will.

Be determined enough not to let this drag you through the muck and mire day after day. Get into the throne room of grace and cry out to Him until you find relief.

This word *cry* is a Hebrew word *qara*, meaning to call, call out, recite, read, cry out, proclaim, and utter a loud sound, to summon, invite or call for.

Call out to God in a loud voice. Read His Word back to Him. Proclaim your situation to Him. Summon God into your flood. Let the tears usher you right into His throne room as your heart calls for His attention. It's a classic case of deep calling out to deep—the depths in you calling out to the depths of your God. It's an invitation for God to invade your fainting heart.

Inquire of Him to lead you. Ask for the pathway out of your emotional distress and trauma. Seek Him that you may advance in the right direction. Engage the Lord to shepherd you through this difficult place.

Where do you want Him to lead you?

You need a heavenly escort to the Rock that is higher than you.

In essence, your supplication is, "Lord, raise me up from this place. Lift me up to where You are. Cause me to stand straight and tall again. Remove me from this valley vision and cause me to be seated with You where You rule and reign. Put me on Your heavenly escalator and transport me to the top where the view is clear—a place where I will see and think correctly once again. It's an abode hidden from my natural eye but in plain view to my spiritual eye. There is renewed hope and vision in Your dwelling place."

This may seem dramatic, but I believe we serve a dramatic God. I once heard Beth Moore, a well-known teacher of the Word, say that God is the King of drama. Just read your Bible, and it won't be long 'til you run into a story where a sea was parted, a dead person came back to life, water was turned into wine or something of that sort. Just a flip through the book of Psalms will take you on a journey with some who knew how to be desperate and serious in their excursion with God.

Your life is meant to be lived out to the fullest. That means you should experience the amplitude of joy as well as the profoundness of sorrow and suffering. Don't be afraid of extremes when it comes to loving and serving God. There is a certain kind of relationship that God desires to have with you. It is one of intimate fellowship no matter your position in life—be it the valley of suffering or the mountaintop of elation. He wants to share it all with you. Out of this kind of fellowship with the Master comes the sweet, satisfying relationship that you need with Him. No other relationship will compare to the one you share with Jesus.

Whatever you are going through right now, find that heavenly escalator right up to the High Rock.

I dare you to ascend in your hope today.

FULL CIRCLE

GRIEF

GRIEVING LOSS AND WHAT WAS
WHAT WAS . . . IS NO MORE
YET WHAT IS HAS COME
READY OR NOT
WAVES OF SADNESS OVER AND OVER
CURTAINS PULLED
PULLED SOLITUDE

TEARS

THEY MUST FLOW
THEY WILL DO THEIR WORK IN THE SOUL LIKE THE RAIN
LIKE A RIVER
LIKE A WATERFALL
A CLEANSING FLOW
THROUGH THE HEART AND THROUGH THE SOUL

COMFORT

*FOR THE MOMENT IT'S WHAT'S NECESSARY
TO SURVIVE … TO KEEP HOPE … TIME MUST PASS
BUT ONLY AFTER IT HAS STOOD MOTIONLESS
FOR A SEASON
HEALING IS OFFERED HEALING IS EMBRACED THEN . . .
STEPPING FORWARD AGAIN STRONGER
DEEPER
MORE COMPASSIONATE*

MINISTRY

*STRONGER NOW PAIN DIMINISHED
EMOTIONS HEALED
HERE COMES ANOTHER WITH SORROW AND TEARS
THERE'S A WEALTH INSIDE ME FOR
THE SORROWING ONE
I HAVE BEEN EMPOWERED TO COMFORT
BECAUSE I WAS COMFORTED
I WAS TOUCHED NOW I TOUCH ANOTHER*

**THIS IS THE CIRCLE OF LIFE THIS IS LIVING
GIVING WHAT WE HAVE BEEN GIVEN
IMPARTING THE LIFE GOD HAS LAVISHED UPON US**

Blessed be the God and Father of our Lord Jesus Christ, the Father of mercies and God of all comfort, who comforts us in all our affliction so that we will be able to comfort those who are in any affliction with the comfort with which we ourselves are comforted by God. 2 Corinthians 1:3-4 (NASB)

SOAK YOURSELF IN THE FEAR OF GOD

Let not thine heart envy sinners: but be thou in the fear of the Lord all day long. For surely there is an end; and thine expectation shall not be cut off. Proverbs 23:17-18 (KJV)

Do you ever wonder if God is really looking? I mean, sometimes it seems that those who love sin are the ones prospering. Do you ever wonder if God sees the injustice in this world?

191

I think we all have thought these thoughts at one time or another. Possibly God knew that, so he had King Solomon pen these words in Proverbs for our encouragement. We have a tendency to calculate the whole according to everything we are seeing at the moment. This is a grave mistake. God sees it all from the beginning to the end. We see it all from history that we have learned to the present moment of our lives. God tells us to remember that there is an end. There will be that final day when God pulls the curtain on everything we have experienced up until that point. No more waking up in the morning. No more reports of murder in the news. No more rapes. No more starvation. No more injustice of any kind. God will probably stand up and announce something like, "Okay, folks, this is the last day of earth as you have known it."

Until then, God has given us a gift:

HOPE

Don't for a minute envy careless rebels; soak yourself in the Fear- of-God—That's where your future lies. Then you won't be left with an armload of nothing. Proverbs 23:17-18 (MSG)

Soak yourself in the Fear of God.

This is crucial to hanging on to hope when our circumstances are dictating other messages to us. This is fundamental to winning in the battleground of our mind. When we soak ourselves in the fear of God, we will prioritize His Word above anything we are feeling or seeing in the natural. We will be able to rise above whatever is pulling us earthward.

The mentality of the world calculates what it can see, feel and touch right now. Our standard of living as a Christian is so very different, or at least it should be. We have been given the assignment of living, not according to what we are seeing with our natural eye but according to what God has said in His Word. We have the Holy Spirit saying, "I know this looks difficult and confusing, but I am working and networking something far beyond what you can think or ask," or, "I have heard your cry, and I am working out the answer—trust and wait upon Me," or, "Your timing is now, but My timing is not yet."

Fear God. Value His thoughts and words above all else. When it's all said and done, remember the end of Proverbs 23:18 (KJV):

And thine expectation shall not be cut off.

There are really no risks in putting all your hope in God. Don't add up the numbers just yet. He is working. He is continually networking. He is causing all the affairs of your life to work together for good. He is keeping extremely accurate records every time there is a rape, abuse, murder, etc. He knows about every time you are sinned against personally.

There is so much truth to the adage, "It ain't over 'til it's over." We have not crossed the finish line of time as of yet. There are people yet to be born. There are people who will go to their graves every day. We are not at the end of all time yet.

So, the next time you wonder if God is really keeping track, just stop and remind yourself—because you have soaked yourself in the fear of God—that one day, everything as we know it will have an end. One day, God will have written the last line in the book of world history, and He will write the words: **THE END.**

Then all the reasons why you kept hoping will finally surface. Faith will give way to sight. Hope will give way to the tangible, continual presence and reward of your heavenly Father. The devil and all who rejected Jesus Christ will get their just punishment, and those in Christ will go on to glory for their eternal reward. The current days as we know them will be no more.

$\mathcal{P}$ITY PARTIES OR PROVISION PARTIES?

But God, Who comforts and encourages and refreshes and cheers the depressed and the sinking . . . 2 Corinthians 7:6a (AMP)

$\mathcal{A}$ren't you glad God has a plan when we're depressed? Isn't it good to know that God knows what to do when we are sinking in life's sea of hardships? He hasn't left. Nothing takes Him by surprise. He knows it all from the beginning to the end.

We get agitated. We get surprised by hardship. We get sideswiped by sorrow and pain. We get impatient and sometimes don't even want God's help. Our rebellious sin nature kicks in and we're "off to the races" in our own pathway of deception and destruction.

Trial, pain, sorrow, frustration, depression, anger, tribulation—all of these will hit us at one time or another. We are the bull's-eye for those kinds of arrows. You see, God is going to allow trials to come our way that are much bigger than we could ever handle. If He didn't, I'm convinced we would never see our need for Him.

Have you been targeted for some difficult challenge today? I want to tell you that God has comfort, encouragement and refreshing for you today. God desires to cheer you up.

Whose perspective are you walking in today—yours, the devil's or God's?

It's kind of a no-brainer. When you believe your thoughts or the devil's thoughts over God's thoughts, it will always get you in trouble. We will always end up in the ditch when we accept lies for the truth; but when we adopt the truth for the truth, we are grabbing onto a Holy Life Preserver.

Sometimes when I have been in deep, dark places of pain or despair, I have cried out to God in this manner:

Lord, if you don't come and rescue me from this place, I will be here forever! I am powerless to help myself; and if You don't come and get me, I'm not sure I will make it.

You know what? He has come to my rescue every time. I know because I have spoken with Him in that place more than once in my life.

The problem is that we have to *want* to be rescued. We have to *want* help. We have to *want* the comfort zone of trouble to be removed. Did

I just say comfort zone of trouble? Yes. We can become comfortable with our zone of unhealthy living. Fear of anything different can serve as a blockade to the new that God wants to bring. *We must start waving that S.O.S. flag before God's face.* We have to reach out for the Rope of Heaven so He can pull us in and comfort us. His rope of hope will pull you from the pit.

Remember, God won't do what *we* can do, and we *can't* do what only God can do.

We co-labor with Him on this journey. We have all of heaven on our side. God has given us a car, but we have to put the key in the ignition and turn it on to go. We have been given everything we need for life and godliness on this earth *(2 Peter 1:3)*. We just have to reach for it and use it.

God will not come to our pity parties. However, He loves to come to our rescue and escort us to His great provision parties.

REAL LIVING IS . . .

. . . embracing all the little moments of life, experiencing all the emotions God created you to experience and growing in love with the Creator of the universe.

. . . forgiving people when they have wronged you, getting down to the "nitty-gritty" of connecting with people, going beyond the surface and learning what makes a person really tick.

. . . raising a family, then opening the door and releasing the children to engage the world for themselves.

. . . when suddenly there is an empty nest, and you look over and see your faithful spouse. There are new adventures on the horizon.

. . . when God brings a real friend.

. . . entering into deep grief when there is loss in your life, letting the tears flow without encumbrance, remembering what was and how beautiful it was.

. . . when you find yourself alone, and you take pleasure in who you are, and you enjoy who you are, and it's okay.

. . . tapping into the power of the Holy Spirit when you have fallen down, finding a hand of a friend reaching out to you to help you up and brushing the dirt off from your fall.

. . . walking in the woods and inhaling the sweet woodsy air, feeling the grains of sand between your toes as you stroll along the Atlantic beach, smelling the sweet pine in North Carolina, listening to the swaying treetops as the wind whips up a storm, losing your breath in the high altitudes of the Rockies.

. . . giving birth—to a child . . . to a dream . . . to a vision.

. . . not copied. You either experience it or you miss it.

. . . understanding the heights of sheer joy, and dancing when the moment requires great celebration.

. . . knowing the discipline of quietness and silence.

. . . speaking the language of love—the spoken word, the loving touch, the giving of a gift, the offering of time, the act of serving.

. . . being content with the moment; making the most of the moment, for a moment is really all that you have.

. . . knowing when to let go and when to hold on.

. . . preparing for death. Death is part of life, and you will land upon its doorstep one day, unless Jesus comes first.

. . . discovering why you were created in the first place—then doing it.

. . . staying consistent by being faithful to God, family and friends.

. . . never letting go of hope no matter what the circumstance, no matter if all hell is breaking loose around your feet.

. . . being an intimate friend of Jesus.

. . . what it's all about.

RESCUED FROM YOUR PERSONAL HELL

He was despised and forsaken of men, A man of sorrows and ac-
quainted with grief; And like one from whom men hide their face
He was despised, and we did not esteem Him. Isaiah 53:3 (NASB)

Webster's American Family Dictionary defines reject this
way: refuse to have, take, use, recognize; to refuse to accept or admit;
to discard as useless or unsatisfactory; to eject; vomit; to cast out or off;
something or someone that is rejected, as an imperfect or unwanted
article.

Rejection can be one of the most painful experiences of our lives.
When we are cast off, there is something that just cuts us to our core.
When we are devalued as a person, it can shake us to our foundation.
When we are betrayed by someone who we thought loved us—how can
you describe that sort of pain? It's very hard to even explain with words
the caliber of pain that comes flooding into us.

To be left alone is a frightening experience. To be ruled out as odd
or useless and imperfect can be one of the most horrendous ordeals.

We were created with a need to love and be loved. When we do not experience that, there is a gaping hole that will be filled one way or another. There will be an insecurity about us that will cause us even more pain and rejection.

Sorrow: Distress caused by loss, disappointment, misfortune.

Grief: Keen mental suffering or distress over affliction or loss; sharp sorrow; painful regret, trouble; difficulty.

The sorrow of loss, disappointment or misfortune can also grip us in a deep winter chill. The grieving process itself can take years, depending upon the relationship with the person lost. Oh, the depths of the human soul. God created us with great care. We were created to think and feel very deeply. We are created in His image. Our God is a very deep thinker. The well of His emotions and feelings is limitless.

None of us have been able to escape the winds of sorrow and rejection in one form or another. The ultimate experience of rejection and sorrow was saved for Jesus Christ. It was our sorrows and rejections that weighed Him down that day. It was the sorrows and rejections of the whole world. Just stop and let that sink in a bit. Verse 4 goes on to tell us, *"Surely He hath borne our grief and carried our sorrows."*

Our physical and mental pains were upon Him that day. There is no difficult thing in our life that has not been carried on the back of our Savior.

Have you been despised? Have you been rejected? Are your sorrows, like sea billows, rolling? It was upon your Savior that day. He was resolutely bearing it for you.

You belong at the foot of the cross for your healing and relief. There is healing, relief and forgiveness found on the bloody, scourged back of Jesus Christ. There is peace and well-being found in the bloody, nail-pierced hands of Jesus Christ. There is a healing balm produced by His bloody, thorn- pierced brow. There is eternal life for you because of His bloody, brutal death. It's all been paid. *You have been provided for in full.* There is nothing missing, nothing lacking in the work of the cross of Christ. The blood of Jesus Christ is enough.

The questions are these: Will you bear your pain alone, or will you draw near to Him and let Him cleanse your wounds? Will you allow Him to wipe your tears? Will you permit Him to touch you where it hurts the most? How long will you insist upon remaining in your personal hell? Don't you know that the Lord has unlocked your prison cell? All you have to do is walk out and be freed.

I pray that you walk out. I hope you take His hand. I pray that you accept what He has done for you. He knows the footpath you should take. Your job is to draw near to Him, listen and obey. He will fill you. He will help you. He will take the edge off of your sorrow. He may even remove it completely. For sure, God will make it more bearable for you.

A Petition to the Most High

Father, you sent Your Beloved Son for me that day. Your pure motivation was love. You saw me swimming in my personal hell and came to rescue me. I accept what You did for me. Come into my life today. Fill me with all the provisions of the cross of Jesus Christ. You have unlocked my prison cell. I choose to come out and be healed. I choose to accept Your comfort for my grieving soul today. I choose to let You come into that place where it hurts the most and apply Your healing balm. Come now, help me I pray. In Jesus' name, amen.

$\mathcal{T}$HE LORD WILL RESCUE ME

*The Lord will rescue me from every evil deed, and will bring me safely
to His heavenly kingdom; to Him be the glory
forever and ever. Amen. 2 Timothy 4:18 (NASB)*

$\mathcal{T}$*he word rescue in the* Greek is *sozo*. It means to save, keep safe and sound, to rescue from danger or destruction, to save a suffering one (from perishing), *i.e.*, one suffering from disease, to make well, heal, restore to health, to save from the evils which obstruct the reception of the Messianic deliverance, to preserve one who is in danger of destruction, to save or rescue.

The Lord will come and get you. The Lord will prepare a way of escape. The Lord will move on your behalf. He will deliver you.

When?—when you are surrounded by the enemy; when the battle becomes swift and heavy; when you are beaten down with the enemy's lie; when circumstances have been crafted against you.

The word *evil* in the Greek is *poneros*. It means full of labors, annoyances, hardships, pressed and harassed by labors, bringing toils, annoyances, perils; of a time full of peril to Christian faith and steadfastness; causing pain and trouble, of a bad nature or condition; in a physical sense: diseased or blind; in an ethical sense: evil, wicked, bad.

The word *deed* in the Greek is *ergon*. It means that which one undertakes to do, enterprise, undertaking, any product whatever, anything accomplished by hand, art, industry, or mind, business, employment, that with which anyone is occupied.

This tells us something of your adversary. Satan is a business owner. The commodity he is after is your attendance in hell with him. If he can't accomplish that, then he will work feverishly to render you an impotent and spineless Christian.

His business is to see to your very destruction. He wishes to steal from you—to kill or destroy anything he can get his filthy hands on concerning you. Satan and his demonic entourage are preoccupied with harassing you, bringing hardships, annoyances, pain and trouble of all sorts.

Okay, enough focus on our enemy. I think you get the point.

There have been moments in my life when I have felt very helpless. Ever been there? There have been times that I have said to the Lord, "Lord, if you don't come after me, I am doomed." You know what? He rescued me—every time.

We must learn to think from the end. Yes, you may be in a mess right now. Yes, the bills may be mounting. Yes, you may be living on the edge, but I urge you to continue calling upon the name of the Lord. Hear the

Lord calling out to you today, "My Child, have faith. Have hope. It's time to grow." Until the manifestation of His deliverance comes, your roots can go down deeper in Him. Your faith tested as pure gold will be refined in the refiner's fire.

Heaven is your final destination. His promise to you today is, "I will bring you safely to your heavenly, eternal destination."

Think from the end, not the present.

THE EPICENTER OF GOD

Where does hope come from? Hope always follows a divine encounter with My heart. As you read and study My Word, hope can't help but attach itself to your core. Hope is a byproduct of absorbing my love into your being. When you truly believe I love you, there also will be pure, organic hope. True hope is not manufactured in this world. There is only counterfeit hope in your world.

Walking in hope doesn't consist of believing that there will never be difficult days. True hope knows the sun is still shining even though there are clouds. Your hope level is an indicator of your health. A hopeless person is truly sick in heart. Hope means there is health in your heart. Hope says, "This situation looks dim, but I love and serve a God who is at work and will do all to bring this into a good expected end for my good and His glory.".

Confidence in the final outcome gives extra strength for the day of trial and tribulation. Hope is not wishful thinking. As you employ true Holy Spirit breathed hope, it is like an anchor for your soul. Hope looks at My promises and says, "That's mine.". The hope I infuse you with is Rock solid.

The epicenter of my existence is love which produces hope in every person who will receive. Hope is necessary for you to not only survive, but thrive in all areas of your life and calling.

The ones who are filled with My hope are the ones in whom I can give the power to influence and expand My kingdom. A strong saint will be strong in the area of hope. The world is populated with millions of hopeless inhabitants. As My people walk the earth and carry the banner of hope, they will be noticed and I will draw people into salvation through the winds of hope blowing through My precious sons and daughters.

So, keep hope my precious one.

ᏔHE EASE OF THE GLORY BUBBLE

Let the godly ones exult in glory;
Let them sing for joy on their beds. Psalm 149:5 (NASB)

Ruth Heflin, who has gone to be with Jesus, used to say, "There's ease in the glory." That phrase has stuck with me ever since I heard her say that. When we are living in His glory bubble, there is abundance, riches, dignity and honor.

It's very obvious when I am participating in His abundance and when I'm not. It's the difference between night and day.

Outside the greatness of God's presence there is struggle, work that takes more energy than necessary and all kinds of fear and ungodly emotions. Everyday life is difficult and more challenging.

Inside the realm of His splendor, my soul is calm and fixed. No, my circumstances might not be peaceful, but yes, my soul realm is walking with faith, ease and confidence in God. Inside His glory realm, there is dignity for my soul that cannot be attained in this world.

God has this "bubble" for us to exist within, and it comes from abiding and dwelling with Him. I enter in every time I meditate upon how He has taken care of me in times past. It encircles me when I saturate my heart with the Word of God. The glory realm surrounds me as I soak in His loving kindness and worship Him in spirit and in truth. It's a secret place. It's a place just out of reach of the enemy.

He who dwells in the secret place of the Most High shall remain stable
and fixed under the shadow of the Almighty
{Whose power no foe can withstand}. Psalm 91:1 (AMP)

No foe of mine or God's can withstand His power in and around me. That's great news.

The word *dwell* comes from a Hebrew word that means to sit down, to marry. In other words, we aren't just coming to the Most High for a visit. We have come to live with Him and make His presence our home. Our trouble is that we come to Him for little visits, yet He has actually invited us to stay with Him and live with Him. This is the deal: If we want 24/7 stability, we must have a 24/7 existence in God's presence.

The word *dwell* also means to be inhabited. *Webster's American Family Dictionary* defines *inhabit* as to exist or be situated within. God wants to situate us within His presence. He wants to consume our very being. When we allow this to occur, we are then living in His "glory bubble," and there is an ease to life that comes in no other way.

Secret place is an interesting term here. The Hebrew meaning denotes a hiding, hence something secret, clandestine, bread to be eaten in secret.

I learned a new word—*clandestine. Webster's American Family Dictionary* indicates that it means to be held or done in secrecy or concealment; stealthy.

Have you ever heard of a stealth aircraft? It was built so that radar couldn't easily detect it. I think this was God's idea first. To dwell in the secret place means we now have the capacity to evade detection on our enemy's radar. It's the "glory bubble" again.

Practice God's presence today. Soak in it. Stay in it. Live in it. Be protected in it. Be guided by it. It's God's highest and best for you. There is heavenly bread for you in His secret place. It will satisfy and empower you to do His will. Do you need to be stabilized? Do you need to be fixed? Get into the secret place.

$\mathcal{F}$RAILTY FILLED WITH SPLENDOR

If you only look at us, you might well miss the brightness. We carry this precious Message around in the unadorned clay pots of our ordinary lives. That's to prevent anyone from confusing God's incomparable power with us. As it is, there's not much chance of that. You know for yourselves that we're not much to look at. We've been surrounded and battered by troubles, but we're not demoralized; we're not sure what to do, but we know that God knows what to do; we've been spiritually terrorized, but God hasn't left our side; we've been thrown down, but we haven't broken . . . .
2 Corinthians 4:7-11 (MSG)

It's pretty clear. We are the clay pot—frail, unattractive and dirty on the outside—yet we are carriers of the glory of God, carriers of a treasure beyond all treasures. Make no mistake. It has nothing to do with us and everything to do with Him. If there's any flicker of shine coming from us, it is emanating from the treasure chest within.

Jesus Christ in us is the hope of glory. *(Colossians 1:27.)* How dare we ever take credit for anything good coming out of us? We can love because we were first loved by Him. We have the ability to do good because we have been filled by the God of goodness. We can encourage because we have been encouraged by Him. We are able to give because we have been blessed. All glory and honor belong to God.

Our vessels know sorrow, trouble and hard times; but *within* is glory and wholeness. We are carriers of a most heavenly germ. We are to transmit this germ and spread it to all with whom we come in contact. How infected are you? How many people have you touched with this divine condition?

You are dressed with frailness, but filled with splendor. God is a God of extremes. The extremely frail are filled with extreme splendor. Your body—a frail, weak and sometimes sick shell—is the very place where God has chosen to reside. You are the container of the presence of the Almighty God. You hold the message that will steer the world right into the presence of God. Imagine that.

The container is nothing to look at, but the contents are spellbinding.

CRUSHED: THE WALNUT EXAMPLE

In the fall, walnut trees lose their leaves. Their fruit, the walnut, falls to the ground, and the outer shell begins to fall apart.

When I was a little girl, my grandma used to collect walnuts and lay them out on newspapers on her garage floor. She would roll each walnut on the concrete floor until the outer soft shell fell off and the hard walnut became exposed. When enough time had passed to dry out the walnuts, the cracking began.

The cracking was necessary in order to get to the meat of the nut. Usually a hammer would do the trick. Then a pick was used to pull out the best part. The nuts were then used for eating, baking or storing in the freezer. What can we glean from this?

Grain for bread is crushed, Indeed, he does not continue to thresh it forever. Because the wheel of his cart and his horses eventually damage it, He does not thresh it longer. Isaiah 28:28 (NASB)

. . . your steadfastness (your unflinching endurance and patience) and your firm faith in the midst of all the persecutions and crushing distresses and afflictions under which you are holding up.
2 Thessalonians 1:4b (AMP)

Okay, let's bring this home now. God's ways are not our ways, right? God's thoughts are not our thoughts, right? His ways are higher, and our natural mind does not comprehend the activity of the Spirit *(Isaiah 55:8-9)*.

One of His ways with us is parallel to how grain is crushed. Every one of His children will go through times when the hammer is coming down, and a season of crushing has come. When the hammer falls, many questions and insecurities can arise in our soul. What is my purpose? Why am I here? Why won't my heart stop bleeding? I feel all alone. Where is God? I am falling apart. I feel useless.

Friend, we must endure the crushing seasons of our life. When we do, what God is already doing and preparing for you on the other side of this season will be precious gold. Stop asking the "why" questions and start just *being* in His loving care each frustrating day. No, your heart may not stop bleeding for a while; and yes, you may feel dry as a bone for a bit longer. But joy does come in the morning. *(Psalm 30:5.)* The sun will rise again, even though the dark night of your soul seems endless.

As the walnut, once you endure the rolling, and hammering, and crushing and picking away, you will become food and nourishment for someone. What He pulls out of you will be useful and valuable. You can count on it.

Your life will be a delicacy. When others taste of you, they will know that they have tasted something not made with human hands. It will be divine. It will satisfy.

The walnut needs to fall to the ground, lay there, maybe be run over by a car or be crushed and rolled around until it dries out. Then the next shell needs to be broken before the inner part can even be useful.

The result is feeding another. God not only wants to feed and nourish you, He wants to feed and nourish others through you. That's one of the reasons why it's so necessary not to fight the processes of God in your life. The sooner you cooperate with His way with you, the sooner you will get to the other side of it and see some of the reason for this crushing season in your life.

It does not please Him to see you in pain. It does not bring Him delight to smash you down. But He looks upon you now, thinking of your future, and exhorts you:

My child, please endure this unpleasant moment in your life. Just trust Me. You will reap, if you faint not. You will become food for many, if you will just endure. Be filled with My Spirit now, and you will be empowered to overcome.

God is all about multiplication. He has this special way of taking just one and turning it into many. God is after reproduction. If you are not reproducing, you're missing part of the kingdom cycle. It's important to declare to others what God has done in your life. A silent testimony will result in a dry and stagnant life.

Yield to the crushing. Make the devil sorry he even messed with you in the first place. Honor your Father in heaven by quieting down and absorbing all the love, power and strength that He has for you right now.

COMPOSE YOUR SOUL

Surely, I have composed and quieted my soul; like a weaned child rests against his mother, my soul is like a weaned child within me. Psalm 131:2 (NASB)

What a picture of true satisfaction. A child, resting against his mother, not wanting anything from her but just content to be with her. How often do we come to the Lord, not wanting anything but to enjoy our union with Him? How often do we simply sit with Him and enjoy the love we share with Him?

Child of God, I challenge you today to compose your storm-tossed soul and allow yourself to be filled with hope. I challenge you to quiet down and wait patiently for the salvation of the Lord. In your waiting, with your composed soul, just rest against Him.

Let your soul enter into a singleness of mind and purpose with Him. Let your heart be harnessed and yoked together with Him. Let your emotions become His emotions. Be as that weaned child who is simply content to sit and enjoy the presence of the one caring for him.

There comes a time in every stormy crisis and trial when one must quiet himself and behave in a certain manner if he is to continue on to the victory.

The psalmist is comparing his composure to that of a weaned child resting against his mother. A weaned child no longer demands milk from his mother but rather is content to be near her and quietly sit on her lap.

A weaned child has come to a level of maturity and can receive from his mother in ways that he didn't experience in his younger days. In his younger days, he depended solely upon his mother for milk. Now he is learning to feed himself and sees that his mother will continue her care, but in a different dimension. He has learned the joy of just being with his mother without the desire to be fed at her breast. He is learning that even though he is getting his nourishment in other ways, his mother remains to protect and nourish his need for love and acceptance. Resting his head upon her breast without feeding is a knowing of his mother in a whole new amplitude.

In our trials, we can become demanding of the Lord. We might tell Him, "Lord, if you will do this, then I will do that," when we probably should have been doing *that* all along. We bargain, plead and beg God; but to sit quietly before Him, silently trusting Him to steer the wheel of our storm-tossed ship, is the better place for us.

Friend, sit quietly in the passenger seat. Learn to behave yourself as the weaned child with his mother. God knows the severity of your storm better than anyone. He's the one with the plan, and He sees the end. You and I are very safe with Him. He will get us to the other side if we will let Him. Stop flailing your arms around like a nursing child putting demands upon his mother. Grow in the grace and maturity to which He is calling you. Grow in the experience of just sitting with Him in all trust, satisfaction and contentedness.

$\mathcal{H}$OPE AND WAIT

It is good that a man should both hope and quietly wait for the salvation of the LORD. Lamentations 3:26(KJV)

The fashion in which I walk through a difficult trial is important to God. Two elements crucial to our spiritual health are keeping hope and the ability to wait. It's not a "call my best friend and vent everyday" kind of waiting, but a certain quietness as I hope and wait. It's valuable to wait and to hope *quietly*.

I must wait; and in the quiet waiting and hoping, I *will* see the salvation of God. When studying this phrase "hope and quietly wait" in the Greek, it denotes some interesting terminology. It means to twist, whirl, dance, writhe, fear, tremble, travail, be in anguish, be pained, to be made to writhe, be made to bear, to be brought forth, to be born, suffering torture, to wait longingly, to be distressed.

When the above words describe the condition of my soul before God, I could be in a place of birthing something new in my life. Before the new comes the travail. Before the next place of serving the Lord comes times and seasons of waiting and hoping. There will be times and seasons of pain, anguish and maybe even fear and trembling of the heart. Before the new can be brought forth, there will be occasions of longing and bearing down. This is a perfect description of a woman in labor just before the child comes forth from the birth canal.

What is God birthing in me today? What is coming from Him for which I must hope and quietly, yet painfully, wait? When the baby is born, there is joy and happiness. When the salvation of the Lord comes, it, too, will be accompanied with joy and happiness. When victory and safety come, the travail of waiting will soon be forgotten, and I will be swept into His marvelous salvation.

I must be careful to be quiet in my waiting season. I must be careful to nurture hope and expectation in my God. I must bear my pain and longing in the secret place of the Most High, for the incubation time of waiting and hoping in God will one day give way to the full salvation and deliverance of the Lord.

$\mathcal{T}$HE SECRET WAY OF PASSAGE

$\mathcal{D}o$ *you know what time* it is? It's time to step closer and not further from Me. Even in your frustrations and pain, step closer. My plan is for your good and not your devastation. My hopes for you include joy and contentment.

Do not fear to draw near to your heavenly Father. Do not look the other way when I come to you. Life has been full of difficulties and hardships. Life has dealt you severe blows of sorrow and pain. My dear child, if you could see what I see when I look at you. These storms—they have formed you. They have constructed a character about you that would have never come otherwise. I have kept you through it all.

I bring comfort to you today. Come and receive it. Come and take the strength that belongs to you. I see your vulnerability, and I want to cover you in this moment. The enemy prowls around to see who is open and bare. Come quickly to Me that I may cover your nakedness and vulnerability and clothe you with My covering. As you come under My wing, you will be invisible to your adversary.

You ask Me to take these moments of sorrow and trial away from you, yet you wish to be formed in My image. I tell you, it cannot be both. The formation of your life to exemplify Christ requires the storms. If My Son learned obedience through the sufferings of this life, then you, too, will learn it this way. It's the high way. It's the best way.

Can you trust Me? Do not look to your future with dread. Do not calculate what's ahead without Me; rather, live in the moment, for that is what you have. Bring your pain and sorrow to Me, and I will place My healing balm upon your wound and ease your pain.

With Me you can do everything. You can walk through trouble, sorrow and all sorts of difficulty. As you remember this, My Spirit will carry you through. When you need to wait, I will empower you to wait. Timing is everything in My kingdom. Waiting can be grueling sometimes, but with Me you can wait for however long it takes.

Endure with Me. Continue to draw near to Me, for in waiting and resting is your salvation. Your soul is storm-tossed. Begin to speak to your soul: Soul, be still and know that He is God. You can speak to your soul, and it must listen to you. You can tell your soul to be quiet and it must. Come up to the heavenly realm, the realm just above your circumstances. Be seated with Me in the heavenly places and see what I see. It's the place just above the clouds of sin and pain and tears—the place of clear skies and victory. Come on, dear one, come sit with Me. Let Me show you real life from My perspective.

Come down into the deeper waters, the place of serenity where the outward looks different from the inward. Circumstances may not change for a while, or they may change suddenly; but the important thing is for you to find deep peace no matter what's happening around you. The imperative thing is for you to find the deeper places of communion with Me. I'm calling you to that right now.

You are so tired and exhausted. Quiet down for a bit. Take time out and do what you need to do to find Me. I cannot be found in the noise and confusion of this life. I can be found in the quietness. Go for a walk. Go into your room and close the door. Sit by a stream. Do what it takes to find Me. I will not let you down, but I will not compete with other noise and commotion in your life. You must decide to go apart to find Me, just as My Son did on many occasions while upon the earth. He went up into the hills to pray. He physically removed Himself from people and noise. That's where His empowerment came. That's where My union with Him flourished. That's where He was comforted and loved upon. It is no different for you.

Come, weary one. Come, exhausted one. Come and see how I will bring rest to your storm-tossed soul. I will show you the secret passageway through. Move toward Me, and I will guide you onward.

QUIET STREAMS

He leads me beside quiet waters. Psalms 23:2b (NIV)

No matter the season or condition of your soul, God wants to take good care of you. He intends to reconcile you to Himself. He wishes to return you to peace. He calls you to compose and settle your soul. God is working to harmonize you with heaven. His heart is to guide you to places of rest and satisfaction in Him.

Life has a way of coming in the backdoor and stealing your hope and peace when you're not looking. The enemy of your soul desires to use your circumstances to lead you to the place of torment and fear. If allowed, he will lead you beside turbulent rapids and then throw you in headfirst.

God has a different plan in mind for you. The path that God will lead you upon is a path not exempt from trial and difficulty, but it is a path where you will certainly enjoy peace and joy along the way.

Wherever we end up, God or Satan can't force us. God created us to be followers. Who you follow will determine in what kind of water you will end up. Will it be a peaceful stream or turbulent rapids?

Quiet waters . . .

Just to read these words has a soothing effect upon my soul. As I close my eyes and remember standing near a babbling brook, I can bring the sound to the forefront of my mind once again.

The storms of life will remain relentless, but there is a secret place reserved for me in God. It's a place hidden and out of reach from my adversary. If Jesus can be asleep, resting on a boat in the middle of a great storm, then when I suddenly find myself hurled into a frightful gale, I can find rest and peace in the chaos. Why? because the Spirit of Jesus lives in me *(Romans 8:11)*. As I surrender to Him, I will always find the power and ability to stay calm in every tempest that comes my way.

His job is to lead.
My job is to follow.
It's simple.

Where He leads, I could never find on my own. He knows the way, and I don't. Clearly, a sweet destination is in store for me as I follow the Master's lead. Sometimes, He wants to lead me beside the quiet waters, for He knows what I need and when I need it.

$\mathcal{O}$HE BABE

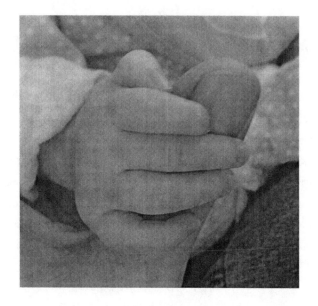

She will bear a Son, and you shall call His name Jesus
[the Greek form of the Hebrew Joshua, which means Savior], for He
will save His people from their sins [that is, prevent them from failing
and missing the true end and scope of life, which is God].
Matthew 1:21 (AMP)

Before Jesus Christ even entered the world, we needed to be saved.
We needed to be healed. We needed hope.

WE NEEDED TO BE RESCUED.

We were on a crash course to the pit of hell. Jesus Christ stepped into this world and became a roadblock between us and hell. Ever since the fall of man in Eden, we've needed a Savior; we've needed to be rescued.

The angel of the Lord told Joseph in this verse what name he was to give this child. The angel gave him the name *and* the purpose of His life.

JESUS

He will save His people from their sins.

When we celebrate the birth of Jesus Christ, we celebrate being rescued. Truly, it was tidings of great joy. Truly, it was peace on earth and goodwill towards men. God's will is good towards us.

Because of Jesus, there is always an avenue of escape. Through Jesus, we have unending hope. At the hand of Jesus, our wounded soul can discover health. By virtue of Jesus, intimacy with God has been restored; the curtain has been torn, and we have free access to the hearing ear of our heavenly Father.

Prayer of the White Flag

Lord, I surrender to Your plan today. I surrender to the heavenly Babe. I surrender to the purpose of His existence on earth. Jesus came as a babe, but He grew up and fulfilled the strategy of heaven. I worship You and the wonder of Your love. It's a wonder to think about the details of Your birth, Jesus. All the foretold prophecies, the shepherds, the wise men, the star, the stable, the holy conception, the angels, the dreams—it's all a mystery and too wonderful for my full comprehension. I thank You for doing it. I thank You for coming to my rescue. Amen.

$\mathcal{A}$S HE IS, SO AM I IN THIS WORLD

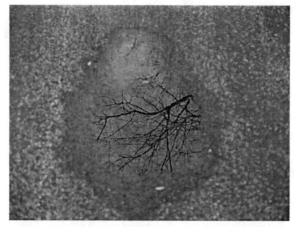

The Reflection of a Tree in a Puddle of Water

*And the child grew, and waxed strong in spirit, filled with wisdom: and
the grace of God was upon him.*
Luke 2:40 (KJV)

Let's examine Jesus in this verse. Jesus came into this world as a
babe. He was formed in His mother's womb just as we were and traveled
down a constricting birth canal to make His entrance upon earth.

And the child grew . . .

He started as a newborn baby and grew into manhood.

. . . and waxed strong in spirit . . .

The word *spirit* in the Greek is the same as *Holy Spirit*. He didn't start out strong, but He "waxed strong," meaning He increased in the strength of the Holy Spirit.

Little by little, trial by trial, crisis by crisis, the Holy Spirit became stronger and stronger in Him. Jesus paved the way for the normal Christian life. A healthy Christian life is evidenced by an increasing strength of the Holy Spirit.

. . . filled with wisdom . . .

Jesus brimmed with wisdom. The Greek word for *wisdom* means broad and full of intelligence, the knowledge of very diverse matters . . . of things human and divine.

Here are several more annotations concerning wisdom:

- knowledge acquired by acuteness and experience, and summed up in maxims and proverbs
- science and learning
- the act of interpreting dreams and always giving the sagest advice
- skill in the management of affairs
- the knowledge and practice of the requisites for godly and upright living
- supreme intelligence, such as belongs to God

This is a clearer picture of our Jesus. He was no dummy. He was at the top of his class when it came to the natural realm of this earth as well as the dimension of the Spirit. What a standard for each and every one of us.

. . . and the grace of God was upon Him.

Grace: pleasure, delight, sweetness, charm, loveliness, grace of speech, favor, thanks, recompense, reward.

From the moment Jesus Christ made entrance into this sin-sick world, there was something upon Him. It was the pleasure of His Father. He had the Father's thanks. He carried the sweetness of God upon Him until the second He took His final breath upon the cross. There was a charisma about Him that could not be denied. Jesus' speech was peppered with such grace. He was very likeable. Verse 40 of Luke 2 speaks of how He grew in favor with both God and man.

. . . as He is, so are we in this world. 1 John 4:17b (KJV)

Now, the point of this encouragement is this: As we see a clearer picture of Jesus, we are seeing a clearer picture of who we are to become. According to 1 John 4:17b, as Jesus was, so are we to be in this world. What a message of hope to us.

The pattern is clearly before us. Grow. Wax strong in the Holy Spirit. Be filled with wisdom. Walk with the grace of God upon you. Friend, study Jesus—then mirror Him.

Take Me, Lord

Father, I give You permission today to cover me in Your grace and open my eyes to the wisdom from above so that I'm walking in it consistently. I choose to increase in strength as I learn what pleases You. I receive a fresh baptism in Your Holy Spirit so that the waxing of strength can occur in my life. I am growing in You and thinking Your thoughts more and more as I walk through each trial and test. The Holy Spirit is gaining more and more dominance in my thoughts, habits and emotions. I surrender to You today. Help me, fill me and use me in violent acts against the kingdom of darkness, I pray.

And as You are, may I be in this world. Amen.

$\mathcal{W}$HAT ARE YOU DRINKING?

Behold, God is my salvation, I will trust and not be afraid;
For the LORD GOD is my strength and song, and He has become my
salvation. Therefore, you will joyously draw water
From the springs of salvation. Isaiah 12:2-3 (AMP)

$\mathcal{I}saiah\ exemplifies\ a\ way\ for$ us to live when surrounded by difficulty. God was three things to him:

- his strength
- his song
- his salvation

Then in verse three, it states, "Therefore," implying *because* He is your strength, song and your salvation, water can be joyfully drawn from the springs of salvation.

Life has a way of making you really thirsty for the waters of salvation. We scurry around sipping on contaminated spiritual waters of the world that simply do not satisfy.

Our busy, self-absorbed lives eclipse our true need. When a crisis hits, we are naked before God. The moment arrives, and we are faced with great poverty of spirit. Our sin-sick soul is in dire need of a deep drink from the springs of salvation. This moment of stripping is a true gift from our heavenly Father.

As we begin drinking from His well, we move from that place a little more sensitive to our deep need for that salvation water. The fresh springs of His salvation cannot be compared to the murky waters of this world from which we've been sipping. Oh, yes, the world offers you many drinks. Think about traveling in a Third-World country. You need to take your own water. A simple swallow of its water can make you deathly ill.

When God brings you into a new realization of the muck in which you've been living, there is now hope for transformation and change.

Thus, the journey of life—traveling, learning and realizing over and over again that God is your true strength, true song and true salvation. You will run more often for your bucket and with great joy draw from the springs of your salvation. It's something to learn; the more you do it, the more you will benefit from it.

Coming to Your Holy Well

Lord God, I'm getting my bucket out today. I'm coming over to Your well, and I'm going to draw from the water of Your salvation. I'm going to draw it up and pour a glass. I will savor it and drink it down. It will quench my thirst today. It will be healing to my thoughts and emotions. Your drink will be cool and satisfying to my dry soul. I will regain my strength. I will stand firm and not be afraid, for You are my source and my deliverance.

A COMPENSATION OUT OF THIS WORLD

And if children, then heirs; heirs of God, and joint-heirs with Christ;
if so be that we suffer with him, that we may be also glorified together.
For I reckon that the sufferings of
this present time are not worthy to be compared with the glory which
shall be revealed in us. Romans 8:17-18 (KJV)

Are you a child of God? Then you are an heir. There is an allotted portion assigned to you because of your sonship. You are a son or daughter of God; therefore, whatever is due His children all belongs to you. In this case, both the suffering and the glory of Christ will be your portion. Christ is the standard; Christ is the role model; He is the elder brother.

. . . if so be that we suffer with him . . .

Adversity will be very much a part of your Christian journey. Christ suffered; consequently, it will be your lot as well. Suffering with Him implies a sharing of the difficulties that arise. There's a co-laboring together in the pain and difficulties—not a removal of them, but a sharing in them, both in persecutions and in all sorts of troubles. We would welcome nothing more than the removal of trouble and pain, but this sort of freedom will be experienced only as we pass over through heaven's gates in death. Until then, we will experience times of relief from intense tribulation but never complete immunity *(John 16:33)*.

Jesus will suffer with us. Our Redeemer will share in our sorrows. He will come and take the other side of the yoke and help us bear our burdens. He will lift us and supply comfort and strength that we may stay on the path. *Together* is His will—*together* in pain, difficulty and tribulation—sharing and fellowshipping in it, not the removal of it but the sharing in it.

. . . that we may also be glorified together.

The Greek word for *glorified* denotes being approved together. As we choose to allow Him to suffer with us and include Him in our hardship, then a day will come when God will raise us up together with the same approval He is giving His very own Son. We will be approved together with Jesus Christ. It's the same glory and approval that Jesus Christ gets.

We are the siblings of Jesus Christ by divine order of God Himself. Paul reckoned (calculated) that the sufferings (misfortunes, calamity, evil, afflictions, both outward and inward) of this present time (the time when things are brought to crisis) aren't even worth mentioning in comparison to the unveiling of splendor that is going to occur in each one of us who has shared in the sufferings.

One day, we who have walked with Christ will experience an unveiling, and what we've been will give way to who we really are, for we will share in the same glory that Jesus Christ Himself actually experienced when He was resurrected and ascended to heaven. What a promise of hope.

This word *glory* is a Greek word *doxa,* meaning that condition with God the Father in heaven to which Christ was raised after He had achieved His work on earth.

When we have achieved our work on earth, there is a glory waiting for us. God will then uncover His masterpiece.

We will be the great unveiling. Right now, we see only glimmers of the splendor God sees in us for the simple reason that we now are in the season of sharing in the sufferings of Christ. It is not yet known what we shall be, but it is known to Him. That's why He stays with us. He walks beside us. He shares with us. As we share with Him in the hardship, there is a guarantee of the sharing of His glory in us as well.

There will be no comparison. It will be well worth every current sorrow and hardship of today. Christ in you is the hope of glory.

Enfold Me

Thank You for sharing in my pain and suffering. Thank You for Your constant attention and supply. I welcome You in this dark place. I take Your hand in fellowship. I see Your gaze towards me. I see Your smile as we co-labor in this thing. I enjoy Your presence, love and embrace as the frigid temperatures surround us. I am dressed with Your garments, and I am protected from the dangerous elements surrounding me—safe in Your shadow, resting in Your shelter—as I am being shaped and formed into the image of Jesus through the steady companion of trouble. I eagerly await the day when I will be glorified together with You.

$\mathcal{T}$HE WINTER SEASON

*I always say that winter is my fourth favorite season. It is not first, to be
sure, yet there is something in it that I favor. I need the scourging that
it brings. I need its toughness and endurance. I need its hope. I love the
way winter stands there saying, "I dare you not to notice my beauty."
What can I say to a winter tree when I am able to see the shape of its
soul because it has finally let go of its protective leaves? What do you say
to an empty tree? Standing before an empty tree is like seeing it for the
first time. Oh, the things that can be seen when one is empty.*
Macrine Wiederkehr, A Tree Full of Angels

The faithfulness of winter can be counted upon. I love this excerpt from one of my favorite books. It's rich in truth. We have all experienced the season of winter in our spiritual lives. It's a necessary, but difficult, season. There is beauty, for sure, to be found if we have the proper lenses. There is warmth to be found if we are dressed properly.

A winter season brings moments of chill right down to the bones. There's more darkness than the long days of sunny summer. The snowy blizzards can bring unwanted immobilization—a great contrast to the fall season of harvest activity and abundance. Life becomes more black and white in our winter seasons.

A winter season in our life is a season to hunker down, press in, stand firm and resist the howling wind. It's a time to cease constant movement and *be*. Take example from the tree. It's an interval of exposure. It's an opening of seeing firsthand just what you're made of, and sometimes in plain view for all to see. You have been stripped down to your bare wood. All the color has fallen off, and onlookers now see your exposed limbs. If your roots are deep, you will last through the winter season with no problem. If you have shallow roots, watch out when the wind whips up and threatens your structure, for the wind will always dare you to just stand there while it swirls violently around you. Will you bear it? Can you find the strength you need just to stand there and not come crashing down? The winter season will prove you, and then it will give way to springtime.

May you stand in your winter and stay strong in the roots of your faith. When the evil winds of adversity come against you, you need to continue to stand—vacant branches and all. May the Holy Spirit of endurance fill you through and through. Just as spring comes after winter, so should your heart remain hopeful for a coming spring season for your winter laden soul.

Embrace the season of winter. Be fixed in your heart to see the beauty of it. Understand the value of it. Grow deeper because of it.

THE JOURNEY REUNION

You sift and search out my path and my lying down,
and You are acquainted with all my ways. Psalm 139:3 (AMP)

Traveler, your thoroughfare is under the continual watchful eye of the Father. The road before you has been first traveled by Him, and He has gone before you to secure your safety—not your comfort always, but your safety. For it is by the hills and the valleys, the rocks and the rivers that you will travel through and gain your heavenly crown. There is no smooth, even pathway for you, but rather, bumpy curves and corners to help develop the level of intimacy with the Father that you need. Sometimes, there will be a fellow traveler who will traverse with you for a season and bring friendship and companionship, but mostly, you will find aloneness on the journey that draws your attention towards heaven. You will be alone, yet very much not alone.

Whether you are walking and climbing or resting and lying down, the God of the universe has perfect knowledge of all your ways and thoughts. Your mannerisms are always before Him. He sees your character, and He knows just what He wants to do with it—thus your own personal road and the great journey before you. Your pathway is best suited for you alone. No one else can travel your passage. No one else will be able to copy you when He's finished. Your pathway is handcrafted by your loving heavenly Father Himself. Yes, your roadway may parallel or join with another for a while; but soon, you'll see that God has constructed His roadway to journey off in another direction. You can be sure that the roadway of those you love who are serving Him also will lead them across the same gates of glory. Eternal glory will be one of the greatest journey reunions of all time.

Take heart. You are in His hands today. It may be jagged and bumpy, uncomfortable and frustrating, but the reflection of His image is beginning to form very beautifully. You must not give up or give in but rest in His loving care and provisions. He will keep you and guard you. He will send His ministering angels to your side.

The process is the reason for your journey. You need the process because by it, you will be crafted. You need all that He allows you to face in order to form you into His marvelous image. Thus, the journey.

$\mathcal{T}$HE PERENNIAL PASSAGE THROUGH

When the enemy shall come in like a flood, the Spirit of the LORD shall lift up a standard against him. Isaiah 59:19b (KJV)

When we encounter an onslaught by our enemy, we are not left to fight alone. There is an arising of a discontent God on our behalf. He begins to open up the way for our safe passage through the warfare. We are never trapped. We are never so tangled up that we can't become free. God will always see to our escape.

When the Lord lifts up a standard against our enemy, one way it's described in the original language is "to fly to the attack on horseback."

Friend of God, we are not immune from the flooding of our adversary. We can count on it just as the sun will rise tomorrow morning. There is something else we can count on even more: our Lord coming on our behalf. The timing of His coming belongs to Him, but you can be sure that He will mount up on His holy horse and fly to the attack on our behalf.

The adversary comes through difficulty or a tight and narrow place. This could be finances, marriage trouble, problems with our children or trouble with a co-worker. It could include emotional frustrations, fears, oppression . . . you fill in the blank. The road can quickly transform into a path of tar. It becomes difficult to just simply lift your foot and take the next step.

As we keep our eyes upon the Lord, there will come a moment in our crisis when God pronounces enough is enough, and the Rescuer will come and bring the deliverance or breakthrough for which we have been searching.

And the God of all grace, who called you to his eternal glory in Christ, after you have suffered a little while, will himself restore you and make you strong, firm and steadfast. 1 Peter 5:10 (NIV)

Even Jesus went through times of suffering, according to Hebrews 5:8:

Though he was God's Son, he learned trusting- obedience by what he suffered, just as we do. (MSG)

In your moment of demonic harassment, God will suddenly become discontent with your situation, lift up a standard and come to your aid. Until He comes to your aid, there is a moment or season when suffering is your constant companion, and your way through to victory is to listen and obey. Your business is to be patient with the process and grab hold of the hem of His garment each day. Your job is to be full of the Holy Spirit so that, having done all, you are able to stand firm and see the deliverance of the Lord.

Are you standing today? Are you keeping hope? Are you lifting up your shield of faith to quench the fiery darts of your adversary? Do you have your breastplate of righteousness in place so your heart is protected and preserved only for the Master?

The enemy will overwhelm you at times, but be on your guard and fight as a son/daughter of the Most High God. After you have fought, suffered and obeyed for a little while, the God of grace will restore you, make you stronger and set your feet in a secure place.

MY TIMES ARE IN YOUR HANDS

My times are in Your Hands . . . .
Psalm 31:15a (NIV)

No matter my struggle and strain difficulties and perplexities
My times are in Your Hands

Be it day or night whatever the season
Summer, Winter, Spring or Fall
My times are in Your Hands

No matter the trap or trick of my adversary, my need, my ups and
downs
I am learning ever so slowly
My times are in Your Hands

As deep sorrows cut like a knife and comfort is nowhere to be
found
I look to You and gratefully remember
My times are in Your Hands

Be it hour by hour or minute by minute in a demon-possessed
valley or a glorious mountaintop encounter
My times are in Your Hands

In life's final breath
When I have lived the last numbered day ordained for me I will
gladly meet You at the gate
For . . .

My times have been in Your Hands
Oh yes, dear Lord . . . my times have been in Your Hands

$\mathcal{B}$UT AS FOR ME

But as for me, I will look to the Lord and confident in Him I will keep watch; I will wait with hope and expectancy for the God of my salvation; my God will hear me. Micah 7:7 (AMP)

$\mathcal{W}$*hat about you?* $\mathcal{I}$*t matters* not what others do. What about you? Will you look to the Lord? Be most concerned with the way you conduct your affairs. When Micah penned these words "but as for me," it implies that there were those around Him who weren't looking to the Lord.

Allow God to make you a standard among your peers. No matter what others choose, remind yourself, "But as for me, I will look to the Lord." Be the light. Be the witness to His great faithfulness. Be the window for others to have peeks and glimpses into kingdom living.

Micah had a very purposeful focus in this verse. Despite what was going on around him, he wasn't allowing it to distract him from eye contact with his God. He was intent upon his focus. There was an utter assurance that fueled him to keep watching for the Lord. That confidence was most likely wrapped in faith and hope. He had seen enough of how God worked to know that he could stand there with great fortitude—looking, waiting and watching for the Lord to bring the answer to his supplications.

He tarried with expectancy. He anticipated with hope. Serving God will include long moments of delay. God watches us while we wait. How will we wait? Will there be grumbling, complaining and murmuring mixed with impatience and unbelief—or will we wait with hope and expectancy for the God of our salvation? I believe that some of our rewards in heaven will be directly linked to what we found to do while waiting on God.

The God of your salvation is all about orchestrating His plan and purpose for your life. Don't be in a hurry. Wait with hope and expectancy, fixing your gaze upon Him, confident that in the fullness of time He will perform on

your behalf. He won't do what He's told you to do, and there's no way that you could accomplish what only He does. It's a holy networking that involves a co-laboring with Him. Truly, He does make all things beautiful in His time *(Ecclesiastes 3:11)*.

But as for me . . . (Now *you* finish this sentence.)

O THOU STORM-TOSSED SOUL

O thou afflicted, tossed with tempest, and not comforted, behold, I will
lay thy stones with fair colours,
and lay thy foundations with sapphires. Isaiah 54:11 (KJV)

"Behold, I will lay thy stones with fair colours . . .."This is the
promise of God for the one who is afflicted, tossed by the storm and
not yet found full comfort.

Friend, you are in one of three places right now: you have just emerged from a storm, you are fixing to enter a storm or you are in the midst of a storm. We are not exempt just because we are God's children—quite the contrary.

There may be moments in your life of deep cutting. You may find yourself in a cavern of penetrating darkness on certain legs of your journey. You will be tempted to ask God where He is, and did He see what just happened to you. On some occasions, you may feel so alone and shivery cold, with no comfort in sight or ease to the pain. You may be tempted to succumb to utter hopelessness.

These are the places where you will find the *treasures* of darkness *(Isaiah 45:3)*. I believe that God stores His greatest treasures for our darkest moments. He can lay the greatest foundations of our faith in the place of our deepest wounding and bleeding.

The word for *afflicted* in the Hebrew denotes poor, needy and weak. *Storm-tossed* in the Hebrew means to be driven by a storm, violently shaken, agitated, disturbed, used of the heart, to be tossed about, dispersed. *Not comforted* means forcing yourself to just breathe, panting, groaning.

Just when you can't breathe anymore and when there are only groans to describe your place of agitation, lift up your eyes to your King. He has not been sitting idly by your side. He has been busy laying your foundations with glistening precious stones. You are being built—not according to the blueprints of this world, but according to the heavenly plans of your Father. Your life is on schedule, just as He purposed.

The workmanship of God in you is eternal, imperishable, immoveable and incorruptible. You are being formed by His scarred hands. They are hands that bled. They are hands that felt the piercing of a nail going in one side and out the other. You are being built by a God who knows what true pain and agony is. You are being remade inside by a Savior who is well acquainted with sorrow and grief.

This world is only temporal. Our pain and sorrow are the same as our life—a vapor in the halls of eternity. Someday, it will end. The enemy will try to convince you otherwise.

We live in today, and we are not yet in our final home; thus, we continue our search for what comfort we can find on this earth. The picture is not complete, and the last page of our life has not yet been played out. We are not yet what we shall be, but we have this promise from God Himself:

Behold I will lay thy stones with fair colors . . .

Keep hope as a close companion always. Without it, your heart will be sick. Are you storm-tossed and not yet comforted? Keep hope. Have faith. One day you will emerge from this, and the beauty of your foundations will shine for all to see.

THE HOPE OF TRUE BROKENNESS

I want what I want when I want it. I want to appear as though I need nothing. I want to live my life the way I want to. I don't want anyone telling me what to do. I will figure things out myself. I don't need anyone, and I am self-sufficient.

The truth is we are the most deficient creatures upon the face of the earth— always have been and always will be. To whatever degree we drape our heart with the above attitude will be the degree that we are fighting life in the Spirit ... thus, the need for brokenness.

God has to take us through many a trial and tribulation just to get through to us. He created us with hunger and thirst. We were created to be in need of God. We need His love. We need His forgiveness. We need His strength, but our absolute greatest need is to know Him intimately.

Why is it that it takes hardship for us to draw near to Him? I don't know, but many times that's exactly what it takes. Brokenness should be viewed as a friend—a lifelong companion assigned by our side to lead us into the fellowship of the Spirit. Brokenness is a tool in God's hand to help us see our insufficiency.

Sin has robbed us of what God truly intended for us. A rebellious attitude will put us on a detour every time. God is always in pursuit of us in order to take us back to the Garden. This, my friend, is God's highest and best thought for us—unbroken fellowship with Him.

Jesus Christ paid the price that was ours to pay. He did it for the joy that was set before Him—reuniting us back into fellowship with God. So, the way is made. It behooves us to search Him out.

Brokenness will smack us in the face once in a while and unmistakably utter, *"Refocus, my friend. Refocus. Get your priorities straight. Remember in whose image you were made. Remember that your life is but a vapor, but God has placed eternity in your heart."*

When difficulties come, we can be surprised to the point of wondering what we did to deserve them. Difficulties are sometimes self-inflicted, but many times they come straight from the strategic planning room of the Holy Spirit. They come as a result of our prayer and devotion to emulate Jesus.

How could we experience true joy if we have never encountered real sorrow? Where would we find the patience of the Holy Spirit unless we had to wait a long time for something? When could we ever taste that peace that passes understanding unless we were in a place that rocked our boat? How would we ever learn self-control if we didn't have opportunities to choose? It would be almost impossible to comfort another unless we have experienced firsthand the deep, abiding, comforting arms of the Savior in the midst of our pain.

When one truly understands the value of brokenness, he has found spiritual wisdom beyond what the natural mind can understand. When you can see brokenness as a friend, you have bypassed your reasoning, logical mind and found an eternal gem of wisdom that only heaven understands.

If you are a child of God, then you can be sure that the discipline of the Lord will follow you all the days of your life. You cannot escape it. It's proof of His love for you. He's in hot pursuit of bringing you to the Mountain of Holiness. He's in loving pursuit of taking you by His right hand and showing you His pleasures evermore. He's coming for you and desires to hear your voice in the Throne Room of Grace in your time of need. He longs to be longed for and seeks to be sought.

Demand less and less for yourself. Yield to the brokenness that will take you on the holy high road.

In the words of John the Baptist himself:

He must increase, but I must decrease. John 3:30 (KJV)

CREASURES OF DARKNESS

Isaac went out to meditate in the field . . ..
Genesis 24:63a (NASB)

A few years back, my father turned over part of his tillable farm to participate in the Wildlife Conservation Program. He has planted all kinds of prairie grasses and wildflowers in many of his fields. One day, I took my camera and quiet music and rode over on my three-wheeler to take pictures and meditate in the field. Such peace and satisfaction entered my spirit. There's something about being outdoors, surrounded by the beauty of God's creation that just soothes my soul.

There are moments in my life that it has been crucial to find the peace of God, to find "the hem of His garment" *(Luke 8:44)* and reassurance of His presence. It's nothing short of a miracle when heaven itself enters into us in the midst of the cruel storms of life.

In times of difficulty, I look for the shelter of the Most High. In times of great personal challenge, I have to find the way of escape. I believe for every time of tribulation God allows us to experience, there is an equal place in the spirit for us to find and occupy. It's the great security blanket atmosphere of God Himself—a place where our storm-tossed soul can find solace and comfort. Sometimes, it takes us awhile to find it, but it is part of the provision of God to His sons and daughters as they tread this earthen sod. There are treasures in the sand to be excavated. *(Deuteronomy 33:19.)*

I will give you the treasures of darkness and hidden wealth of secret places
So that you may know that it is I, The LORD, the God
of Israel, who calls you by your name. Isaiah 45:3 (NASB)

The word *give* in the Hebrew means "assigned." The word *darkness* denotes an underground prison, a time of sadness, misery or adversity. *Hidden wealth* in this verse means something hidden or underground, having the feel of an underground storehouse.

Child of God, you have been assigned certain treasures that can be discovered only in dark places. What appears to be an underground prison may in fact be the very place of buried treasure and hidden wealth toward which God is trying to lead you. We must not fight Him on this. If we want to experience the fullness of God, we must not kick and scream the whole way down to the hidden treasury of God. If we are patient with the process of God in our lives, I am convinced that we will see every dark, underground prison in our lives be transformed into a great storehouse of treasure and wealth.

Why does God go to such great lengths to get our attention? Well, sometimes we would never know the call of God on our lives unless we went down under, where it's dark and cold and sometimes scary. The call of God to us is a beautiful treasure to discover. You are chosen, and you are known by your very own name before God Himself. Sometimes, it's not until we are whipped around by a storm and come to utter helplessness that God can lead us to the treasures of darkness and the wealth of secret places.

That day in the field I found the wealth of the secret place. As I stopped in the midst of my whirlwind of circumstances, I found the hidden wealth of God. What is that wealth?

God Almighty, who knows me by name.

What peace came swooping down on my soul that day. What satisfaction I found in just fellowshipping with Him. The union I have with my God is crucial in propelling me forward. It's vital to my safe arrival to the other side of the storm.

When you are in your little storm-tossed boat of life, remember your union with Jesus Christ. Remember that He calls you by your very name. He is very interested in taking you on a treasure hunt. The jewels will be worth the journey, my friend. Don't give up.

$\mathcal{G}$OD IS IN THE MARCHING BAND

You are my hiding place; You preserve me from trouble;
You surround me with songs of deliverance. Selah Psalms 32:7 (NASB)

Selah. What does that mean?

Selah means to pause, to interrupt, a technical musical term probably showing accentuation, silence, to rest. It is used in marking a short pause in singing the words of a psalm so that the singer would be silent, while the instrumental music continued.

God chose to keep that word in place when it was penned down for us. We must give heed to this five-letter word. It's really a power-packed little word. For us it means: Don't skim over what was previously written. Stop; pause; think about this for a minute; meditate; ponder; chew.

Therefore, let's do that for this verse:

You are my hiding place.

Did you ever have a secret hiding place when you were a child? We all have a need to hide and be alone sometimes. When we are troubled or fearful or upset by something, sometimes we prefer solitude. The psalmist states that God is, indeed, the place of hiding. God is the secret place where no one else can find Him. God is his shelter and covering. We are safe when we are eclipsed in God. He will keep our secrets to Himself and share them with no one. Did you ever ask, "Can you keep a secret?" The only one with whom your secret is truly safe is God. You can be covered in Him.

The words *hiding place* in Psalm 32:7 are also the same as the Hebrew word used in Psalms 91:1 (KJV) for *secret place*:

"He that dwelleth in the secret place of the Most High shall abide under the shadow of the Almighty."

I find it very comforting when God speaks in terms of "secret place" and "under the shadow." There's a sense of security and protection, and that's exactly what God is trying to convey to us in these verses. Can you hear His whisper— "Child, if you will come running to Me, I will cover, protect and hide you from the enemy's eyes."

You preserve me from trouble.

There are certain troubles that we will be kept from when we find our secret hiding place in God. *Preserve* here means keep, guard and watch over. It's true that in this world we will have tribulations of all sorts, *but we can add to those troubles by not staying under God's shadow.* We can actually increase our troubles when we are not living in that "secret" or "hiding" place. Every once in a while, God has to remind us, *"You're making this more difficult than it needs to be."* By making the Lord our hiding place, there are moments that He will place us just out of the reach of our enemy.

You surround me with songs of deliverance.

We are going to have some fun with this word "surround." It has a very full meaning. Here are some of the Hebrew words describing surround: change directions, encircle, change, to march or walk around, transform, reverse, to be surrounded.

The word "songs" means "shouts."

The word "deliverance" means "liberation" or "escape."

Okay, here's a scenario: I'm in trouble. The enemy is after me. My sinful nature is flaring up. I run into God's secret hiding place. I go where it's safe. Instantly, God gets up and starts marching around me, encircling me and just surrounding me. I am completely covered by Him. There's no way my enemy can even get to me. Next, God begins to shout and sing songs of liberation over me. I have escaped the enemy's snare. I have been liberated from what was crouching at my door to do me harm. God is singing and marching around me, and He is full of joy as he covers me and marches around me. Something else is occurring while I am being immersed by God. I am being changed. I am being transformed. There is a reversal in the way I am thinking and acting. I emerge from this place different: maybe stronger, but certainly more Christ like.

Friend, there's a whole lot that goes on in the realm of the Spirit. There is so much to learn in His presence. Don't calculate by what you can see with your physical eye. Learn to step into the atmosphere of heaven. Train yourself to be moved by what you *can't* see with your physical eye. The unseen realm is the *real* realm.

God will not do what He's asked us to do—in this case, run to Him when we are in trouble. We certainly can't do what only God can do.

He loves you today. Your Father in heaven cares for you very much. Hide in Him as He covers you now. Go in to Him as He dances and marches around you in a victory parade.

GOLD IN THE GLOOM & DIAMONDS IN THE DARKNESS

The earth was without form and an empty waste, and darkness was upon the face of the very great deep. The Spirit of God was moving (hovering, brooding) over the face of the great waters. And God said, Let there be light; and there was light. Gen. 1:2-3 (AMP)

God has this certain specialty. One thing He is really good at is speaking into dark places and creating light. Another thing He specializes in is brooding, moving and hovering over empty, formless areas.

Are you His child? Could it be that you are in a season that is "without form and an empty waste"? Did you know that God has made darkness His secret hiding place?

He made darkness His secret hiding place; as His pavilion (His canopy) round about Him were dark waters and thick clouds of the skies. Psalm 18:11 (AMP)

If you are struggling right now, the shades have been pulled, and your room has darkened—if life seems empty and formless at the moment, please take heart and understand the perspective of heaven.

God is with you in the dark just as much as God is with you in the light.

If you can wrap your mind around this truth, it will help you fight the negative thoughts that God has left you alone in this difficult place—because nothing could be further from the truth.

There is a mindset that when all is well, God is with us, and when things turn sour, it means only one thing: God has stepped out of the room for a minute.

Isaiah 45:3 (AMP) tells us:

> *I will give you the treasures of darkness and hidden riches of secret places, that you may know that it is I, the Lord, the God of Israel, Who calls you by your name.*

There are treasures in dark places that we will *never* discover in the light. We will have no way of knowing about these hidden riches if we always live where it's easy and pleasant.

Darkness and light both have benefits for the child of God. Darkness has the potential of pushing us right into His arms. Think of your bedroom. In the daylight, you see clearly where everything is. At night, if you get out of bed in the dark, everything is still there where it was in the daylight. The memory of where things are helps you navigate through the dark room. So it is when things darken for us spiritually. We can't really see what is around us, but we remember that God was with us and continues to be there even when we can't see Him clearly.

It's the ebb and flow of life. The tide comes in, and then it goes out. We need both the ebb and flow to keep us alive. We need the ups and downs to form us into His image.

Change your way of thinking. Don't be on such a downer when the tide is out. Don't give in to depression when all looks gloomy. Rather, start looking for the hidden riches that belong to you in Jesus. Put your spiritual headlamp on, and soon you will discover the gold in the gloom. You will find the diamond in the dark. It's there, but you must search for it. He is there, but you must discover Him.

Remember: God is brooding over you in this difficult place. He is hovering over you, watching over you as a hen resting upon her nest. Soon your hope will be realized. He will speak into your darkness, and you will emerge into the light.

GET OFF THE EMOTIONAL MERRY-GO-ROUND

Be quiet and know that I am God.

Be confident that I will do what no human being can do. Be still and let Me heal your heart.

Be comforted and let Me hold you.

Be peaceful and see the storm from inside its eye. Practice stillness and hear My voice.

You will cross over on dry soil. The mighty flood will not swallow you. The weapon formed against you will not prosper.

Knowing comes out of inward quietness. Knowing is birthed out of waiting.

Knowing is the mother of hope.

All of your answers are in Me. All of the keys you need are in My hand. I have every key for every door that needs locked or unlocked.

Look upon My wounds, not your wounds. Stop receiving hurt and start receiving help. Your attention will dictate your direction.

I am all about turning water into wine, coal into gold, night into day, weeping into joy, war into peace, swords into ploughshares, a desert into an oasis.

The elements around you have come that Christ may be more clearly formed in you.

The elements must not be your focus. Jesus, your hope, is to be your focus.

I want eye contact with you, dear one. For therein is your way through.

JUST ABOVE YOU, WAITING TO INVADE YOU

Come, and let us return unto the LORD: for he hath torn, and he will heal us; he hath smitten, and he will bind us up. Hosea 6:1 (KJV)

A Cry from the Fire

Lord, I'm in the fire. Help me see. Give me Your vision. Grant me Your perspective. Save me from my thoughts. Release me from my own emotions.

Take me to the place where You are. Furnish me with the vision I need to make my way through this place of confusion, pain and disappointment.

An Answer

My Child, I hear your cry and plea for help. I answer you with My loving kindness. I envelop you in this moment of shattering. I stand with you in the fire.

I have allowed this moment in your life. I see your need to be near Me; and when the enemy asked if he could buffet you with this, I said "okay." I said okay to your adversary because I saw how it would better equip you and strengthen you and bring you closer to My heart. This thing will not devastate you. This pain will not destroy you. This fire will not burn you. As you draw near to Me in it, you will witness how I will uphold you. You will observe firsthand the emerging wisdom in your heart. You will see My blueprints and how I am using this thing to build My kingdom in you and all concerned.

New heights, new victory and fresh understanding of My ways hover all around you, seeking to invade your heart and soul today. I am pleased with your heart cry. I am happy to reply to your request. I am here to raise you upon My wing today.

Disappointments are appointments with Me. I care deeply about what touches you. Take heart. We will rise together, and what the enemy sought to destroy you with will be used as the very wing that will cause you to rise with new strength and power in Me.

Don't be afraid but continue stepping through the fire in communion with Me; and when you come out of this place, the smoke of it shall not even be upon you, but the glory of it shall shine all about you.

ℳY DARKNESS ILLUMINATED

*For thou art my lamp, O LORD: and the LORD will lighten my
darkness. For by thee I have run through a troop: by my God have I
leaped over a wall. 2 Samuel 22:29-30 (KJV)*

ℊod is my candle, my lamp and the only hope of seeing something
in full truth, but I must strike the match or flip on the switch for the
desired light. It may be a still, small voice whispering "trust Me." It may
be a quiet inner voice that gently calls out, "Be still and know that I am
God." However, He comes to me with light, I must "find the switch"
and position myself to hear. I must unburden my soul with the baggage

it carries, deafening me to His voice. However, when His light comes, I will be liberated from my fears and anxieties. I will enter a level of peace that surpasses the need to understand. I will encounter a supernatural power to prevail against my adversary.

What is "my darkness"? What is it that God will "lighten"? *Darkness* in the Hebrew is the word *choshek*. It means obscurity, secret place, night.

You know the station. It's that area no one else sees. It's the spot you find yourself in time and time again. It's the ground where God breaks you, forms you and makes you into His image. It's the platform of death to self—the battleground for your soul.

It's a place where vision can grow dim—maybe even downright confusing—a place of uncertainty. Sometimes, you find yourself in a corner of gloom or depression. It's that place between the setting and rising of the sun. You can't really see much. Understanding has escaped your heart.

. . . and the LORD will lighten my darkness.

My Lord will lighten my darkness. He might not completely take it away, but He will sure come in and help me to see more clearly. He will help and assist me to get through it.

When the light comes in on my darkness, I am going to begin running instead of tripping and stumbling over everything. I am going to gain the ability to start running. It will be a run very similar to that of an animal finally set free from a trap.

And the troops who were engaged in raiding me for plunder, ravaging me, roaming around me or attacking me will suddenly be split in two as I run through them and disappear before their eyes.

The wall that was before me, blocking me, stopping me or hindering me will become a hurdle that runners love to leap over in the race. It will no longer stop me from making progress. I will jump over it as a deer that leaps over a hedge and keep running with my God.

I can do these things because God has come to me and illuminated my darkness. He has caused me to see the journey with true sight.

He is with me. He will never abandon me or leave me without support. He loves me. He is leading in triumph over my adversary. He is ready to empower me in any moment of time, enabling me to stand and not faint. The road is no longer lonely.

Running and leaping with God always means that there is hope in my soul. Hope is my flashlight to see where I'm going when darkness surrounds. Because I have hope, I will have light. God is light, and as I am in Him, there will be vision and sight for each step of the way.

$\mathscr{T}$HE PRESERVATION PLAN

And the Lord shall deliver me from every evil work, and will preserve me unto his heavenly kingdom: to whom be glory forever and ever. Amen. 2 Timothy 4:18 (KJV)

$\mathscr{D}$*emons have been assigned to* harass and annoy, and to cause pain, trouble and disease upon every inhabitant of the earth. The demonic structure of hell thrives and survives on turning us aside from our faith in any way, shape or form . . .

and God has allowed it.

God, on the other hand, has laid out a plan for every single person who is looking to Him for their strength and sustenance. The plan is simple: I will be delivered from every scheme the evil one has planned against me. I will not only be delivered, but I will be kept safe and whole all the way across the finish line of heaven. My soul will be kept alive through every fire.

This implies that evil will be at work, and there will be a need to be delivered. I am not exempt from evil influences, but I am preserved and brought safely to my home in heaven. I may have a few bumps, bruises and scars, but I will be all the better because of them because my God will see me through each and every hardship. I have not been delivered *from* but *through* the rising floods of difficulties. What the adversary thought he was doing only got used to further my intimate walk with Jesus. Isn't that glorious?

The difficulties that God allows to touch me are meant to better equip and strengthen me. God will never give permission for a trial that will destroy me. As I trust in Him, I will have strength equal to the trial and grace to face the challenge. Ultimately, God will deliver me from every work of the evil one *(2 Timothy 4:18)*.

Think of some of the heroes of our faith.

Jesus obtained my salvation through a torturous death. Paul was beaten many times while advancing the gospel to those who hadn't yet heard it. Job was deeply afflicted physically and emotionally but came through knowing God more intimately. Joseph was misunderstood and unjustly thrown in prison, only to be strategically placed second in position to Pharaoh. David was hunted down by the madman, Saul, while all the while he was anointed by God to be the next king of Israel.

Do you think you have it hard? Think twice as you contemplate our forerunners in the faith. Whatever the difficulty in your life that has you sighing and moaning inside, offer it to the Author and Finisher of your faith. Stop convincing yourself it will go on for eternity. It's His workmanship in your life at this moment. It's His business. You have no idea what the completed work will look like. Now trust Him and remember His promise to deliver you. It will be His timing, not yours. It will be His way, not yours. It will be for His purpose, not yours.

This deserves our praise to the Glorious One, today and every day for the rest of our eternal lives.

$\mathscr{I}$N MOMENTS OF WAITING

$\mathcal{W}$ait: to postpone or delay in expectation, to remain inactive or in a state of repose, as until something expected happens; linger, abide, delay, to remain temporarily neglected, unattended to, or postponed; to watch; to observe; to take notice, to stay or rest in expectation; to stop or remain stationary 'til the arrival of some person or event; to rest in patience; to stay; not to depart.

Times of waiting fall upon us all. Days when you feel temporarily neglected can come upon you suddenly. There are intervals when there's nothing to do but abide in Him, occasions when what you want is being delayed for some unknown purpose, moments in life when you are just the observer and not the participator. Seasons come when you are virtually forced to stand quietly because you don't know what else to do. There are times in life when you scratch your head and look up to God in absolute perplexity.

The Word of God is very specific for these times, and we should not become surprised when they come crashing down upon us. As a matter of fact, we should expect pockets of these types of seasons regularly visiting us.

What we do in these divinely orchestrated moments will make or break us. It's in these times that our true maturity level will be known. Let's look to the psalms for some direction and comfort.

> *Let integrity and uprightness preserve me; for I wait on thee.*
> *Psalm 25:21 (KJV)*

The word *integrity* denotes simplicity and innocence. While I'm waiting on the Lord, I must not fall into sin. I must not entertain confusing thoughts. I must keep the simple trust of my Lord ever before me. These acts will be ingredients to my preservation while I wait.

> *Wait and hope for and expect the Lord; be brave and of good courage*
> *and let your heart be stout and enduring. Yes, wait for and hope for and*
> *expect the Lord. Psalms 27:14 (AMP)*

In this psalm, God is encouraging us to take courage and be brave while we have to wait for Him. He calls us to expect Him to come; yet while we are waiting, we must find courage and hope. This implies that we are going to find ourselves in some tough spots. We will be greeted by difficulty and pain, thus the need for courage and hope while we wait.

Rest in the LORD, and wait patiently for him: fret not thyself because of him who prospereth in his way, because of the man who bringeth wicked devices to pass. Psalms 37:7 (KJV)

Rest in the Lord. This word *rest* is really a prompt to become dumb and still. Stop talking and quiet yourself down. Show forth one of the fruits of the Holy Spirit—patience. Don't worry about the next guy who seems to be having success no matter what he does. It's not over until it's over. One more in Lamentations 3:25-26 (NASB):

The LORD is good to those who wait for Him, to the person who seeks Him. It is good that he waits silently for the salvation of the LORD.

When we have to wait for God, it's a sign of His goodness to us. If you are a seeker of God, you are going to have to wait for Him. We must learn not to be in a rush. God does everything on time and in His way. Salvation will eventually come to the soul who has learned how to be motionless and silent in times of waiting.

Confessions of a Storm-Tossed Soul

Lord, there are circumstances in my life that bother me. I am discontent. I come to You and ask that You help me. Pour Your fresh supplies over my tired soul. Give me Your courage. Infuse me with fresh hope. Convict me when I am sinning. Empower me to wait in innocence. Let me taste the rest that You have promised me while my flesh is screaming that You are neglecting me. Take me into deeper realms of simple abiding in You. Thank You for listening to my thoughts. I receive fresh bread and water from You now. Thank You for preserving me. Thank You, Lord. I love You. Amen.

ℐHE HEAVENLY CORD, *TIQVAH*

For surely there is a latter end [a future and a reward], and your hope and expectation shall not be cut off. Proverbs 23:18 (AMP)

Don't for a minute envy careless rebels; soak yourself in the Fear- of- God—That's where your future lies. Then you won't be left with an armload of nothing. Proverbs 23:18 (MSG)

Expectation: We need it for every deep, dark trial. We must stay stirred up in it. We must soak ourselves in the fear of God. The Hebrew word for *expectation* is *tiqvah*. It means cord, hope and outcome.

Expectation is your cord to heaven. It's the thing that keeps you connected when the violent winds of tribulation are whipping at your feet. It's the lifeline that will keep you in the will of God if you hold on to it.

The Word of God predicates that our cord of hope will not be cut off. We could let go of it, and we do sometimes, but God affirms that as long as you hang on, it won't be cut.

The King James Version states, *"For surely there is an end . . ."* Speak to yourself right now, "Surely there is an end . . ."

Say it once more. Surely there is an end.

Just declaring that to my soul brings comfort and strengthens the cord of expectation and hope. We must keep ourselves stirred up in hope every day. The days of our trial are numbered. There will come a day when God insists "ENOUGH." and circumstances will have to give way to His authority. Hell will have to bow down, and torment will no longer be allowed at our doorstep.

Until then, however, we have a cord on which to hold. God teaches us how to walk in the dark. One way He does this is to give us a cord of hope. As we hold on to it, we will find our way around when we can't see. The cord of expectation is a gift from God.

We can expect the ending of trouble and sorrow and trauma. Until then, we must grow through every wind and gale. Until then, we must stay focused to hang on tightly while our faith turns to gold before God.

"My soul, wait thou only upon God; for my expectation is from him."
Psalm 62:5 (KJV)

Keep your chin up, saint. It's a test of endurance. It's an assessment that we need to pass. It's a scrutiny to strengthen our faith. It's an exam that has an ending.

Oh Lord, Do It Again.

Lord, I continue to hang onto Your cord. I revere Your Word, and I humbly submit all my thoughts and feelings to You today. Cleanse me of all that would lessen my grip on the cord. Baptize me with Your Holy Spirit as I cling to You. Then I will be empowered again today to stand strong and hold on. Thank You for Your provisions. Thank You for Your hold on me. Thank You for leading me back to the cord in the times I let go. You are gentle and patient with me. I bathe in Your love now and receive from Your hand the supply of hope needed for today. Amen.

ONWARD HO!

To go through something—I mean go *through* it—is how I will grow. My faith will never become stronger if it has no opportunity to flex its muscles. The place of difficulty is a perfect workout room for my faith to gain strength and spiritual muscle.

God has not promised exemption from hardship. There is no "pass" card dealt to me when I enter into the realm of the salvation of my soul. I will not be overlooked by the devil just because I now belong to Jesus. No, no, absolutely not. As a matter of fact, my choice to deny myself and take up my cross may attract my adversary. Furthermore, you may experience heartache, misunderstanding, loneliness, fears, anxious thoughts and the like.

Oh, but the glory that's coming my way will not be compared to all the devils and darkness that crossed my earthly path. There is one journey that is worth the trouble and one journey alone. This journey is the one I take with my Master and Savior Jesus Christ. All other ways of walking end up in darkness. Yet this one path, the narrow path, will lead me to a golden gate. I will one day walk through this heavenly gate on to the sight of all sights. It will be the reward of all rewards. One day, I will enter into the reward of seeing my Savior face to face. I will lay my crown at His feet. I will receive the embrace of all embraces and finally be home.

I don't belong here. I can't settle here. My heart wants more than this old world can offer. There are sights and smells and colors that I long to see and smell because I was made for there and not here.

Here is where the metamorphosis of my heart is occurring. Here is where my love for Him is proved. Here is where my faith is turning to gold. This journey upon earth is gaining for me the salvation of my soul. Through the fire and flood, my soul is proved and tested for Him.

I have His love and presence, and that's really all I need. People come in and out, but He comes in and stays. He has made His home with me; and while I'm traveling upon this dark sod of earth, I have a continual heaven in my heart because of the continual presence of my God with me. At any moment through the storm, I can go into His shelter and fellowship with Him. He always keeps the home fires burning and is always anticipating my fellowship with Him. It's a secret place—that place between Him and me—a place of safety and rest, a place of satisfaction and assurance, and a room where I always experience the embrace of my heavenly Father.

It's vital that I experience all the hardships of this life. For in this experience, I get to understand more and more the depth of His love for me. When I fall down, He will pick me up. The more darkness that envelops me, the more glory that is heading my way, and oh, the glory of His presence when compared to the darkness—it's magnificent. It's unsearchable and indescribable. It's worth the hellhole in which I sometimes find myself.

I must go through all the divine testing. I must enter into all the suffering and sorrows of this world. If my Lord was a man of sorrows and acquainted with much grief, then I will suffer as well. As I endure the baptisms of the tribulation of this world—oh, the joys that will be mine on the other side. Oh, the certain joy that is mine now. For this joy that is set before me, I can endure, just as my Savior did *(Hebrews 12:2)*. Yes, I can endure.

My flesh will just have to fight and squirm because I'm going after the prize. I'm going after the prize of knowing Him in the sorrow and the joy. I want to know my Lord in the fullness of it all. Jesus showed the way; and as He is, so am I in this world *(1 John 4:17)*.

So, try as you may, devil, and squirm all you wish, my flesh, but the God who made me and crafted me in His image is going to use the very things that want to trip me up to shape me and mold me into the image of Christ.

For the image of Christ is being formed in me. One day—one very special day—when my Lord looks upon me, there will be a clear, undeniable reflection of Him. My life will be well hidden in Him. Oh, what a day that will be.

Until then, onward ho! Yes, onward ho! Into the flame and into the flood I will go. Let the immersion of tribulation come, that the total immersion of knowing Him may be perfected in my soul until He has increased and I have decreased—completely and altogether—until my light is as bright as it was meant to shine. Onward ho! My flesh will not care for it, but my spirit will revel in it. Onward ho! My road will be hard, but my victory will be sweet. Onward ho! Days of confusion and depression will come. Onward ho! My soul, your reward is traveling towards you now. Onward ho! Let hope keep you in its grip.

CASTING OUR PAST INTO OBLIVION

Forget about what's happened; don't keep going over old history.
Be alert, be present. I'm about to do something brand new.
It's bursting out. Don't you see it?
There it is! I'm making a road through the desert,
rivers in the badlands.
Isaiah 43:18-19 (MSG)

Do not call to mind the former things, Or ponder things of the past.
Behold, I will do something new, Now it will spring forth;
Will you not be aware of it?

I will even make a roadway in the wilderness, Rivers in the desert.
Isaiah 43:18-19 (NASB)

I wanted to use two versions of these verses. God is very intentional about what He wants us to do with our past. Good or bad, ugly or amazing, we are not to walk through life looking over our shoulder. True, we cannot completely forget the past. Only God has that ability concerning our sins. Yet He tells us not to think about it and ponder it. God asks us to dwell upon what's ahead and not what's behind.

God asks His children to be forward-thinkers. He has tests yet ahead of us that require our front and center gaze upon Him. When we walk with our head turned back, we put ourselves in a dangerous position. Even in the natural, it won't be long 'til we run smack dab into a wall or something that isn't going to step out of our way just because we are moving towards it.

Our Creator gave us eyes to look ahead and be safe as we walk. Our vision is not for viewing our past mistakes, hurts and wounds. Yesterday has too many mistakes and shortcomings to add them to today's burden of life. If you have sinned in your past, repent of it and move forward. In the same way, we can't take on tomorrow's worries and add them to today's troubles *(Matthew 6:34).*

We were meant to carry only what needs to be carried for today. Too much baggage will hinder our journey and prolong the reward and blessing that the good Lord has prepared for us.

God is saying in essence here in Isaiah:

Look, I want you to stop considering what happened to you yesterday and think about what I am working for you now. I want you to be aware of something I am making for you. I am building a road for you to make it across the wilderness of this earth. I am planting rivers for your refreshing in this dry desert habitation. I won't leave you without supply. I won't have you just barely getting through. I have paved a way for you, and all that you need is here today and will be there tomorrow. If you keep looking back, you won't find the road I have made for you. If you keep looking over your shoulder, you will miss the river that I have prepared for you. Sometimes there is no way you can fully understand what happened in your past. Stop trying to tally it all up. It's hindering your ability to move into your future with Me. What's done is done, and now I will show you new things that will bring healing and strength so you can finish your journey home. As you look forward, you will find new healing and power even in the current pain and bleeding of your dear heart. Where you fix your eyes is a critical factor in your destination. You can end up in the ditch or on a detour, or you can walk on the road I have made just for you. It will be a road that will be best suited for you. Even now, if you find yourself in the ditch or on a detour, begin to look forward; and soon you will be back on the path.

This is not an Old Testament instruction. The apostle Paul also encourages us by the Holy Spirit to look forward and not backward. Saint, there is a goal. There is a prize, and there is a reason to run forward and not backward. It's simply natural to walk forward, look forward and see what's ahead. Spiritually speaking, it's the same. Yes, the memory of yesterday will remain, but how much focus we give it is critical. Too much focus on the wrong things is unhealthy for anyone.

Brethren, I count not myself to have apprehended: but this one thing I do, forgetting those things which are behind, and reaching forth unto those things which are before, I press toward the mark for the prize of the high calling of God in Christ Jesus.
Philippians 3:13-14 (KJV)

This word *forgetting* in the New Testament is used only one time. It literally means to neglect, give over to oblivion or no longer caring for. Past things are just that—they are over. You no longer have the past. It's gone. God asks us to put it out of our minds and cast it into oblivion. Neglect the thoughts of it. Stop caring so much about it.

Friend, if God asks this of us, then He will empower us to do it. Some things simply require a supernatural intervention in order for us to get out of neutral and put it in gear. If that's the spot you are in, then begin to beg the God of all power and ability to fill you with the power you need to obey His Word. What kind of a God would ask you to do something beyond your ability and then not supply you with the power to do it? This is not the way God operates. Instead, He has all the supernatural supply you need to whip the devil on every corner and down every dark alley. He offers it freely to every born-again believer on the earth.

There is a mark to attain. There is a finish line to cross. There is a prize of which to lay hold. Whatever has got you pegged to the floor is not worth the trouble of memorializing. The only memory and picture worth pondering is the picture of the death, burial and resurrection of Jesus Christ. From this perspective, all other memories shadow and pale in comparison and power. For in the meditation of the cross comes any and all supply you will ever need to look forward and not backward. The power of the cross of Jesus Christ is unparalleled to any other memory you have ever idolized.

"Re-member" is truly putting back the picture of what happened. "Re-membering" is only beneficial when God is in the middle of that remembrance. At the end of each year, we have a tendency to remember the past year(s). Ponder what God says about your past, present and future. Forget it. Reach forth. There is a road being built for you even now upon which to travel.

For those who are walking through severe emotional/physical pain and trauma, God is patient and will take you through most gently and graciously—but take you through He will. It will involve some time, but that's okay. Be as patient with yourself as God is, and the severe pain and trauma of the thing will one day (either here or in glory) be softened and bearable to your soul. Until the day breaks and the shadows flee, keep looking forward. Search for His embrace. He will be faithful to you, and His sweet presence will continue on with you to your own finish line.

EVERYONE WHO RUNS TO HIM MAKES IT

photo credit Christy Repasky, used with permission by Sarah Forry (runner)

Psalm 18 is a wonderful passage of scripture. King David is revealing some secrets about his personal life with God. We would do well to pay close attention. I have picked out a few verses from this chapter, but I encourage you to read the whole chapter to see if the Holy Spirit might show you more.

> *In my distress I called upon the LORD, And cried to my God for help;*
> *He heard my voice out of His temple,*
> *And my cry for help before Him came into His ears.*
> *Psalm 18:6 (NASB)*

*He reached from on high, He took me; He drew me out of many
waters. Psalm 18:16 (AMP)*

*He brought me forth also into a broad place;
He rescued me, because He delighted in me. Psalm 18:19 (NASB)*

*Suddenly, God, you floodlight my life; I'm blazing with glory, God's
glory!
I smash the bands of marauders, I vault the highest fences.*

*What a God! His road stretches straight and smooth.
Every God-direction is road-tested. Everyone who runs toward him
Makes it.*

*Is there any god like God? Are we not at bedrock?
Is not this the God who armed me,
then aimed me in the right direction?
Now I run like a deer; I'm king of the mountain. He shows me how to
fight; I can bend a bronze bow!
You protect me with salvation-armor; you hold me up with a firm
hand, caress me with your gentle ways.
You cleared the ground under me so my footing was firm.
When I chased my enemies I caught them; I didn't let go 'til they were
dead men.
I nailed them; they were down for good;
then I walked all over them. Psalm 18:28-36 (MSG)*

*For You have girded me with strength for battle; You have subdued
under me those who rose up against me. Psalm 18:39 (NASB)*

*The LORD lives, and blessed be my rock;
And exalted be the God of my salvation. Psalm 18:46 (NASB)*

Because we are human beings, and because we are upon this sin-sick earth, we will regularly encounter times of distress. The Hebrew word for *distress* is the word *tsar*. It means narrow, tight, enemy, oppressor, hard pebble, flint.

It's guaranteed that you will enter into the narrow place of oppression and enemy pursuit. Distresses of all sorts will come that will feel similar to a pebble in your shoe—times of discomfort and times when you feel squeezed on all sides and totally surrounded. King David remembered such times.

"He heard my voice," and *"My cry for help before Him, came into His ears."* Child of God, let me remind you right now that your *Abba* Father hears *your* voice. His ears are attentive to your cries. Your God is not deaf. He is listening for your voice and waiting for you to cry out to Him. When was the last time you really cried out to Him in your distress? How long does it take when you are in the waters of trouble for you to fall on your knees and make known your voice in His Throne Room of Grace?

Oh, my. The undue burdens we bear when we keep the lid on our heart of hearts before the Lord. The weight we carry only because we refuse to unburden our souls before the One who formed us in our mother's womb. He waits to hear from His children so He can answer. How many times do we have not because we have asked not?

God, in answer to your cries when you are in a place of distress, will *"reach from on high,"* He will take you and He will draw you out of many waters. Wow. That's my God. Did you ever see a rescue mission over deep waters? They send in a helicopter, let down the line and basically snatch that person out of the water. That's the picture. God, in His loving kindness, brings His Holy Helicopter over you in your distress and lifts you away with Him to the secret place of protection and fellowship.

He rescues me. He lights my lamp. He causes me to run through a troop that formerly harassed and sickened my soul. He causes me to leap over the wall that I kept beating myself against in defeat. I can hide behind His shield now because He has plucked me out of my pit of despair. Oh, dear saint, are you encouraged yet? This God, to whom you have given your life, loves you deeply and passionately—so much so that He wants to rescue you out of your discouragement today.

He wishes to gird you with strength and arm you with power. *Everyone who runs to Him makes it.* I used to stumble and crawl in despair. After He rescued me, I can run like a deer. He has given me supernatural power to rise above what held me down.

My God is alive. I worship Him. He is a Rock. The God of my salvation is worthy of all my adoration.

$\mathcal{L}$IGHT ALWAYS PREVAILS

You, LORD, are my lamp; the LORD turns my darkness into light.
2 Samuel 22:29 (NIV)

God has delivered me from going down to the pit, and I shall live to
enjoy the light of life. Job 33:28 (NIV)

You, LORD, keep my lamp burning; my God turns my darkness into
light. Psalm 18:28 (NIV)

*I will lead the blind by ways they have not known, along unfamiliar
paths I will guide them; I will turn the darkness into light before them
and make the rough places smooth. These are the things I will do; I will
not forsake them. Isaiah 42:16 (NIV)*

*The light shines in the darkness, and the darkness has not overcome it.
John 1:5 (NIV)*

God's whisper ...

*Child, you are in the night season. The season of day and clarity is yet
ahead of you. For now, lean against My breast tonight in trust and confidence.
I hear your cry for help. Your voice in My chamber touches me to the core.
Never believe that I am deaf to your cry. Never imagine that I don't care.
My affection for you runs deeper than you will ever comprehend. Even in
your wonderings I understand.*

I do not condemn you.

*We are walking together. I am with you. Never are you alone. What
concerns you concerns Me. There are places of challenge that are in your life
for you to grow and understand My love for you. I am teaching you now, just
how to walk by what you can't see or feel. Life can seem empty and void of
direction. Wait. Listen. Absorb my love into every fiber of your being while
you wait and listen.*

*Go into My creation and be refreshed by My presence. Feel My love for
you as it breezes against your face. Absorb My love as the sunrays shine down.
A rippling brook reflects the refreshing that belongs in your soul. There is
much to learn by studying My creation.*

*In darkness, there is food for you. In the shadows, I have a table prepared.
Come. The resistance in your heart is robbing you of a lavish meal that I have
ready for you. Let Me love on you. Allow yourself to bend into Me. Could
I perform a miracle in your heart? Can I bring light into the dark places?*

Just as the nighttime is swallowed up in the sunrise of each day, so shall the darkness of your soul be chased away in the light of My glorious love shining upon you. Remain transparent with Me.

Pain paralyzes people.

Your pain must propel you forward into My arms.

Demons want to demoralize you.

I have already affirmed and glorified you.

The Father's love will fill you and take you places that will amaze and astonish you.

Every day, light overcomes darkness. Every day, there is light for you to embrace to combat the darkness of this world. No day is filled with pure darkness if you belong to Me. No day is so hopeless that there isn't a way through.

My children are called children of the day. Even in their night seasons, there are places of dwelling that bring light and warmth in the dark and cold. I have provided well for each of My dear ones.

You are My dear one. Take heart. Be filled in your soul with the light of My love. Be infused and then go shine. I am with you always. No matter what you feel and no matter what you see, I am with you always. My Spirit of counsel lives within you. Learn my voice and you will shine and soar when there is no logical reason to shine and soar. You will be a miraculous wonder in the earth as my glory-glow surrounds your life.

THE GIFT OF DELAY: A DIALOGUE

Father, I want to express how grateful my heart is for the blessings and gifts You have given me recently. At times, there is challenge and difficulty and struggle, but at other times, like now, there is an enjoyment of answered conversations we have had. There is a fresh satisfaction blowing over my soul. I am comforted. I am living in the pleasures found only at Your right hand.

My child, it was My good pleasure to bring you into your answer, fully. I had the answer before you even thought it. I knew what you were going to ask Me and I knew exactly how I was going to answer you. There is an ebb and flow for each of My dear ones. There is a time of instruction and testing, and then there is a time for recreation and enjoyment. I have dismissed you to your "recess" and I have been enjoying watching you play in your newly-answered request.

For many years we had many conversations about a certain desire in my heart. You said that I should let my request be made known. I did. You said that I should surrender that desire. I did. I asked You to take my desire away if it wasn't in Your plan. You didn't. Since You didn't, the place of unfulfilled dreams and unanswered requests became my existence.

Yes, I gave you the gift of delay. The gift of delay is not always perceived as a gift. You carefully and lovingly opened your gift of delay in the atmosphere of trust. My daughter, you trusted Me. Even now, that stirs a beam of pride for you in Me. You trusted Me in the pain. You trusted Me in the sadness. You surrendered and even came to the road post of saying "yes" for the sake of My perfect plan and will which could include not receiving what your heart was longing for. You embraced My gift of delay and you occupied your place of living like one who didn't skip a beat. I never once heard a rant of anger towards Me. You never once demanded your way. By your spiritual posture, I was able to move heaven and earth to grant the desire of your heart. I was able to move on hearts and open doors that no man could shut. You postured yourself in such a way that allowed for the heavens to be opened on your behalf.

Lord, I am convinced that by the time a specific answer is in my lap, You will have accomplished so much more than just a simple answer to my prayer. The answer is such a gift, but the gift began to be unwrapped the moment I had that first dialogue with You. How did You do that? Yes, You are God, but wow, I mean, at times the details that You included as I waited. In these last years of waiting, I have seen Your handprints over and over again. I really do live in a continual state of awe concerning You, Lord.

My dear one, yes. In the waiting, you worked for Me. You labored out of your love for Me. You saw many miracles of the heart, just by allowing My atmosphere to swirl around and rest on you on so many occasions. It was my joy and delight to have this "dance" with you as we worked and co-labored together. The yoke we share is sweet and as we continue to walk in step, there is yet more that I will teach you. As you learn, you will teach. Many will find great value in the lessons you learn of My Holy Spirit.

Papa, I love You. I am humbled to walk with the Creator of the universe. I am having difficulty finding words to express my love and gratitude towards You. I thank You for the gift of delay. I have found strength that I would not have found if You hadn't given me the gift of delay. People were influenced by Your heavy hand upon me. In that season of ebb and delay, You taught me how to labor in your kingdom. I learned at Your feet. You showed me how to run through a troop and over a wall that was set up to stop my spiritual progress. You took my tears and put them in Your bottle. Not one of my tears was shed in vain.

Now, dear one, look around and discover your new land. Take it slowly, but begin walking. Look around. See what I will say. Just do the next thing I give you to do. It will be simple, yet the impact will be profound. You hear Me. You know Me. Keep the trust flowing even in the face of unanswered requests. The gift of delay will be given to you over and over again, but it has become like a friend to you now. You understand it better. It will serve you well, My child ... Let's go make history.

Yes, Lord, let's go make history.

STUDY/DISCUSSION QUESTIONS ON "LESSONS IN HOPE"

1. In one sentence, define what hope means to you. Share a Bible verse that encourages you with hope.

2. Read "Full Circle." Have you ever come "full circle"? How is our pain linked to ministry?

3. Have you ever been in the "zone of comfort" of trouble and really not desired help? How can fear keep hope away from us?

4. Read Romans 4:18-22. What does it mean to hope against all hope?

5. Why is hope critical to our stability and well-being? Share some scriptural reasons.

6. Why are we sometimes afraid to get our hopes up? Is there ever a reason to be hopeless? Explain. Use scripture to back up your thought.

7. When you feel hopeless, how do you travel towards a place of hope? What is helpful in stirring up hope in your heart?

8. Proverbs 13:12 says that hope deferred makes a heart sick. Explain how heart health and hope are related.

9. What would be the first thing you would say to someone who was acting hopeless who was not a Christian? How about someone who was a Christian?

ℒESSONS IN LOVE

Place me like a seal over your heart, like a seal on your arm; for love is as strong as death, its jealousy unyielding as the grave. It burns like blazing fire, like a mighty flame.
Song of Solomon 8:6 (NIV)

"The beginning of love is to let those we love be perfectly themselves, and not to twist them to fit our own image. Otherwise we love only the reflection of ourselves we find in them."
—Thomas Merton

COME CLOSER

Did you hear Me call your name as the breeze touched your skin? *Did you see Me smiling at you through the face of your dear friend the other day? Did you know how refreshing that glass of cool water tasted to Me when you gave that child a drink? Did you know that I was comforted by your hospital visit? When you sent that money in, My empty stomach was filled by your care and concern; and I was no longer naked. When the preacher preached, did you hear Me whisper to you how I love you and have a certain plan for your life?*

Did you know that I have painted many pictures in My creation just for your pleasure?

Do you have any idea how often I have longed to take you in My arms to hold you as you travel upon your weary road? Many times, you didn't notice I was there. I was the unseen companion with you.

Would you.... could you... allow Me to really hold you when your world is falling apart? It's My heart. It's My desire. Did you know that? I'm here. I am not far away. I am close to your broken heart. I am near you in your sorrows. Every single disappointment you experience echoes in My soul, and I reach out to comfort you and help you through.

Go for a walk. Hear Me in the song of the birds. Be filled with My comfort and joy as you listen. Grab hold of My peace as you watch the sun set into the horizon. Immerse yourself in My love for you as you watch a storm brew up. Touch Me and know Me through My creation. There are many more things I want to tell you. There's so much more for us to experience together.

When you laugh, I laugh with you. My ear is bent to the sound of your laughter.

Your laughter is a melody that fulfills one of My desires to bless you.

I'm writing a book. This book brings Me much joy and delight to write. For I eavesdrop upon your conversations about Me. I take notes and write down the conversations you have about Me. Did you sense Me listening the other day when you were on the phone to your comrade in the faith? Did you sense My companionship when you walked with your friend? Oh, I did enjoy that conversation. I take great pleasure in your pondering and musings of My Word.

Look for Me a little harder today. See Me in the eyes of a stranger. Look for Me in the one who struggles with sickness. Watch for Me in the eyes of your child. Gaze at Me in the arm of your spouse. I will be making eye contact with you in all sorts of places and faces.

Child, I am real. I am calling you and drawing you into My bosom. Come close. Don't be afraid. I am here. I am with you forever. I want you to know Me more intimately.

Come in to My shelter. Be safe from the storms of life. Dine with Me. Let Me hold you. Allow Me to escort you to the secret place—out of the wind, out of the scorching heat of the day—for times of refreshing and renewal.

You need it.

And I want to give it to you. Forever Yours . . . Jesus

$\mathscr{S}$URROUNDED BY SONGS

You are my hiding place; You preserve me from trouble; You surround me with songs of deliverance. Selah. Psalms 32:7 (NASB)

$\mathscr{D}$*o you ever wake up* in the morning and there's a worship song going through your mind, or just going about your day and you suddenly notice a spiritual song running around in your heart? I have thought of this verse when that happens. However God is doing it, He is encircling me with songs of deliverance. It could be through putting these songs in my heart, or maybe He has the angels that are around me singing over me. Their angelic chorus is finding its way into the walls of my soul. Maybe He comes Himself and just sings as He encircles me.

It's truly something to ponder.

One of the things I read when I was looking up *hiding place* was the thought, "bread to be eaten in secret." Bread to be eaten in secret can be found in His hiding place. God has a heavenly place for us to come in and be sheltered and nourished. How often do you find that place prepared just for you? When I was young, I often escaped into my deep clothes/storage closet just to hide away and be with Him. It was a safe place to talk to Him. Any sounds I made were muffled by the clothes hanging all around me on the racks. I felt surrounded by Him. It was a secret hiding place. More often than not, I emerged from that place strengthened by the bread He had just given me in secret.

God is guarding me and watching over me. He won't let the enemy near me; but as in Job and Peter's cases, when Satan gained permission, there are times He allows a certain nearness of the adversary *(Job 1:6-12 and Luke 22:31)*. Even then, it is for our growth and advancement—never to harm or injure us. Heaven only knows how much misery we are spared just because of His watchful eye upon us. Ask Him if there's anything for you to repent about, and then just let those songs of deliverance wash over you. Let them rise in your heart. Hear the angels singing over you. Listen for God Himself to dance and sing around you with songs of deliverance. Look around for your way of escape. You are surrounded by a God who loves you and loves to sing over you. Today you are surrounded by songs of deliverance. Take heart; your liberation is coming.

GREATER INTIMACY THROUGH GREATER RESTRAINT

For the love of Christ constraineth us . . .
2 Corinthians 5:14 (KJV)

Love is an extremely big deal in God's heart. God's take on love is extremely important in our vertical relationship with Him as well as our horizontal relationships with one another. Is it no wonder that the first and second greatest commandments have to do with loving Him back with our whole hearts, then loving one another in the same way we love ourselves *(Matthew 22:37-39)?*

This verse is a wonder to me. I want to focus on the word *constraineth.*

In the dictionary, the word is defined: to confine forcibly, as by bonds. As followers of Jesus Christ, the affection of God is a force around us that confines us. We are a prisoner of His undying benevolence and goodwill. We can't get it off us. We can't walk away from it. The love of God will be with us always. When we receive it, life goes much better for us. When we try to shut it out, life can turn into a pressurized pot on the stove.

In the Greek, this word *constraineth* means to hold together, lest it fall to pieces; to compress, to press together on every side with the hand; a besieged city; a strait that forces a ship into a narrow channel; a cattle squeeze that pushes in on each side, forcing the beast into a position where it cannot move so the farmer can administer medication; a prisoner; suffering of the soul.

Dear soul, you will fall to pieces if He stops holding you together with His hand of love.

When we are born again, we give Him permission to transform us into His wonderful image. We are giving Him permission to compress us on every side. In essence, we are stating, "Okay God, I am Your besieged city. You can surround me and hem me in." We are now that beast that needs to be confined on all sides so we can receive the divine medication for our wounded souls. We are now enrolled in the Holy Spirit boot camp where we will suffer for the exchange of knowing Him more intimately. We will find ourselves in places that our minds will take offense, but our hearts will begin to swell with satisfaction from our union with Him.

God will do with us as He pleases. Our reward will not necessarily be the removal of tribulation. It will be finding Him—more of Him is less of us.

Our God is jealous for us. When we love what we love in a lustful sort of way—I mean when we want what we want more than what God wants—He will take the ship of our lives and cause it to enter into a tight place, forcing our selfishness to the surface like dross. When you don't get your way, how do you handle it? How often does this happen to you? Maybe you should stop fighting it and think of it as God confining you in His love or as God taking His tool of choice and rooting out the weed of selfishness in your life. For when we are selfish, we are not walking in His love vertically (with Him) or horizontally (with others).

I am thy shield, your exceeding great reward. Genesis 15:1b (KJV)

Friends, our reward is finding Him.

If we go through our journey and always fight the process, we will never find Him. We will lose the reward of a fresh encounter with God Himself. Understand His love today. It doesn't always mean that you will get everything you want. It means that you will get everything He wants. Believe me, it's better than anything we could ever want for ourselves in the first place. Our natural minds cannot comprehend the properties of the Holy Spirit dimension, but we can discern them by the Spirit *(Romans 8)*.

Step out of *your* mind when you are trying to process and understand what God is doing. Put on your spiritual glasses, enabling you to see more clearly into the divine realm. Even then, there are moments when you won't be able to dot all the *i*'s and cross all the *t*'s. The wonderful provision of peace and faith will carry you right into the middle of where God would have you to be, and that's a place prepared just for you and Him alone—a place where you are bound with the constraints of His marvelous love.

A PRIVATE LOVE FEAST WITH GOD

. . . I meditate on all thy works; I muse on the work of thy hands.
Psalms 143:5b (KJV)

The psalmist understood the value of putting a halt to the everyday grind of life in order to meditate. We don't use this word much today. Actually, we don't even hear a lot of teaching on the discipline of meditation. As a matter of fact, when you hear the word meditation, your mind might directly think of it as a practice in the eastern religions. Stop for a moment and understand that meditation was God's idea first.

It's another classic case of something God created for good that the devil took and twisted.

One of the first records of meditation in scripture is found in Genesis 24:63 (AMPC):

And Isaac went out to meditate and bow down [in prayer] in the open country in the evening. . . .

"And Isaac went out to meditate . . . ."

If I were to read between the lines a bit here, I think this was a normal practice of Isaac. It was in the open country and in the evening. He went out, meaning he didn't stay indoors. Outdoors is a great place to meditate. Creation is the perfect place to think about God and talk to Him.

Why meditate?

This Book of the Law shall not depart out of your mouth, but you shall meditate on it day and night, that you may observe and do according to all that is written in it. For then you shall make your way prosperous, and then you shall deal wisely and have good success. Joshua 1:8 (AMP)

Right here are four great reasons to meditate.

Obedience, Prosperity, Wisdom, Success

Meditation is compared to chewing. Think of the cow who swallows its food, then after a time it comes back up and he chews some more. It's called "chewing the cud." This is exactly the concept of meditation. First, we read the Word, and it goes down into our spiritual belly. Then, we bring it up later for more pondering and chewing. This can happen over and over again just with one single word or sentence of the Word of God. The more we meditate on God's Word, the more we are feeding our spirit man. When our spirit man becomes stronger, we are empowered to hear and obey the voice of God. Keeping God's Word near in our thought life serves as a weapon of defense when a lie tries to enter.

Meditation was very much a part of David's life. One place in the Old Testament tells how he strengthened himself in the Lord. No one else was around to give him a spiritual pep talk. As a matter of fact, those around him wanted very much to stone him to death. Let's read the verse:

And David was greatly distressed; for the people spake of stoning him . . . but David encouraged himself in the LORD his God.
1 Samuel 30:6 (KJV)

How do you think he did that?

I think he thought about God and the words that God had spoken to him; or maybe he was in a beautiful corner of creation and through the beauty of the scenery before him, he was able to meditate on Who was there with him, in this place of difficulty and danger. Most likely, as he stood there surrounded by people with stones in their hands, he couldn't just flip out his copy of the Law and start reading it. The Word of God had to already be in his heart, ready to be spoken or thought upon at will.

The word *encouraged* here means to strengthen, prevail, harden, be strong, become strong, be courageous, be firm, grow firm, be resolute. When we truly meditate upon our God or upon His Word, we will find ourselves rising up to face the moment. We will be instantly fortified and enabled to continue the long, sometimes steep climb of life. Meditation upon God and His Word will harden us against the onslaughts of our enemy.

Every one of us should practice the discipline of meditation for that very purpose. One day you will be in need of encouragement, and if you have hidden the Word of God in your heart, you will be able to bring it up and chew on it for a while. Soon your spirit will be lifted, and you will be refreshed in God's presence once again.

Look at Psalm 1:1-2 out of The Message:

How well God must like you—you don't hang out at Sin Saloon, you don't slink along Dead-End Road, you don't go to Smart-Mouth College. Instead you thrill to God's Word, you chew on Scripture day and night.

Another great time to meditate is when you are awake in bed. The time before you sleep, during the night if you awake, or just when you are waking up in the morning are wonderful moments to talk with Him.

I lie awake thinking of you, meditating on you through the night. Psalms 63:6 (NLT)

There are numerous times in the day when we can step away in our minds, go to the Rock and share in a private love feast. I encourage you to make it more of a discipline and habit in your life. Go ahead. Get out into creation as Isaac did. Get into God's creation. Breathe in the fresh revelation of His thoughts towards you today. Encourage yourself in the Lord as David did, and may God harden you against the attacks of the enemy. May your intimate journey with Him deepen and intensify.

$\mathscr{Y}$OU HAVE A VOICE AND GOD HAS SOMETHING TO SAY

Pursue love, yet desire earnestly spiritual gifts, but especially that you may prophesy. 1 Corinthians 14:1 (NASB)

$\mathscr{P}$ursue love . . .

The Greek word for *pursue* is *dioko*. It means to run after, to run swiftly in order to catch a thing, pursue (in a hostile manner), to follow after (someone).

To walk successfully in God's kingdom, love is not an option. We are commanded to walk in it no matter what. We are instructed to not only walk in it, but run after it, eager to win the prize. Love is not a feeling. Love is an action and a choice of the will *(1 Corinthians 13)*. Feelings will come and go, but godly love is a constant. Even more than that, Love is a person. That person is Jesus Christ.

Put in that context, we could state: Pursue Jesus Christ. Run after Him. Pursue Him at all costs (in a hostile manner). Go after Him who is the prize of your heart.

. . . yet desire earnestly spiritual gifts . . .

The Greek word for *desire* is *zeloo*. It means to burn with zeal. The Greek word for *spiritual* is *pneumatikos*. It means belonging to the Divine Spirit, one who is filled with and governed by the Spirit of God, pertaining to the wind or breath.

Even though we are to run after love, yet there is more for us to consider. In pursuing love, we must burn with a zealous fervor to be filled and governed by the Spirit of God. That means that as we yield to Him, His breath will blow through us; it can only touch others in a positive way. Yet there is a part three to this verse:

. . . *but especially that you may prophesy.*

The Greek word for *especially* means more, to a greater degree, rather, more willingly, sooner, more readily. The Greek word for *prophesy* means to speak forth by divine inspiration, to teach, refute, reprove, admonish and comfort others.

As a Christian, you are to be able to readily speak for God. Since our words have the power of life or death, then I can understand why the gift of prophecy would be towards the top of God's list for us in which to consider to participate. After all, every one of us opens up our mouth every day of the year. What comes out of it is of prime importance to God.

The Word of God will teach us, it will correct us, it will admonish us and it will comfort us. Whatever our need, God has a word for us. As we are receiving God's Word for ourselves, it should be simultaneously flowing out to others.

Sometimes, we put too much emphasis on the words *prophetic word,* thinking it's some high and mighty thing that happens to only a select few. No, no, no! Let's bring it close to home. Each one of us has the ability to hear God's voice. Each one of us has a voice for God to use. God is exhorting: Learn to love as I do, desire to be used, but especially in the area of your vocal chords. He can only do that when we are yielded to His Holy Spirit. When we are yielded, then all we have to do is open our mouth and He will fill it.

In Numbers 11:29 Moses said, *"Would that all the Lord's people were prophets."* He said this just after he was told that someone in the camp, other than he, was prophesying. They wanted Moses to stop him, but Moses was glad about it. Let's put a stop to wrong thinking. It's for you. It's in the Bible, and God says do it.

Sometimes, when in a conversation, I will sense the Holy Spirit slipping in, and even though I am not speaking "Thus says the Lord," I sense a fresh confidence and authority to my words that I know are not my own. I know that at that very moment I am prophesying. I am teaching, correcting, admonishing or comforting by the very breath of God through me. It's a wonderful experience, and I "burn with zeal" to experience that more and more.

$\mathcal{T}$HE UNFREQUENTED HIDEAWAY

$\mathcal{G}od's$ whisper ...

The vapor of your life is always before Me. Do you realize how short it is? Be careful not to live your life like there's no tomorrow. Just as your physical life had a day of beginning, so it shall have a day of ending. You were given a first breath and you will most assuredly be given a last breath upon this earth.

I want you to value your life more. I need you to understand that every word, every deed, every action or lack of action is noticed from the Divine perspective. Carelessness costs. It costs you, it can cost any person who has ties with you and it costs our relationship.

The Divine perspective is simply this: God-thoughts towards you. You are conceived, you are born, you live and then you take your last breath on earth. Multitudes go to the grave never understanding why I created them. Myriads take their last breath rejecting My love.

YOU HAVE PURPOSE.

YOU MATTER.

YOU HAVE WORTH.

There is beauty inside and out.

Whose opinion is most important to you ... theirs or Mine? When you live out of Divine perspective your thoughts and actions will be much different from one who is shortsighted and relies upon opinions of man. The opinions of man are offensive to Me. The opinions of man—when not based upon My heartbeat—cause Me to want to wretch. I am a God of hope, peace, strength and love. Any voice telling you otherwise is a lying spirit.

As long as life as you know it proceeds, there is always hope. There is always a way to lay hold of peace. There will most assuredly be strength for you equal to your challenge and there will never be a moment that I am not intensely in love with you.

GET THAT.

I have not asked you to be plain. I have asked you to shine like a star in the backdrop of darkness. I have given you a personality that reflects Mine. When your personality is filled with My Holy Spirit, the uniqueness that will emanate from you will confound the demons of darkness that wish to derail you. I have asked that you sparkle with the glitter of My glory all over your life. Ordinary never describes the life of one walking in step with My heartbeat in the earth. Come forth from your mediocrity. Dare to stand out because of My glory glare upon your life. Getting out of the boat and placing your next step upon the water, belongs to My champions in the earth. A winner in My kingdom listens and then moves and has their being in Me.

Ok ... you have fears. Let me take those fears and overwhelm you with My love. The power of My love invading your heart and soul drives out fear.

If you give me your fear, then there will be room for My love. To the degree that you are saturated with My love, will be the same degree that fear has no power over you.

In the chaos of your life, My whispers speak to you. I purposely speak in hushed tones that you may incline your ear and come close. My words and thoughts come to greet your heart that you may be revived and refreshed in this difficult and cold world. My words will bring warmth to your chilled soul. My love brings reassurance and security to your worth-challenged frame.

Dear, I'm holding you this day. I bring comfort to your sorrowing soul. I bring healing to your injured heart. Hurry ... come close and I will wrap you in My loving grip of kindness and the shelter you will find in Me will be a place you will want to run to often. The place of secret. The place of seclusion. It's off the "beaten path" where not many travel. The unfrequented hideaway.

The shelter that is secret is for you. The place where darkness cannot grip you is in the bosom of my covering. You are invited. You are separate from the world of darkness. You are different. You are blood-bought. Your life in Me will reflect that.

The dying world is hungry for real.

Be the real you. Nothing more and nothing less. For when you reflect Me through your personality, there will be a magnetic attraction in such a way that cannot be refuted. Your life in Me will feed and nourish many.

So take heart this day and remember that the vapor of your life must have impact. You must succeed and you must discover every reason and purpose that I created you. I created you for greatness. I created you to enjoy the holy exchange of love and to share it with another.

Be seated at My table. There is a lavish spread before you. Eat, be nourished and go forth from the table I have prepared into your world to rescue and call others in to the secret place of My loving kindness. For there are many empty seats at My table. Go. Call them in. Compel those who are wayward and see how I will use you in the earth at this time.

$\mathcal{T}$HE SECOND GREATEST COMMANDMENT

Teacher, which is the greatest commandment in the Law? Jesus replied:
"Love the Lord your God with all your heart and with all your soul
and with all your mind." This is the first and greatest commandment.
And the second is like it: "Love your neighbor as yourself." All the Law
and the Prophets hang on these two commandments.
Matthew 22:36-40 (NIV)

$\mathcal{J}$*esus was asked what the* greatest commandment was. He replied
by explaining what the first greatest was and the second greatest as

well. *One would do well to note that.* He answered a question that wasn't asked.

People are on top of God's priority list. Whenever people aren't top on our priority list, we are failing at obeying the second greatest commandment that God ever gave mankind. One cannot confess that he loves God and then live his life excluding others or ignoring their needs. It's the same as water and oil. They just don't mix. Out of our union with Christ, we will love and care for people—period. It has nothing to do with their worthiness of our love, just as God's love for me has nothing to do with my worthiness of His love.

Jesus wasn't asked what the second greatest commandment was. He just spoke it because it was important to link it to the first greatest commandment. If your relationship isn't properly lined up with God, then don't count on having the power to love people the way God calls you. What God has asked of His people is to love others as we love ourselves. This, my friends, is an impossible task outside of a holy infusion of love and power flowing through us. What we need is birthed out of loving God with our whole heart, soul and mind (the first greatest commandment).

I cannot love anyone selflessly without God's help. My human love comes with strings attached. It's the "if you love me, I'll love you back" sort of mentality. What reward is there in this? I will tell you where the reward is. There is honor prepared for you when you love as a choice and not an emotion. There is eternal compensation when you have been filled with the Spirit of Christ, and you love the one who has injured you. There is a fulfillment in God's heart when you show His love to the outcast. God's advice concerning the "odd or strange" one is love them the same way you love yourself. No questions asked.

Beloved, we can't give what we don't have. If your walk with Jesus is off kilter, then your horizontal relationships will be off kilter as well.

Practice absorbing God's love into your being. It's simple—not always easy, but simple nonetheless. God's truth is always simple.

The Bible also reads that we should bear one another's burdens and thus fulfill the law of Christ *(Galatians 6:2)*. Fulfill the Law. Obey the top two commandments, straight from Jesus' mouth. Love God. Love people. Get your eyes off yourself. Align yourself with God today. Receive the supplies of power and love to walk in obedience to the first and second greatest mandates from heaven.

Love God. Love people.

$\mathcal{A}$ POWERLESS CHRISTIAN IS A POINTLESS CHRISTIAN

Love is patient, love is kind. It does not envy, it does not boast, it is not proud. It is not rude, it is not self-seeking, it is not easily angered, it keeps no record of wrongs. Love does not delight in evil but rejoices with the truth. It always protects, always trusts, always hopes, always perseveres. 1 Corinthians 13:4-7 (NIV)

There is a lot of meat in these four verses. What is this love that God has exemplified for us?—to not envy, to not be proud, to not seek its own, to not be easily angered, always protecting, always trusting . . . this is humanly impossible.

For the Christian, though, this is the standard, and this is the plumb line from the mouth of God Himself. How, then, can we ever hope to attain such a standard?

We must be full of the power of the Holy Spirit.

It takes the power of God at work in our hearts for this to even be possible. God has told us how He wants us to act. The problem comes when we fail to connect with the spiritual current of heaven. We fall flat on our spiritual faces. We are doomed to fail and fall short when we act *apart* from the power of the Holy Spirit. It's an impossible mandate from heaven when we ignore the provision of ability to do His will. You might as well put your coat on and go on home if you separate God's mandate from God's power to do it.

How do we attain such aptitude? The only way it will happen is through our intimacy with God—through walking with Him and talking with Him all through life's journey. A form of godliness *without the power* at work is dead, dry and works-oriented *(2 Timothy 3:5)*. Godliness *with the power* is life and victory. Let's take a portion of these verses and focus a bit on it. Love is not easily angered. Are you easily provoked, irritated or aroused in anger? Are you easily offended? Do people walk on eggshells around you for fear of ruffling your feathers? Do you get your feelings hurt often?

You are not walking in love.

Offense is one of the biggest traps of the enemy. It can run rampant, *especially* in the church. Offense causes much trouble and heartache.

Offense exists because forgiveness doesn't.

It's so much easier to let our flesh have its own way rather than pound on the door of heaven for the holiness of God to invade our lives. It's easier to get mad and walk away. It's much more fulfilling to our flesh to hold that grudge or maybe give them the silent treatment. Proverbs 12:16 (NIV) says, "*Fools show their annoyance at once, but the prudent overlook an insult.*"

As a Christian, you have gigantic, awesome spiritual voltage available to you 24/7 to love, hope, believe, persevere, forgive, behave wisely, walk in humility and much more.

If you decide to do things your way, then you will be that unsalted, bland piece of food God can't feed to anyone. You will be as a rudderless ship, going in no direction—aimless, visionless. If the power of God is not at work in you, then you are missing the whole boat, my friend. You are no different than the world around you that operates on an unrestrained whim with every evil thought and action. Your faith, my friend, is dead, and you are useless to the Master. Why should a person going to hell be attracted to you? What is it that makes you different from them? When you are operating in your flesh, letting it run wild and giving it everything it demands, your faith is pointless. One must ask oneself, "Why am I a Christian?" Why profess Christ when you walk in your own way? It's a huge contradiction to the message of the cross *(Luke 9:23)*. Either you are for Him or against Him. There's no middle ground with God *(Matthew 12:30)*. Either you are yoked with Christ or not. You can't ride the fence and be all that God is calling you to be. Be restored to your intimacy with God, and He will "turn the power back on."

A powerless Christian is a pointless Christian. These are tough words I know, but it's time to grow up, get off the milk of the Word and start eating the meat.

$\mathscr{A}$RE YOU STUCK IN THE GATE?

For the gate is small and the way is narrow that leads to life, and there are few who find it. Matthew 7:14 (NASB)

What? A narrow gate that leads to life?

The Greek word for *narrow* is the word *thlibō*. It means to press (as grapes), press hard upon, a compressed way, metaphorically, to trouble, afflict, distress.

Wow. Does this mean that to find true life, I will have distress and trouble, be afflicted and pressed hard upon?

Yes.

Why do you think few find it? Many are looking for life, but few actually find it. Few are willing to pay the price of endurance.

By your steadfastness and patient endurance you shall win the true life of your souls.
Luke 21:19 (AMP)

The true life of your soul will be gained by making it through hard stuff. When you accept Jesus Christ as your Savior, get ready for the pressing. Get ready to be squeezed. To find real life—the life God intended for you—nothing will be handed to you except the power to find this life. You are equipped. You are holding all the supplies you need to find this life for which you were created. You will be tested and tried 'til you are at the end of your rope. When you are at the end of your rope, look around. There's more strength and power to be found in Him.
. . . seeing that His divine power has granted to us everything pertaining to life and godliness, through the true knowledge of Him who called us by His own glory and excellence. 2 Peter 1:3 (NASB)

God has made sure that we have everything we need for this marathon we call life. There will be ups and downs all along the way, but there will be heavenly supply each time a fresh provision is needed.

. . . His divine power has granted to us everything . . .

What is this power?

It's the word *dunamis*. It means ability, power for performing miracles, moral power and excellence of soul, the power and influence which belong to riches and wealth, power and resources arising from numbers and power consisting in armies.

My dear reader friend, there are heavenly resources available to you 24/7. There is no limit to what God has promised. The only limit to God's power is us. When we don't trust Him, we are handicapped in the

Holy Spirit. When we don't believe His Word, then we are downsized to an impotent child of God. Everything will be overwhelming, and life will feel hopeless.

There is a gate, my friend, through which God is calling you. It's a gate not of ease but of pressure. Beyond this gate, you will find an absolutely amazing life. Proceeding through this gate will require you to find the power of God. Once you tap into His holy might, you will find the armies of heaven behind and before you. No demon of hell will be a match for the infusing strength coming into you from God.

His strength will supply everything you need at each point of tribulation and sorrow. His promised power will cause miracles inside your heart. The places you thought you'd never escape will turn into places of abundance. When you allow Him to place His robe of authority upon your shoulders, you will find safe passage through the narrow gate.

The gate is comparable to a birth canal. Pressure on all sides but moving through, there will be an entrance into a life you've never known. New freedom to move and act will be unlike any other time in your life. No one can avoid the pressure to get to the life promised. Don't be miscarried, my friend. See this thing through to the other side. Call out for the power. Cry out for the miracles that belong to you in God. Grab hold of what is rightfully yours. Strength and ability belong to you. There is no trouble that is bigger than the omnipotence of God.

The lie is this: What I have gone through is too big for even God. Friend, there is a God full of love and power extending His hand to you right now. Hear His thoughts:

My child, you are stuck in the gate. You haven't applied My power. You have struggled on your own. Now, take what I have for you and proceed through the gate. I will help you. You are not alone for My love for you exceeds all your trouble.

I NEED YOUR LOVING CARE TONIGHT

Emptiness . . .

. . . going and going 'til I can't go any longer. Knowing I need to stop and listen and breathe . . . Oh God, this is where You and I need to meet— At the crossroads of my tension and fatigue. I'm here. Please join me.

Come, O Holy One, into my unholy world and be the transforming entity of my soul.

You are the only One whom I can trust with my life. Today, Lord, I am in need of Your salvation once again. I receive by faith into my soul a fresh portion of grace. I receive by faith the infusion that my tired heart needs today.

My spirit says, O Lord, how wonderful You are.

You are worthy of all my adoration.

I worship You and lift my thoughts to Your throne.

You formed me and knew me even before I drew my first breath.

Your ways are much higher than mine . . . Teach me Your ways that I might not stumble.
My spirit knows that in Your presence is fullness of joy.

Let me taste and see Your goodness.

Bid me to come to You and be filled with Your joy.

Escort me, O Holy Spirit, straight into that place where You are . . .

Where Your glory is . . . That's where I want to be.
Take me, O Holy Spirit, into Your secret hiding place That I may feast with You at that table . . .
Where is that table, my Lord? Show me, and I will go there with You now . . .

Holy blood of Jesus, wash over me.

Wash over me and cleanse me from all unrighteousness, All unrighteous thoughts and deeds,
O cleanse me, precious blood of Jesus. Make me to know Your truth and mercy. Truth . . . that lies may not win over me, Mercy . . . that love may rule over me.
O Savior, come and carry me into Your loving care today.

ᑌNFORCED RHYTHMS OF GRACE

Are you tired? Worn out? Burned out on religion? Come to me. Get away with me and you'll recover your life. I'll show you how to take a real rest. Walk with me and work with me—watch how I do it. Learn the unforced rhythms of grace. I won't lay anything heavy or ill-fitting on you. Keep company with me and you'll learn to live freely and lightly. Matthew 11:29-30 (MSG)

Take My yoke upon you and learn from Me, for I am gentle and humble in heart, and YOU WILL FIND REST FOR YOUR SOULS. For My yoke is easy and My burden is light. Matthew 11:29-30 (NASB)

Anytime I find myself striving and struggling, I must ask myself, "Whose yoke have I put on?" A yoke is something that couples or binds together. A yoke is a bond or a tie. To what do you bind yourself: fear, anger, religious works, depression? You fill in the blank.

Jesus teaches that we are to become coupled with Him; and if we do, we will find rest. These verses simplified say: put My yoke on and you will find rest.

The Greek for *rest* is the word *anapausis*. It denotes intermission, cessation of any motion, business or labor.

When we hook up with the Master, rest will follow. *He does not expect constant movement and motion from us.* As a matter of fact, when we are bound with Him, there will be moments of intermission and regular junctures of pause. The atmosphere around Jesus will be the same atmosphere around us when we yoke up with Him.

Is there an ease in your step that causes others to see the lack of rest and refreshment in their own lives?

Do people want what you have?

The yoke of Jesus Christ upon our shoulders is not heavy. When we become burdened, it is proof that we have added to the yoke that He has asked us to bear with Him. The yoke of Jesus brings energy and causes us to be agile. There are no heavy weights with the Master.

There is a religious yoke that is heavy and oppressive *(Matthew 23)*. Beware of it. It is based upon righteous works to gain favor with God. The only righteous work that God accepts is the work that Jesus performed upon the cross. When we accept Jesus as our Savior, we begin a love relationship with Him. Out of our union with Jesus, acceptable righteous acts will occur. Your choice is this: Would you rather do something for God because you love Him (relationship), or because you are afraid if you don't He will be displeased with you and withdraw His love (rules)? The way of love is always the correct path with God.

The bond with Jesus is a connection of beauty and freedom. The bond with the world (or religion) is a chain of hardship and imprisonment. There is a way that God works for His dear ones. He is interested in creating moments of rest and refreshment for us along the way. It *is* possible to be in this world but not of it. We are here, but when we are hidden in Him, we are in other places at the same time. Being seated with Jesus in the heavenly realm has heavy benefits that cause us to override and overcome every earthly trap.

With the yoke of Christ around our necks, we will outwit the devil every single time. We will leap over walls and run through a troop without injury when we are bound to Christ in mind and spirit. Oh, that we would see it and walk in it. Oh, that we would remember what belongs to us in Christ when we are sore-footed and weary. He offers us all we need to be on this earth. He reminds us that He will dress us for victory and success (success in terms of the kingdom of God and not the kingdom of this world).

Hear His whisper to you now . . .

I will give you rest and cause My ease to fill you when you take My yoke, put it on and listen to My instructions for life. Learn of Me.

Rest belongs to you, my dear one. Go ahead. Slip on His yoke today and begin experiencing His "unforced rhythms of grace." Why don't you change into something more comfortable today? I guarantee you it will fit perfectly.

$\mathcal{V}$ENTURE OUT! MEET GOD ON THE WAVES

$\mathcal{W}$*hether you realize it or* not, *I am orchestrating your life circumstances. I am creating ways for you to know Me more intimately. I am allowing situations to touch you that you may turn to Me and exercise your faith. I am permitting things to bump against you that you may comprehend your true need for Me. It's all good, even though it feels difficult.*

Sometimes, it's simply a matter of reaping what you have sown. There will be times and seasons when you will have to walk through the consequences because of unwise choices. The fact is that no matter what, there is always a new morning each day filled with new mercies for you to lay hold of. Each day you wake up, there is fresh grace and mercy from heaven to find Me and receive what you need from Me for that day.

It makes no difference what you have done or not done. I love you always with open arms. If you seek Me, you will find Me. It's that simple. If you call on My name, I will answer. There may be a season of waiting, but I will come to you in the perfect time and way. When I don't bring an immediate answer, I will always bring immediate peace for the one who is searching and trusting Me.

I am after you. I am in love with you. I am focused on your growth. I am concerned that you know Me. I have created you to know Me. You came into this earth with an instant adversary. Satan desires to distort your picture of Me. Grab hold of My heart for you. See and believe that I am for you and not against you. As you lean into Me and allow Me to hold you when your heart is breaking or when you are full of fear, I will calm you and comfort you as a mother does for her distraught child.

Trust Me, child. Let go of all that you are clinging to for comfort and security. Child, you are safe with Me. My shelter will provide all that you need to survive and even thrive in this cold, dark, confusing world.

I am not a God who always protects His children from the storms. I am a God who walks with His children through the storms, that they may know Me and learn to love Me. For when I do return for My people, I will find faith. I will find a people of strength. I will find a people who love Me and are working exploits in the earth. I will find those who have chosen to trust, despite what they have seen or felt.

Emotions cannot always be trusted. Your understanding of a thing cannot be relied upon for I am a behind-the-scenes God. I am a God who brings beauty in time. True beauty cannot always be created in a second. True beauty can take lots of time. Time is on My side. Eternity is on your side when you belong to Me.

Will you give up this senseless feeling of hopelessness? Will you venture to trust in ways you never have before? Yes. Venture out. Meet Me upon the waves of the mighty storm. Stop trying to protect yourself, and step out of the boat of comfort. For what has become a comfort to you has actually turned into a hindrance to knowing Me.

The new day has arrived. Come and see the new sights I will show you. Come and dine with Me at My table. Let Me show you how to taste and see that I really am good. Come enjoy the pleasures that are at My right hand.

For the orchestration that I am performing for you is beyond anything you could think of or imagine.

THE EYE OF THE LORD IN THE FIRE

Beloved, think it not strange concerning the fiery trial which is to try
you, as though some strange thing happened unto you . . .
1 Peter 4:12 (KJV)

Dear one, worthy of love and highly esteemed, are you surprised or astonished with what's happening to you? Are the trials of your life creating a meltdown in your soul? Good. This is the purpose. He cannot increase in you unless you are decreasing. It's not pleasurable, but it's the right road for you. Make no mistake about it—the heat has been turned up for your purification and His glory.

Fiery trial in Greek is the word *pyrōsis*. It means the burning by which metals are roasted and reduced, calamities or trials that test the character.

Remove the victim mentality, and put on a garment of thankfulness. You stopped being the victim the day Jesus died on the cross for you. For this thing which has come to you has come for your refining. You are not exempt from the love of God; thus, you are not exempt from the fiery furnace of refining. You are not exempt from the melting pot of self-reduction. As you bow in the fire and melt, your heavenly Father is carefully controlling the temperature, faithfully skimming the dross off and bringing a purity you have not known as of yet. Only He sees what is coming in you. Your job is to surrender and yield to Him, the One who loves and esteems you more than anyone else.

Why do we act so surprised when hardship hits? Why do we ask why? As sons and daughters of the Living God, we would be better off seeing pain as our friend and not the enemy. Pain has the potential to be the vehicle that will carry us into greater realms of intimacy with the Father. Pain has the potential to transport us straight into the arms of Jesus. When you accepted Jesus Christ as your Savior, that was only the starting block. The rest of your life will be the school of the Holy Spirit with plenty of tests along the way. The remainder of your time on earth will be the "proving" of your commitment to Christ. The devil will be allowed to test you, dear one, but your heavenly Father will control the level of testing and proving. What you can handle and overcome with Him will be what comes your way. Is the pain great? You've been entrusted, dear one. Your heavenly Father has allowed it because He sees the glory coming all over you as you overcome by the word of your testimony, the blood of the Lamb and loving not your life even unto death *(Revelation 12:11)*.

The proving is the process. When you accepted Christ, you also accepted His empowerment to live and move and have your being in Him and in Him alone *(Acts 17:28)*. He knows the power of your flesh, but He loves you so much that He has moved in with you and offers you constant power to prevail.

Be patient with Him. Be patient with yourself. He will form His image in you over the course of your lifetime. He will finish what He began in you from day one. Continue yielding. Continue surrendering the best you know how.

You will get there. He will see to it. Cease treating pain and hardship as a stranger, but look for the eyes of your Lord in the pain. See His searching eye looking for you in the form of pain and suffering, perplexity and frustration. Search Him out. He is that "other man" in the furnace with you *(Daniel 3:24-25)*. He is on deck to comfort and coach the one who has found himself in the fire. He is the "man of sorrows" and "acquainted with much grief" *(Isaiah 53:3)*. What better companion to have when the valley of trouble desires to swallow you up?

He offers comfort and love. He offers kingly authority and desires to place His scepter in your hand.

Therefore, as trouble and difficulty accompany you as two faithful friends, remove the surprise. Put on His garment of strength and power to travel forward and not backward. Remove the victim mentality garment, and put on His royal robe of power to overcome. Put on the garment of praise for the spirit of heaviness *(Isaiah 61:3)*.

One day, the purity that has been formed into you will be a blinding, reflective light to your enemy's eyes as the glory of the Lord shines from you. You will come forth from this fiery furnace chaste, purified and transformed into His wonderful image.

$\mathcal{L}$IVE AGAIN BY RETURNING AGAIN

God—You're my God! I can't get enough of you! I've worked up such hunger and thirst for God, traveling across dry and weary deserts. So here I am in the place of worship, eyes open, drinking in Your strength and glory. In Your generous love, I am really living at last!
Psalms 63:1-3 (MSG)

$\mathcal{T}$*raveling across dry and weary* deserts today? Thirsty? Tell your soul, "Remain fixed, and know that He is God." Worship Him . . . get on your face.

Drink in His strength and glory. Open your eyes.

Stop being angry with Him. Surrender.

It's generous love that calls for you.

It's the voice of love for which you have been looking. The love of your heavenly Father is waiting for you.

He waits patiently for you to come home. Dinner's ready. Surrender.

Die.

Be reborn. Be.

Stop living for other people.

Live for Him, your high supreme God.

Living for Him will settle all you need to be concerned with here. You will answer to Him and to Him alone.

Absorb His love into your soul like rain showers upon the parched earth.

As you do, the empowerment to love others will fill you through and through.

Return to simplicity. Return to your first Love. Love is cold?

No matter.

Run—no, race to Him!

The fire will be rekindled, and you will burn hotter than ever. It's His specialty.

Turning what is *not* into what *is*. It's what He loves to do.

Now settle down in His loving arms today, and do what you need to do. Then you will be who you need to be.

There are ocean waves of love waiting to break over you.

$\mathcal{D}$O YOU WANT TO DEVASTATE HELL IN YOUR LIFE?

$\mathcal{D}$*o you want to devastate your adversary? Do you tire of his harassments?*

This kind of defeat requires a tenacity of violent proportions. Lean in to My presence and hear My Voice, and then go do My will. For this is what will upset hell's plot against you. Hear My voice. Become one with My will. See a great ambush in the camp of your enemy.

Who will pay the price of drawing close enough to hear? Who will sacrifice what they want to do for what I want to do? Who will spend more time in their prayer closet? Who will offer themselves as one set apart?

Those who desire true victory; those who desire to see the head of their enemy trampled upon.

The power is yours. Heaven's resources are at your disposal. Many will hear the call, but few will actually choose what it will truly take to live life to the fullest on their journey with Me.

You cry out, "There must be more." My answer to you is, "Yes, My child, there certainly is."

Many temptations are being released in the earth by the adversary. Many stumbling blocks are being set in place ahead of you on your path. Many stones of offense have been hurled upon your pathway for you to trip over. I tell you in advance to arm yourself for readiness. I tell you beforehand so that when you come upon them, the blocks and stones the enemy has laid up for you to stumble upon will become the very stepping stones that bring greater opportunity for Christ to be formed in you.

It's the way of the kingdom of heaven. What was meant for evil concerning you is the very thing that I choose to use to advance My kingdom in you. See it. Realize it. Embrace it.

I see a radiant Bride being prepared. I see an incomparable beauty. I see gems and precious stones lining your heart as you continue on with Me in the fire. I see greatness in your soul as you give over your pain and sorrow for My use. I see the formation of gold as your faith comes to the surface of your storm-tossed sea. I see precious garments being laid upon you by the angels as you choose the more difficult but righteous road on your journey.

I have asked you to not be moved by what you see, but to let what you don't see move you. For the wind blows and you know not where it has come from nor where it is going. Similarly, My Holy Spirit will carry you along to the places I have prepared for you. You will be led by what the natural eye cannot see, nor can the natural mind comprehend. You will be carried above and see what others cannot, enabling you to do what others cannot.

Oh, how My heart is enthralled with you. I sing and dance over you often, and I await with great anticipation your arrival into your heavenly home, framed by My hand.

You have every reason to cheer up. For greater testimonies of My faithfulness belong to the one filled with childlike trust. I call you forward, My Child. I call you upward. I call you onward. Arise from your place of frustration and see the horizon of glory and promise. Keep hope in your heart.

For you are Mine, and I am yours.

$\mathcal{J}$S YOUR UMBRELLA UP OR DOWN?

$\mathcal{M}$*y love is raining upon* you today. It comes to cover and saturate *you. These showers come to wash away the fears that contaminate your soul. My rain comes in the form of comfort to ease your pain. It comes to assist you with peace. My love is falling, and I ask that you put away your umbrella. "My umbrella, Lord? How can I put up an umbrella to protect myself from Your love? I would never do that."*

There are several ways you can protect yourself from the rain of My love touching you. Spiritual umbrellas come in many shapes and forms. Busyness and noise are two factors that will block your reception of My love for you.

This umbrella will cause spiritual deafness, and you cannot hear My voice telling you how much I love you. Becoming quiet will put this umbrella away.

Another type of umbrella used is pain. Your pain can become such a focus that it becomes more important to you than receiving My loving, healing oil. There is no reason to suffer and suffer and suffer, and not understand My love for you. When your pain becomes bigger than My love for you, you have enthroned it; and it becomes a type of umbrella, protecting you from My love raining down on you. For My love will bring relief. My love will soothe. My love will bring healing.

Then there is the umbrella of distrust. This is a strong umbrella that can be difficult to put away; but once the choice is made, it comes down easily. Man will fail you. I will not. As you realize this, it will assist you in putting down this umbrella of distrust.

Hopelessness is another type of umbrella that shields My love from raining on you. As my child, this enemy should never have a hold on you. Hopelessness belongs to those who don't have Me in their life. There is never a reason to be without hope. My love dissolves hopelessness like water on sugar. As you embrace hope, the umbrella will come down; and you will know and feel My droplets of love coming down on you.

My love is raining down today. Is your umbrella up or down? When the sun's not shining, it might be raining.

THE TRAP OF COLD LOVE

And the love of the great body of people will grow cold because of the multiplied lawlessness and iniquity. Matthew 24:12 (AMP)

This is a sobering verse. These are the words of Jesus just before He left earth for heaven. When someone is gone from this world, we tend to look upon his last words and actions as some of the most important messages he was trying to send before he left.

Jesus is speaking of the end times. We are closer than ever. One of the top strategies of hell in this hour is to trick as many as possible to become cold and indifferent to their fellow human beings. When one is sinned against, the easy reaction is to put up a wall and never trust again. The wide road of response is to get even and return sin for sin.

This is how the love of many will grow cold. It will happen in conjunction with the increase of iniquity in the earth. Many people will be sinned against; thus, many people, because of hurt, will choose the pathway of cold, indifferent love. This is a sad truth of what is happening and will continue to happen.

People will become offended. The seed of offense and wounding, if allowed to be nourished, will grow into a great tree by the name of cold love. Jesus said there will be many whose love will wane and grow cold.

Saints, watch out. Offense is a trick from hell. Forgiveness is a solution, as well as a mandate, from heaven.

If the powers of darkness can mess with your love capacity, then you have been bound and are handicapped in your witness for Jesus.

Now all these things are from God, who reconciled us to Himself through Christ and gave us the ministry of reconciliation.
2 Corinthians 5:18 (NASB)

Sons and daughters of God have been given a charge from heaven. You have been given the task of representing God to the world by your thoughts, words and actions. Your job is to be a road sign of how favor from God can be given to every human being on the earth. You have a godly responsibility to keep the hot embers of love in your soul.

This is your ministry. This is your task until you take your last breath. Judging people is quick and easy. Restoring people takes time but brings great reward. We tend to shun those who have hurt us instead of calling for the power of God to fill us in order to love with His love. We have it all backwards. God is the Judge, and He will do His job well. We are to be focused on restoring people to God. If they refuse our service and ministry, then they will answer to God, not us.

Let's bring this all together. If our adversary can get us filled with offense, then we will not be focused on getting them reconciled to God. The iniquity of others will blow on us like a wind until the God-breathed love in our heart will flicker and become snuffed out.

If you are so mad at how evil the world has become—and that is your focus—then God has no use for you. We can have a faultless claim, but mixed with an unholy attitude, we go nowhere with God. When we have truth mixed with a wrong spirit, the bit of truth we have will not be heard or breathed upon by the Holy Spirit who brings life to the truth of God in our hearts.

Hurt people hurt people. Healed people heal people.
It boils down to that.

$\mathcal{A}$ LOVE LETTER

$\mathcal{I}$ am searching the earth for the one who has separated himself for Me. I see each one who loves Me with all their heart. The furnace has become hot for My dear children. It's necessary for the preparation of coming days. If I would take you into the coming seasons and not prepare you, you would think and believe that I have not loved you; and it would be true.

But I have loved you with an everlasting love; thus, I must drive you into the desert places just as I did My Holy Son after His baptism. Look at His impact in the earth, then and now, and for all eternity. You will experience the same. I will not spare you of anything that could bring us closer and make you stronger in the end.

Dear one, every trial, challenge, sorrow and flaming dart that I have permitted to come your way is a direct link and specific tool for the formation of Christ in you. The ebb and flow of easy and hard is perfectly timed by My design.

I give you all you need for every life circumstance. Learn to pick up the weapons I have provided for you. Learn to use the tools I have placed in your hand to stay strong and do the work. Darken My doorsteps often and come in for times of intimate loving. You desire to hear My voice, yet have you forgotten how I long for your voice in My inner courts?

Rest assured today, and be reminded of how I'm holding you. I am caring for you and loving you in ways no other can or is even willing to. Bring to Me your sorrows. Present your wounds to Me. Let's walk this thing out together, arm in arm. For I have provided for you My very own Holy Spirit to be in you and all around you. This should bring you much comfort in your day of trial and pain.

Trial and pain will continue—and even accelerate—but with the accompaniment of My glory and strength. For as your days, equal shall your strength and stamina be. It's My promise to you. You will be strong enough in the power of My might.

Lovingly,
Your heavenly Father

$\mathcal{R}$AIN UPON THE MOWN GRASS

He shall come down like rain upon the mown grass: as showers that water the earth. Psalms 72:6 (KJV)

Come, let us return to the LORD for He has torn us, but He will heal us; He has wounded us, but He will bandage us. He will revive us after two days; He will raise us up on the third day, that we may live before Him. So let us know, let us press on to know the LORD. His going forth is as certain as the dawn; And He will come to us like the rain, Like the spring rain watering the earth. Hosea 6:1-3 (NASB)

Every true child of God will experience times of cutting, tearing, wounding, pruning and as the psalmist put it, times of being mown like one would mow a field of grass. These moments can be identified as moments when your spiritual life is all but snuffed out. Things were going along just fine until happened. You felt as though you could die. There was no sense or logic to it at all. You were just sideswiped. The sharp blade of the "circumstance mower" just leveled you out, and you were swiftly cut—straight across.

None of us are exempt.

After this sort of an experience, He comes down upon us ever so gently. He has promised that He will come down upon our bleeding edges in the form of heavenly rain and refresh, replenish and prepare us for our new growth. He will come to us with the spring rain, lest we die in our cutting. He will certainly come cascading upon us; and as the rain saturates the earth, in like manner shall we enjoy the holy saturation of His rain. He will shower down upon us, causing us to thrive once again and grow into the new realm of what we are becoming.

He will heal us. He will bandage us. He will revive us. He will raise us up that we may live before Him and not die. Then multiplication and new growth come. Then the greater realms of glory arrive. Promotion will accompany the hand of God. After the cutting comes the rain. After the pruning comes the rain. Times of healing and recovery will follow times of wounding and cutting.

Do not think that your present fiery trial will have no end. Do not calculate without God as you walk through the floodwaters. O child of the Most High God, there is a greater ending to your beginning. There are larger dimensions and greater glory just ahead of you. Do not make camp in your present day. You are just passing through. Jesus promised to take you to the other side, not to take you to the middle and let you drown.

ᝨHE TAILWIND OF GOD

There is no fear in love; but perfect love casteth out fear: because fear hath torment. He that feareth is not made perfect in love. 1 John 4:18 (KJV)

"Fear hath torment." Fear can hang on to you like an unrelenting cold north wind. Fear is **F**alse **E**vidence **A**ppearing **R**eal! Fear is

the darkroom where all our negatives are developed. How often have you read in scripture the words, *Fear not*? Many, many times, God has spoken these two words to His beloved children. They are sprinkled from Genesis to Revelation. It's human nature to fear. Fear is one of Satan's chief weapons. If he can get us to doubt God's love for us, then fear will come running in and overtake us the way water runs into a dry, empty hole.

Why do we fear? Well, according to 1 John 4:18, we have not been fully perfected in God's love. It would behoove us, then, to become rooted and established in God's love. The more rooted and established we are, the less likely we will become moved by the winds of emotion and circumstance and the less likely we will give ourselves over to fear dressed in tormenting thoughts.

We could even think of it this way: To the degree that you fear is the degree that you have not accepted God's love.

If you truly believe God loves you, you will be less inclined to embrace the lying whispers of your adversary. When a person isn't confident in God's love, he is wide open for other deceiving thoughts that the enemy is happy to send his way. More than likely, the lies will then be embraced as a "truth" in his soul. God created us with a vacuum. That vacuum is always looking to be filled. God meant it to be filled with Him. But when we make choices to be moved by our feelings or circumstances rather than meditating and soaking in God's love for us personally, we are flinging the door wide open to all kinds of demonic torment.

Another way fear can grab us is if we feel we aren't measuring up to everything a Christian should be—you know, all the rules and high standards by which we should be living. Fear could overtake us, and we could dupe ourselves into believing that God is going to punish us and condemn us if we don't measure up to every "jot and tittle" of the

Word. Yes, we need to stay in obedience, but a big NO, we don't need to accept the condemnation of the enemy to belittle us and hammer us down to nothing when we fall short. There is a big difference between condemnation and conviction. We would be wise to understand the difference.

Condemnation is not from God *(Romans 8:1)*. If you are a born-again believer, you are never condemned by God. Condemnation brings with it fear and torment *(1 John 4:18)*. It is a fear that one of these days God is going to really whack you because you are just not measuring up to Sister So-and-So. Condemnation brings no hope or way of escape. It's just a doomed feeling that stirs up all sorts of other ungodly emotions—fear being at the top.

Conviction is very much of God *(John 16:7-8)*. When we *do* sin, and fall short, the Holy Spirit will convict us. He will lovingly call us back on track. There is a way of escape and returning provided for us when we sin and fall short. There is always a way to return in repentance. We are disciplined of the Lord only because we are deeply loved by our Father *(Hebrews 12:6)*.

There is no torment in conviction, just love, mercy and grace to come back home as quickly as possible. As we obey the conviction of the Holy Spirit, we will always find ourselves in the forgiving arms of our Savior. Repentance will always lead us to a place of restoration.

Therefore, as we reflect on fear versus love, it's very clear what God is communicating. We need to focus on being rooted and established in His love each time we are confronted with a new test and trial. The perfect love of God is the starting block as well as the tailwind in the race. Yes, love is the tailwind of God—that force that moves us along in peace and confidence as we run for Him. As we become perfected in this divine love, fear will have less and less power over us.

Bathe Me in Your Love

Lord, I come to You today. I need to soak in Your perfect love. I need to live, eat and breathe it. My enemy stands crouching at my doorstep, waiting for an opportunity to pounce upon me. I acknowledge my need to be perfected in Your love. Come now. Perfect me more and more as I choose to believe and as I meditate on Your incomparable love that always extends to me. Amen.

ᏨHE BLAST OF COLD LOVE

Because of the increase of wickedness, the love of most will grow cold.
Matthew 24:12 (NIV)

ᏨHe fierce winds are blowing. Can you feel the chill in the air? Can *you feel the arctic blast? What is this fierce wind you may ask? What kind of "chill," Lord?*

I speak of the chill of hatred and abandonment—you know, the blast of subzero self-centeredness.

The high test of My saint in the earth is the test of true love. There is a strategy from hell brewing and spewing all over the earth in this day and hour. *The tactic is this: to cool down the living embers of love in My people. There is great temptation in My house right now to become offended with another. There is great desire in the kingdom of darkness to cause My people in My house to stumble and wane in their love for Me, and to wane in their love for one another.*

Take up your shield, My saint. Take up your sword, and do battle with your adversary. It's him you must fight, not your brother.

Examine your level of patience. How kind have you been? Do you know that it's My kindness that leads to repentance? There is no good fruit that comes out of a rude spirit. Are you wishing for something I have given someone else? Please don't do that. Do you often find the need to defend yourself and exalt in your accomplishments? This is not what true love practices.

In your example of My love, does your tongue slip into fits of anger? My child, this does not exemplify my loving character. Love—true love—doesn't even keep track of wrongs. Why do you insist upon stacking up all the wrong your brother has done? What hope, then, is there for the one who is falling from grace?

My love protects, hopes, trusts and perseveres.

The love of many will wax cold. See to it that you not fall into this slimy tactic of Satan; but rather, guard the love you have for Me and protect the love I have in you for the world around you.

As darkness increases in the earth, part of what separates My people in the earth will be the love that I have put in their hearts. This kind of love does not even love its own life but is willing to die for whatever the cost of My love requires.

Love the Lord your God with all your heart, soul and mind. Love your neighbor as you love yourself.

There is nothing else that will continue on with you into eternity. Work on it. Study it. Soak in it. Receive it for yourself. Give it out to others. Wear it as a garment. Don't leave home without it.

For I love you, my dear one. You don't even know in your heart how much. It will take all of eternity for you to fully understand just how much I love you. I freely give it to you. You must freely give it to others. Do not become a dam that stops My love in the earth.

Be careful not to follow the crowd whose hearts have become cold with My love. For there are many now and many more to come who will choose this road of cold love, and My heart sorely grieves for this. Don't let your love grow cold, but let it wax hot even all the more as you see the day of My coming approach.

WHEN I FIRST THOUGHT OF YOU

When I first thought of you, *I thought of how much I would love you and watch over you. I thought of the plans that I had for you and how you would fit in the earth at this.*

When I first thought of you, *I thought of how you would be able to reflect my love and beauty to others. I thought of the children I would give you and how they would reflect Me in the earth. I thought of your spouse and how I would have him take care of you and love you.*

When I first thought of you, *I saw your heart that would be pliable in My hand. I saw how the difficult places I would have to take you would actually help to form you into My likeness. I saw the times of your weeping, and I wept with you. I saw the times of your celebrations, and I danced with you. I saw the times of your sorrows, and I held you.*

When I first thought of you, *I thought of the gifts I would give you—gifts that would be just right for you. I gave you a specific personality. I gave you a personality that would reflect an aspect of Myself. When I thought of you, I thought how "worth it" it would be to* *have My Son die for you and redeem your life back to Me. I saw your wanderings and questionings, and I smiled because I am keeping you safe in my arms, no matter what. When your whole life was laid before Me—valleys and mountaintops—I smiled, for you have chosen to keep walking with Me no matter what. I saw you in times when you didn't quite understand Me and My ways, but you continued the walk. You continued to invite Me to speak and lead.*

When I first thought of you, *I saw how your faith in Me would keep you. I saw you trusting when there was no real evidence that I was close. And I smiled.*

When I first thought of you, *I saw how we would be partners in the earth. I saw how we could love others with no strings attached. I saw how we could walk down the path and converse and laugh as we went along. I saw times when I could just touch you so deeply that you would never doubt My existence.*

I am pleased. I am happy that I created you. The race will end one day, and you will cross the finish line; but until that day comes, I wanted you to know these things and to hold them close in your heart. When you think of Me, remember that I am with you always, even to the end and beyond.

ℬOUND TO THE ALMIGHTY

But they that wait upon the Lord shall renew their strength; they shall mount up with wings as eagles; they shall run, and not be weary; and they shall walk, and not faint. Isaiah 40:31(KJV)

I must return to a position of waiting upon the Lord when I am faint. If I find myself too weighted down, it is an indication that I have lost eye contact with the One who has all ability and strength ready to pour upon my tired head. Hope lost means I have stopped waiting for Him and have turned to take things into my own carnal hands.

In the Hebrew, the word wait also means "to bind together." In waiting upon the Lord there is a binding of my heart and soul to Him. That means I am fastened to His plan and purpose. That means that try as he may, the enemy of my soul will not succeed in tearing me apart from the One who loves me most. In my waiting, I am binding myself to Him. My thoughts are becoming His thoughts. My ways are becoming His ways. We have been united together and our union is strong. In my waiting, I am tied to the God of the universe. There I am safe. In that place, I will become strong in the power of His might.

Bound to Him, my strength is renewed. The choice to wait upon God is the choice to become renewed in power and ability to journey on. When I am lacking in strength, it is a sign that I have disassembled myself from Him. When I stray from His Word, when I detour from what He has told me to do, it's as though I am inviting weakness and exhaustion right into the living room of my soul saying, "sit down for a while."

It is only when I return to the One who loves me most and bind myself to Him in watchful waiting, that I become draped in fresh abilities to mount up as an eagle would, and take off in the wind of adversity and challenge.

The bald eagle is a vision of great strength. They can carry up to four pounds as they fly. Their wingspan is up to seven feet. They can fly to an altitude of 10,000 feet. They sit at the top of the food chain. The sharpness of an eagle's vision is almost four times that of a person with perfect vision. One more thing I found out: eagles do not sweat. That in itself should tell you something. Stop sweating about life.

When I wait upon the Lord, there is no need to sweat. When I bind myself to Him, great strength will overtake me. As I attach my mind, will and emotions to His sovereignty, I will find myself at the top of the spiritual "food chain" looking down upon my adversary and using the clutch of my feet to devour him instead of him devouring me.

God's whisper ... *Come under My wing this night, dear one. You have wandered and have stepped away from the comfort of My shelter. You are chilled in your meditations of things I haven't asked you to think about. You have allowed your thoughts to entrap you. Release all and come over here for the rest that you so need. My thoughts of you are as a canopy of love over you. Come under My thoughts. For My thoughts are for your good and for your welfare. Dismiss the how's and why's of life and release your childlike faith.*

Understanding is not always going to fill your mind. What will bring peace is trusting when you can›t see or feel or touch. I know it is dark. The key to strength is slowing down a bit and pausing in My presence. Pause in My presence. Linger, delay and sit awhile. There is a misunderstanding that to labor and push and work will always get what you need. Sometimes that is important, but often an exhaustion comes in that is not what you were built for. There is ease in My presence. Find it. It's my gift to you in a world full of demands and challenges.

Finally, remember that you are loved to the core of your being. You are cherished, valued, accepted and longed for. I miss you. Wait upon Me. Be renewed in your strength. When you need to walk, you will. When you need to run, you will. You will live and move and have your being in Me. As you bind yourself to Me, you will lack no good thing. And the strength you will find will be supernatural, going beyond the limits of human strength and understanding.

Bow before Me. I will take you straight into your destiny.

CELEBRATE JESUS

Then the King will say to those on His right, "Come, you who are blessed
of My Father, inherit the kingdom prepared for you from the foundation
of the world. For I was hungry, and you gave Me something to eat; I was
thirsty, and you gave Me something to drink; I was a stranger, and
you invited Me in; naked, and you clothed Me; I was sick, and you
visited Me; I was in prison, and you came to Me." Then the righteous
will answer Him, "Lord, when did we see You hungry, and feed You, or
thirsty, and give You something to drink? And when did we see You a
stranger, and invite You in, or naked, and clothe You? When did we see
You sick, or in prison, and come to You?" The King will answer and say
to them, "Truly I say to you, to the extent that you did it to one of these
brothers of Mine, even the least of them, you did it to Me."
Matthew 25:34-40 (NASB)

If you have ever uttered, "Lord, where are you?" then these verses will bring a bit of clarity to that prayer. Did you see the Lord the other day in the eyes of that lonely person? When they announced that Brother or Sister So-and- So had to be admitted into the hospital—that was the Lord calling for your attention to come a bit closer and visit. Our God resides with the sick, needy and rejected in society. Our God requires that we look for "the least of these My brethren."

Least in the Greek denotes smallest in size, in importance, in the estimation of men, in rank and excellence.

You will see the eyes of the Lord looking straight at you through the eyes of a developmentally disabled person. You will see the eyes of the Lord gazing upon you in great delight as you care for that sick or dying one. You can't miss it. You can't help but be fulfilled in Jesus as you make it a point to go out of your way to love the unlovable, the outcast of society. Remember the Good Samaritan? When everyone else—including two religious leaders—passed by a fallen, bleeding and dying man, he stopped to help him. This is what we're talking about.

Look for Jesus today. Don't look at the prideful, self-sufficient person— the comfortable one, or the one who sees no lack in his life. See the Lord in the gaps—in the places of pain and need. Hone in on those places, and make eye contact with your Lord.

Does Jesus suffer want? He most certainly does, according to verses 35 and 36. Imagine satisfying Jesus' hunger pains. What could I do to quench His thirst? How can I comfort Him in His loneliness with a visit to the prisoner? In His nakedness, I can cover Him and shelter Him who has no place to stay. He is in these places, my friend.

It's in satisfying the needs of our Lord that our needs will be met. It's the paradox of being the answer to someone's cry for help that you will find the answers to your secret supplication. The law of "giving and it will be given" applies to all areas of our lives.

Do you want to see more of Jesus? Then go where He said He is and celebrate His presence in the very least of these.

$\mathcal{W}$INDS OF CHANGE

$\mathcal{W}$*inds of change are blowing. Can you feel the breeze of My Spirit blowing around you? The wind and the breeze have come to blow out the old and bring in the new. The old was good for its day but will no longer suffice for the new day. Will you let go of the old, or will you keep clinging to it? If you could see what I have in store for you, you would never think of hanging on to the old way. Cling to Me, and the new day will greet you like a kiss. It will be pleasant to your soul, and you will know Me in ways you never dreamed.*

Even creation is in birth pains for the new. The new is a place of promotion and expansion in My kingdom. It's a place of greater impact and advancement upon the kingdom of darkness. If you insist upon the old way, then you will find a place of great stagnancy in your walk with Me. Winds of change are here. I am here. Won't you ride with Me? Won't you let go of that which you tightly clutch? Let Me carry you along. Let Me help you transition. What you tightly cling to will only be a burden and heavy weight in the journey as you transition with Me. Give them to Me, for I delight in daily bearing your burdens, and you will see that what is lost to you is present only with Me . . . and I will keep safe that which you have entrusted to Me.

There is great anticipation in My heart for you to see the new thing that I will do with and in you. Fear desires to hold you. Come to Me, and the fear will dissolve. Come out of your comfort zone. Come to Me, and you will see that I am embracing you and holding you close. It's a day and an hour to remain in My love. For My love will hold you together when it seems everything is falling apart. Soaking in My love will help you to walk right through the transition . . . and into the new day.

Then Moses stretched out his hand over the sea and God, with a terrific east wind all night long, made the sea go back. He made the sea dry ground. The seawaters split. The Israelites walked through the sea on dry ground with the waters a wall to the right and to the left. Exodus 14:21 (MSG)

THE SIN OF SELF-ABSORPTION

. . . and weep with them that weep.
Romans 12:15b (KJV)

The funeral procession seemed about three miles long. It was a large funeral. I was not in a passing car as a spectator but an active participant in the long trail of sorrowing relatives and friends. The journey to the gravesite took about 25 minutes. I watched as the oncoming traffic approached us. Some sped along as though life was calling them to the next appointment without thought of passing a hearse with trailing grievers. Some just slowed down as if to "tip their hat" to the mourners.

Then there were some who just plain pulled off the road and stopped dead in their tracks to honor us as we traveled to the final destination of what was left of our deceased loved one here on earth. All at once, we came upon a man who had been walking his dog. He stopped, standing there with his dog, just watching with his hands folded. It seemed he was uttering a prayer for us as we inched along.

I marveled at the diverse attention to the mourning parade. What motivated the variety of response? I suppose the motivation was based upon where they were in life. Did they just lose a loved one? Were they battling a terminal illness, or had they never lost a loved one and entered into that deep searing pain of grief? At any rate, I was strangely comforted by those who just took a couple minutes to stop what they were doing and pause as we made our trek to the cemetery.

God has told us to *"weep with them that weep."* We don't have to know the person directly to weep. It can be in the form of simply stopping your car and pausing for a moment as those who are in great sorrow move along. Just a wordless hug can express great comfort. Send a card in the mail telling of your sadness with them as they pass through the valley of weeping—a flower sent, a meal prepared.

Weeping with those who weep is not a suggestion for the Christian, but a direct command from God Himself *(Romans 12:15b)*. Christians should set the example, but Christians are sometimes the ones who handle this area of life with the least care and respect of all. This world is full of great pain and sorrow. Make room for the expression of the Great Comforter to flow from your life. Don't wait for someone to die. Look around you. People are suffering every day, all day long.

Repent from self-absorption.

Someday, you may be the one who has entered the deep night of sorrow and in need of the loving arms of Jesus. We are His arms. We are His feet. We are His hands. We have been chosen to represent Him in the earth.

$\mathscr{P}$OLLYANNA CHRISTIANITY

In the midst of a conversation with a trusted friend, the term "Pollyanna Christianity" popped up. When she said that, something clicked on the inside of me.

I've noticed that there can be a mindset in the church that causes an atmosphere of condemnation. Follow me here: What? You still hurt over that? What? You are still stuck in that place? You must not have enough faith, or there must be sin in your life. How about this: You shouldn't be sad, they are in heaven now. Friends, some grief is so deep that we will probably carry it to our grave, and heaven will be the only place of total healing and relief to the heart.

I've also observed a "if you won't be fixed quickly, I will leave you alone" sort of mentality. Or this one: It's all good . . . just push it under the rug, and it will go away. That's a very hurtful, out-of-sight out-of-mind, way to think.

It doesn't just go away, and that person has to go on somehow with or without help.

Do we really know how to walk with someone for the long haul? Do we even want to do so? Sometimes, there are things in people's lives that won't go away. Do we walk away from them out of our own discomfort, not knowing what to say or do? Sadly, it happens more often than not.

Although there are times in our lives when we need reproved and exhorted, there are also times when we need someone to walk with us through the fire. Where are the firewalkers today? It is just as much of a miracle to walk through the fire, finding hope and comfort along the way, as it is to get an instant miracle of deliverance. There are numerous times in a person's life when there is a need for a fellow firewalker to come alongside to encourage in hope and bring the comfort of God. Frequently, there are times when I don't need someone to say, "It's going to be all right." Heaven is my finish line, I know, but I'm still on the earth and in need of comfort and understanding at times. As a good friend of mine says, "I just need some 'Jesus skin' (someone full of Jesus) to walk with me."

Are you a safe place for anyone? Are you present—really present—to listen to someone's fears, pain or difficulty? Maybe you have experienced this too, but there have been times when I have been in a conversation with someone (I thought), and the feeling surfaced in my heart that they weren't really listening to me and were somewhere else. Isn't that a sinking feeling?

If Jesus was a man of sorrows and acquainted with much grief *(Isaiah 53:3)*, then who do we think we are to believe that we will have a "Pollyanna" sort of life that nothing will ever bother or touch us? Have you ever told someone that he just needed to have more faith, or maybe there was sin in his life, and that's the reason he suffers so? Be careful, my friend, how you walk with someone in deep grief or relentless trouble. Job had a few friends whom, I'm sure, he wished would go away. (Job 42:7)

When you are in the midst of great sorrow or tribulation, offer it to God as a sacrifice. Ask Him to make something beautiful of it and of you because of it.

> *But King David said to Ornan, "No, but I will surely buy it for the full price; for I will not take what is yours for the LORD, or offer a burnt offering which costs me nothing." 1 Chronicles 21:24 (NASB)*

As you offer the thing that is costing you deeply, God will be honored and pleased with your sacrifice of worship. He may or may not lift the pain or burden of it, but He will receive your sacrifice and the costly offering you present. You can be sure of gaining heavenly reward when you offer to Him what costs you. What gift means more to you from someone—something that costs them dearly or something that costs them nothing?

I sort of chased a rabbit there, but we have to learn how to walk with God where the rubber meets the road with ourselves and with one another.

> *"Stoop down and reach out to those who are oppressed. Share their burdens, and so complete Christ's law." Galatians 6:2 (MSG)*

Did you realize that when you walk with someone who is oppressed, you are directly involved in carrying out the law of Christ? Jesus Himself is being honored in your burden-bearing.

There is no place for Pollyanna Christianity right now. This is a serious hour. We are being attacked on every side, and it would behoove us all to stay real and honest with one another. It would be a good idea to learn how to become a burden-bearer. Are you a safe place for anyone right now? Have you walked in a way that someone could feel safe in confiding in you, or is the "spirit of Pollyanna" on you so that you appear as though nothing in the world ever bothers you?

Don't get me wrong . . . we are to have the joy of the Lord like a fountain flowing in our life, but we have to *do life* with God. In this world, we will have trouble. It's a promise straight from the lips of Jesus. (John 16:33) We will overcome but not without trusting Him and standing with one another in the hard places. We will not overcome by ignoring the fact of pain and struggle. Nowhere in scripture are we told to pretend that hard things aren't happening, but we are to find those who will stand with us and support us in our growth.

Bearing one another's burdens is like being a tomato plant stake for someone. The plant will grow heavy and fall over if it is not tied to the support stake. The best fruit will come when the plant is staked and has the support it needs. Be the stake for someone. Attach yourself to the one God is showing you, and stake yourself there as long as it takes. Ask God for someone who can act as a stake for you—one who will encourage you to stand straight and tall in God, one who will be a support as you grow and bear fruit for God.

Galatians 6:2 talks about bearing one another's burdens. This word "bear" means to carry, support or take up.

There is a time when we need to bear our own burdens *(Galatians 6:5)*, but then there is a time when others are needed for our support. It's wise to know when you need to be alone and when you need to call for help. It's also important to understand when to leave someone alone and when to run to his assistance.

Life on earth has lots of troubles. Beware of Pollyanna Christianity. Walk in true love with God and your fellow traveler.

$\mathscr{A}$ GOD OF LOVE WHO HATES?

These six things the Lord hates, indeed, seven are an abomination to Him: A proud look [the spirit that makes one overestimate himself and underestimate others], a lying tongue, and hands that shed innocent blood, A heart that manufactures wicked thoughts and plans, feet that are swift in running to evil, A false witness who breathes out lies [even under oath], and he who sows discord among his brethren. Proverbs 6:16-19 (AMP)

$\mathscr{Yes,}$ $\mathscr{God}$ $\mathscr{hates}$—$\mathscr{not}$ $\mathscr{people,}$ $\mathscr{but}$ sin. There are at least seven things that God loathes. I find it very interesting that He takes time out in His

Word to make a small list for us. When debating scripture, my rule of thumb is this: I try to major on the things God majors on and minor on the things He minors on. This passage of scripture seems to clutch my heart and communicate God's truth with an exclamation point. When I wanted my children to do something around the house, I usually made a list. There would be no questions about what I wanted them to do, so, when I checked on them, I could compare what they had done to the list I made for them. Let's dissect this "list" from God a little bit.

The first thing that God abhors is a proud look. I appreciate how the Amplified reads: *"the spirit that makes one overestimate himself and underestimate others."* That pretty much captures it for us. Also, I noticed in the Hebrew that it means "to be rotten or wormy." So, think twice the next time you are tempted to exalt yourself over another in any way, shape or form. In the New Testament God explains that He will resist a proud person. *(James 4:6.)*

Next, the Lord detests a lying tongue. This is anything that comes out of the mouth that is not the truth. It includes *everything* that deceives. Whatever does not represent the truth, God hates, especially when it's coming out of your mouth.

Third, He despises hands that shed innocent blood. When our hands are upon something, good or evil can occur. In this case, when someone injures or murders someone who has done nothing wrong, God's head is turned, and His heart hates this act. Right away, I think of a couple examples: abuse of any form and abortion.

Next, God resents a heart that manufactures wicked thoughts and plans. This means not only devising and planning but also remaining silent when there are wicked thoughts and plans in the works. This refers to any invention that would bring trouble and sorrow on someone else.

Fifth, He hates feet that are swift in running to evil. *Evil* meaning distress, misery, injury or calamity. This speaks not only of doing evil, but doing it with swiftness and speed. You can't get plainer than that.

The next thing that is an abomination to God is a false witness who breathes out lies. When someone knows otherwise about a situation and flat out chooses to deceive, God hates that. That's pretty black and white. The truth is always the correct path.

Finally, God is repulsed by one who sows discord among the brethren. The Lord thought of six things and then said, "No, let's make it seven things that really disgust Me" Discord means lack of harmony, disagreement, any confused or harsh noise. In the New Testament (John 17:21), one of the ways Jesus says that the world will believe that He has come is by the harmony Christians will display. It serves to show why God would hate this sin so much. It causes the world to have a dim, foggy view of why Jesus Christ came in the first place. Unity, then, is a form of evangelism.

On God's list of *do's* and *don'ts*, this list would be a good one to merit our serious attention.

The good news is that if you have ever been guilty of any of these God- hated acts, there is forgiveness for you through the blood of Jesus Christ, His Son. Even this list of horrible things cannot separate you from God's love. Confess them as sin, and God will cleanse you, forgive you and bring you into right relationship with Him. Here we have the beauty of loving and serving Him. He desires you to be right with Him.

$\mathcal{D}$O YOU COVER OR HARP?

He who covers and forgives an offense seeks love, but he who repeats or harps on a matter separates even close friends.
Proverbs 17:9 (AMP)

$\mathcal{W}$hen you are offended, many times you want the world to know what has happened to you or why you were hurt. The temptation is to tell it, and tell it and tell it again.

Another thought on this is when someone you know has stumbled into sin, the temptation is to gossip and expose that person. The temptation is to uncover them before all to see.

But the way of heaven is to literally cover it. Cover that thing that is exposed. Cover that thing that is ugly. Cover that thing that would embarrass. That word cover literally means to clothe or hide. That is the way of love.

If God wants it exposed, let *Him* be the one to do it.

Repeating and harping on a matter has the power to separate even the closest of friends. Covering and forgiving brings in the power of true godly love. Take time to think about this principle and equip yourself for the next time you are tempted to become offended.

$\mathcal{G}$OD'S PURPOSE FOR KINDNESS

If you only love the lovable, do you expect a pat on the back? Run- of-the-mill sinners do that. If you only help those who help you, do you expect a medal? Garden-variety sinners do that. If you only give for what you hope to get out of it, do you think that's charity? The stingiest of pawnbrokers does that. Luke 6:32-34 (MSG)

But love your enemies, do good to them, and lend to them without expecting to get anything back. Then your reward will be great, and you will be sons of the Most High, because he is kind to the ungrateful and wicked. Be merciful, just as your Father is merciful. Luke 6:36-37 (NIV)

Jesus gives us a hard pill to swallow here. He is telling His followers to do what doesn't come naturally. He's admonishing, "Don't go with the flow." The flow of what? The flow of what feels good; the rush of revenge and retaliation. Why? Because even God Himself is kind to the ungrateful and wicked. If I am a child of the Most High, I will walk like the Most High.

REALLY?

Ever wonder why the ungrateful and wicked get good things?

God is kind.

I will show kindness if I am the offspring of a kind God. It will be part of the proof that I belong to Him.

Let's look at the word *kind*: of a good or benevolent nature or disposition, considerate, helpful, mild; gentle; a sympathetic attitude toward others and a willingness to do good or give pleasure.

Part of the true nature of God includes kindness to the ungrateful and wicked. There is no reward for being kind to those who are kind to you. The world isn't very good at showing kindness to the ungrateful and wicked. The reward for the child of God comes when kindness is extended in the face of wickedness.

Or do you think lightly of the riches of His kindness and tolerance and patience, not knowing that the kindness of God leads you to repentance? Romans 2:4 (NASB)

The purpose of God's kindness is to lead one to repentance.

S.O.S. Lord!

Father, cleanse me of all unkindness today. Convict me when I sink into revenge mode. Open my eyes to my own corruption. Fill me with Your heart of kindness. Remove the need in my heart for everything to make sense at this moment. Make me into You. In Jesus' name, amen.

$\mathscr{K}$EEP ON MY CHILD, KEEP ON

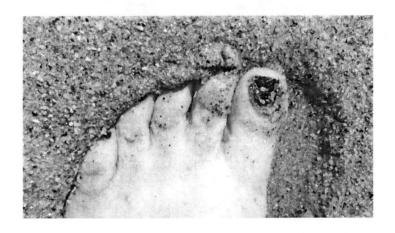

My breath is sweet upon your soul. It is life when you are lifeless. It is energy upon your weakness, for I am near in your sadness. I am here in your helplessness.

Look My way and not in other directions. Look My way and you will find that for which you yearn. Sometimes you don't even understand what you are longing for . . . you just know you are longing. I made you completely for Me. When you think, you find things that satisfy outside of My presence, you will soon be empty once again . . . longing all over again.

Learn how to drink deeply from the wells of My salvation. If you don't, life will seem futile and empty. My breath and My living water will sustain you through any valley you find yourself in. My wind blowing upon you causes miracles in your heart. What could take years to accomplish in a counselor's office can be instantly settled in My healing presence. Find Me every day. Look to Me in the mornings. Live for Me each day. This is why you were created. You were not formed and fashioned according to anyone else's image. You were made for Me. You were desired for fellowship.

Draw up the living water from the wells of My salvation . . . stop putting it off . . . give yourself what you truly need . . . ME. For I will carry you when you need carried. I will forgive you when you need to be forgiven. I will patiently wait for you when you are walking slowly or even dragging your feet. For My love is eternal and bottomless. My grace is upon you as a cloak . . . it is sufficient to keep you warm and filled in My presence.

You are loved and valued in My kingdom. It's a joy to walk with you as you walk with Me. Keep on, My Child, keep on.

$\mathcal{I}$ AM BEING YOUR GOD ON PURPOSE

The pressure all around you is divinely orchestrated. I am being your Lord God on purpose. You have invited Me into your life. You have asked Me to be your Lord and Savior; now I am acting in answer to your call in very deliberate, purposeful and passionate ways.

The pressure is on purpose. The pressure is for a purpose. The pressure is the purpose.

There is a goal. There is an end result. There's a finish line. There's a last page.

You and I aren't there yet. We are here, in the fire. You and I are at the point of the reproduction of Myself in you. You have given Me permission, remember?

Work with Me. Take steps with Me. Stifle continual movement in the compression. Be quiet in the confinement. Stop fighting the constraint. Fellowship with Me in the heat. Turn your ear to Me in the boiling pot. It's going to work, and you're going to come through. My grace is enough, and My power is perfectly formatted to your need right now. I have placed just the right supplies in your hand to come through this with My image more clearly seen in you.

Distractions are coming at you from your adversary. Lies from his dark throne spew forth—it's not worth it. Give up. Let go of hope. Stop being so courageous and valiant. Who do you think you are, anyway?

My beloved, you are a child of the King of the kings. You are a joint heir with My Son, Jesus Christ. You are the apple of My eye, My beloved.

The encumbrance is forming you. The heat is melting and purifying and causing much reason to hope for your future. This is our moment together . . . in the pressure . . . in the dark . . . in the uncomfortable, lonely places. This is the time for you and me to prevail together. The unseen is eternal. The seen is temporary and only useful for the moment. Eternal reward comes out of surviving the compressing I allow—not only surviving, but thriving. For I have not asked you to merely exist. I have asked you to be My personal representative in the earth. Will you do that for Me?

If so, then let Me help you be the champion I see every time I think of you. Let Me take you from here, and let's go over to a place that I have prepared for you to rule and reign over your enemies in greater dimensions.

I'm placing in your hands today fresh strategies from heaven. Turn your ear to My voice, and I will unfold the plan each day you listen. I will tell you to go here or go there and do this or do that. Take time to perceive Me in the pressure. Take time to listen in the heat, for the fire is forming you. The fire is growing you. The fire is increasing your dependency upon Me.

Yes, the fire is all that I intend. I control the temperature, and I control the pressure; otherwise, you would be destroyed. I will not let that happen. Trust Me, believe Me and most, importantly, obey Me.

For I am proving you in this hour for such a time as this.

Your Eternal Lover

COME UP HERE

I am sending rain down upon you. *I am sending fresh supplies. Receive it today, My child. Breathe in My breath that you may live in hope and not succumb to discouragement. Come away, My beloved, and understand that I am for you and not against you. The winds of controversy swirl around your heart, but come up here and be renewed in thought and purpose. Come up here, and I will teach you. Come up here and learn of Me and gain a fresh view and perspective.*

The path narrows for you now. This is good in My sight . . . trust Me. For there is not room for excess baggage. There is only room for the two of us. You don't need anything else now. Strip yourself of fear, worry and anxiety.

Remove the bitterness as I soften you. Take part in the healing process as I pour My oil upon your head. Let it penetrate and have its full effect.

Enter now into the joy of your salvation as you come up—joys unspeakable and full of My glory. The showers are now descending upon you. The rain comes to soften your parched ground—Your thoughts becoming My thoughts, your ways becoming My ways. Together, we will unite now and enter into new territory together.

Together now, we will write history.

For you are My gem. You are My dear one. You have endured thus far and will continue on. Your roots have gone way down, and you are firmly planted by My hand. Nothing can pluck you from the palm of My hand.

Take heart today, My friend. Stay focused when the wind strengthens. Keep eye contact with Me. We will go to higher heights, and we will touch greater realms of My glory together.

I breathe upon you now. Inhale—yes, inhale—take My breath as your very own. Be saturated now in My rain of refreshing. Come up here, I beckon you. Come up here.

$\mathscr{T}$HE BROODING OF GOD

$\mathscr{S}$*pending a concentrated amount of* time with God is a very rewarding experience. There are hardly words to describe it completely, but I will attempt it; and with His help, I will share some things now. There are the outward activities such as listening to a sermon, singing, talking to God, waiting, fellowshipping and reading, and then there are the inward workings of the Holy Spirit.

The inward work is what interests God the most. He wants truth way down in the depths of my soul *(Psalm 51:6)*. Where falsehood exists, where I'm not walking in reality with Him in my inner man—that's where the Holy Spirit will nosedive in times of His divine pursuit of me.

There is the notion (in my mind) that what I am experiencing in God is all there is. It's business as usual. It's life as we know it. It's comfortable and cozy with no real reason to look for something else. Thus, every so often, if I am truly listening, I will hear the depths of God crying out to the depths of my soul. He is not satisfied, even if I am. I will then begin noticing a stirring and prickling of my heart. I will become restless and discontent. I may feel irritated and confused. During this state of unrest, I must go to God and begin the relentless pursuit of finding Him in the new dimensions because He has prepared for me a place of greater anointing and effectiveness in my service to Him. More importantly, He desires a closer place of fellowship with me—one of sweeter intimacy and union with Himself.

Frequently, as I stretch my ear to listen to His heartbeat, there is disquieting that comes upon my spirit. This unsettling is from Him. It originates from Him and will continue to produce a holy discontent in my heart. I must be careful what I do at this point. If I do not notice it as being from Him, I will carry on in the flesh and not only do damage to myself but to others as I react to this unsettledness. I must respond to God rather than react to my flesh. It's a choosing to find Him. It's a decision to go into the greater realms of His presence. My cunning adversary will be there every step of the way to whisper whatever lies I might choose to believe, thus derailing me from the present moment of finding God.

Some of his lies may sound like this: You don't need more of God; you can't handle what He wants to do with you; people will think you are crazy; this is too much work; no one else is doing this; you are unworthy for what God has for you; this is just plain silly; you are going to stick out like a sore thumb. I must choose to bypass the fears and whispers of the enemy—then I'm on my way to meet with Him.

During one season of my life, God was doing such a new and different, but difficult, thing that I was in need of His comfort and reassurance. In worship one day, I suddenly saw a picture of Him standing before me. He was much taller than me and was wearing a robe that was very thick, soft and the epitome of luxury. His arms opened wide, and I went in for His embrace. I felt as though I melted into His wonderful loving kindness on the spot, and I was instantly comforted and freed from my fears. I have since then returned to that vision in my mind several times, only to find the same loving comfort of His arms over and over again. On another occasion, the vision came to me again, only slightly different. I was before Him again, and He had on the same thick robe. Only this time I saw him open His robe, and I went straight into His bosom—His heart of hearts—and He then proceeded to wrap His robe around me 'til I was no longer visible but just covered up in Him. It was a wonderful moment with Him.

Now, I not only take comfort and strength from Him, but I know way down in the depths of my being that I can never exhaust all of the beautiful dimensions of His love for me.

There is a ring in my heart that can't stop thinking:

"THE NEW IS UPON US ALL!"

There are more dimensions of Him yet undiscovered by us. In the midst of my stirring and confusions and wanderings, I hear a clarion call: "There's much, much more for you." Discontentment can be a gift. Frustrations can be the very launching pad for greater realms of glory. The key is having the discernment to recognize the place to which He's brought you. The old will give way to the new only as we let the old go.

We are promised that the glory of the Lord will increase upon us with each passing day *(Isaiah 60:2)*. However, this cannot occur if we haven't positioned ourselves for the new glory. We need to be transparent and naked before Him if we are to enter into the new. We need to release what we tightly clutch in order to experience the new that is coming from His hand.

The Lord has given me three things I am to do in order to be propelled into the new of what He has for me. As we press in, it will be different for each one of us. Ask Him what He wants you to do. He is no respecter of persons, but He will advance those who choose to pay the price of self-denial. He will increase His power and anointing upon those who choose to have clean hands and a pure heart *(Psalm 24:4).*

Pay the price, and your reward will be with Him.

$\mathscr{L}$OVE FROM ANOTHER COUNTRY

*See how great a love the Father has bestowed on us, that we would be
called children of God; and such we are. For this reason
the world does not know us, because it did not know Him. Beloved,
now we are children of God, and it has not appeared as yet what we
will be. We know that when He appears, we will be like Him, because
we will see Him just as He is. And everyone who has this hope fixed on
Him purifies himself, just as He is pure. 1 John 3:1-3 (NASB)*

The King James Version states, "*Behold what manner of love the Father hath bestowed upon us* . . . ." The word *manner* in the Greek is a word that denotes *from what country*. I find that very interesting. What John is really saying is: How in the world did this kind of love ever find its way to us? How did it happen? It is coming from some foreign place, a place we have never known before. From where is this kind of affection and brotherly love originating? The benevolence of God is so otherworldly that we can barely grasp it with our finite understanding.

Bestow: to present as a gift, to put to use, apply.

God literally came from His own country and presented us with a gift of His love. He has applied and put to use all of His godly, fatherly affection upon all of us. Truly, we have been lavished upon. Wow. Because of this great and glorious act of kindness, we now have His name on us. We are His children—His sons and daughters.

Whoever has not acknowledged this holy love and received it is of this world. The world cannot understand this love; therefore, it has trouble understanding those who have received this love. We will be rejected and despised in this world until the day we die. The natural mind, plain and simple, does not comprehend the things of the Spirit. Spiritual things are spiritually discerned.

We are constantly growing, changing and being formed into His image. Picture this: Once we are conceived in Him, we live in the womb of this world. It is a dark place, but it is here that we are being formed and developed. While in the dark womb of this world, it is not yet completely known what we are becoming *(1 John 3:2)*. However, on that day of His appearing, we will come into the full light of His appearance and emerge in Him. The transformations that happened in the dark places will now be showcased for all to see.

Seeing Him for the first time will resemble turning on the brightest lights you can imagine. All that was hidden and opaque now becomes crystal clear and unavoidably focused. What a day that's going to be.

*T*HE DAY JUSTICE WAS MISCARRIED

Justice miscarried, and he was led off—and did anyone really know what was happening? Isaiah 53:7a (MSG)

By oppression and judgment He was taken away; Isaiah 53:7a (NASB)

What should have happened didn't, but what *needed* to happen did. Justice *did* miscarry that day when Jesus Christ was led off to the place of the skull *(Matthew 27:33)*. Something went horribly wrong but gloriously right at the same time. Can it be?

Have you ever been oppressed? Have you ever felt condemned? Jesus was led away to His death with these two companions on His shoulders. He bore oppression and condemnation *in our place.*

The next time you are feeling trampled and oppressed, *make yourself* remember Isaiah 53:7a. You are taking on something for which Jesus already paid. To continue in it is a rebuke to the One who took it away. In essence, you are saying back to Jesus, "I would rather be oppressed than freed. I will ignore what You did for me."

The next time the lies of guilt and condemnation are flying all around you, trying to penetrate your heart and soul, remember Isaiah 53. The condemnation and judgment of *your* sin is what carried Jesus away that day to His death. To hold that guilt and condemnation to your breast as a possession is the same thing as saying to your Lord Jesus Christ, "I won't be needing Your assistance. I do not acknowledge Your love and sacrifice for me that day when You were led away in judgment *wrongly.* Even though You did it for me—thanks, but no thanks. What You did for me is not powerful enough to remove this guilt and condemnation I am feeling right now."

Friend, the blood of Jesus Christ is the most powerful love force in heaven and earth. His blood is proof of His love. The absorption of God's agape love into our being will catapult us into a realm of loving and living with others that will shake hell.

I hope you tap into it. I hope you apply it.

I hope you let it have its perfect work in you today.

OUR BENIGNANT GOD

But they, our ancestors, were arrogant; bullheaded, they wouldn't obey
your commands.
They turned a deaf ear, they refused
to remember the miracles you had done for them;
They turned stubborn, got it into their heads
to return to their Egyptian slavery. And you, a forgiving God, gracious
and compassionate, incredibly patient, with tons of love— you didn't
dump them. Yes, even when they cast a sculpted calf and said, "This is
your god Who brought you out of Egypt,"
and continued from bad to worse, You in your amazing compassion
didn't walk off and leave them in the desert.
The Pillar of Cloud didn't leave them; daily it continued to show them
their route; The Pillar of Fire did the same by night,
showed them the right way to go. Nehemiah 9:16-19 (MSG)

God is a most incredible God. I cannot fathom His love for me. So often you and I love with strings attached. God does not. He just loves. No matter what condition we find ourselves in, God is standing ready to pardon. He waits for us to repent so He can extend grace, for God is a gracious God. He is a kind and courteous Father.

The word *gracious* in the Hebrew is the word *channuwn.* It means merciful and benignant. I had to look up the word benignant and, to my surprise, it means kind, especially to inferiors. That pretty much defines every inhabitant of the earth. We are all inferior to the holy Almighty God.

God is slow to anger. Good thing. We would do well to follow His example. If there is one person who could be one hundred percent justified in venting His anger and judgment, it's God. Instead, He chooses patience.

The King James Version says this of verse 17:

> *. . . but thou art a God ready to pardon, gracious and merciful, slow to anger, and of great kindness, and forsookest them not.*

Take a good look at the heart of our God here. Really. Go ahead and climb into the cavern of His loving kindness. Take a peek. No, be *immersed* in His heart for you. How often do we portray Him as a God ready to judge and call in the cards? He could at any time, but for now He has chosen not to do so. It would behoove us to take comfort and understand just who we serve. How often are we in judgment mode, and God hasn't even gone there yet? The scriptures say He is ready to pardon, gracious and merciful, slow to anger and of great kindness. This is how he related to the rebellious nation of Israel. Wow. Far too often, I venture to say, we place ourselves on God's throne to cast a careless critique of someone we only pass by on the street. *How dare we?* We, who are inferior to God, are called to love every other inferior that He brings across our pathway.

Who is it that condemns you? No one of importance. Your adversary will be quick to slap you in the face, but your God will not. He will not even leave you when you turn from Him in your stubbornness. His love for you is inexhaustible. You're stuck with it whether you acknowledge it or not.

So, go ahead—throw your fit. He is with you. Go on, ignore Him. He cannot ignore you, the apple of His eye. You cannot be loosed from His heart. He loves you, He thinks about you and He desires you. You can't earn His love or work for it. You can't be good or bad enough to alter His love coming toward you.

For God loved every inhabitant upon the face of this earth so much that He came down to save us in the form of His Son *(John 3:16)*. Love is the greatest.

Love should be the emblem of our life. God has set the standard. The plumb line is love—period.

Go ahead—inhale a fresh dose of His loving kindness today. You need it so you can give it. You can't say you belong to Him and then walk in selective love.

Even in your desert place, if you look you will find the pillar of cloud by day and the pillar of fire by night. He who is totally in love with you is also your immutable escort. Just as He was with Joseph in the pit and prison, so is He with you, sitting near, loving you and caring for you in your confining difficulty. You may not have favorable circumstances, but you have what you need most—God's love and care for you. You have His Holy Spirit at home in your heart. Acknowledge Him. Love Him back. Repent from resistance. Enter into the pardon of your God and take a big sip of His grace and kindness today.

$\mathcal{I}$NHALE THE ATMOSPHERE OF HEAVEN

$\mathcal{M}\!y$ *arms are open to you. My embrace awaits you. Bring Me your tired soul. You've been working hard. It's time for Me and you. Come in for some time of rest and refreshment. You need a time of relief and recovery. We will do this together, but you must trust Me. I am calling you into My heart of hearts. See yourself in My embrace. Your weary soul will reap great benefit in My embrace. My embrace will bring healing to your broken heart. My arms around you will give you exactly what you need to put your tired foot into the next step. You've done it alone too long. You are missing the*

point of why I died for you. Fellowship with Me has been restored through the cross. Come now, haven't you heard the Good News?

Yes, come on in now. It's what you need; it's what I want to give you today—a holy embrace. Your Abba Father is here. I haven't left you. I have always been near. Bring Me your tears. Bring Me your broken heart. Give Me your anger and disappointment. I want it all, so I can give you all. There are many things in My treasury that belong to you. It's My joy to give them to you as you give Me your things.

Take in a fresh breath of My love. Inhale the atmosphere of heaven. You are My beloved, and I am yours. The cold winds of this harsh world are whipping around you, looking for a crack or crevice. You need the warmth of My presence. You need My warm blanket of acceptance around you. I have a garment of righteousness on you. You are marked for My purpose. This purpose includes times of intimate fellowship with Me. This purpose includes an invasion of My holy love into your soul. One taste of My true love will wreck you forever. For My love is intoxicating and will soothe your soul.

I'm calling you, My dear one. Can you hear Me? Come close. Be near Me. My Spirit inside you is willing, waiting and looking for you. Your adversary would try and convince you otherwise, but shut him out. Close the door on discouragement and fear. For his greatest fear is that you would come close to Me and have a taste of My goodness. Satan trembles when you draw near to My heart. He fears it when you begin looking My direction—for he knows that if you and I could just make eye contact, that it's over for him—and his power over you is dismantled. As long as he can keep your focus on your pain, he has you right where he wants you. As long as he can keep you in the cold place of fear, worry, anxiety and loneliness, you will be paralyzed. You will remain immobile.

Break out. Break out of his grip and come in. Be seated at the table I have prepared for you. Just as you look forward to a time with an intimate friend, so do I look forward to your presence at My table that we may dine and drink together in sweet harmony.

My arms are open. Come, sweet one, come.

THE LOVE FEAST DYNAMIC

So many depend upon you for different things, dear one. Come over here where I am. In a time when the world is busy, barren and full of unbelief, understand that what little you have tasted and known in My presence is very real and palatable for others nearby. You have proceeded with Me in the hard times, and the things that have become agreeable with you in the Holy Spirit are things that will touch others as they search for Me on their journey.

Do not disqualify anything you have gone through and call it useless. For all can be used to advance My kingdom when it has become surrendered in My presence. What confuses you now will give way to peace and understanding after you have weathered the storm with Me. Together is better, my dear one. I never intended anyone to travel solo. However, there are those that do. Two are better than one—much better. Be careful that you don't find yourself alone. You need others, and others need you.

Others need what I have put in you. Others need the wisdom that I have developed in you. Yes, it's true. Do not question this. There is also wisdom in others for you. Remain teachable. Look for the one that I will show you and see what you can glean from their walk with Me. See how it will help you. *See how another can bring clarification at moments when your heart is wandering.*

I love you, My dear one. Come to Me that we may enjoy a love feast. Come to Me that we may enjoy sweet communion and fellowship. Then go forth from our fellowship and touch another. As I pour My love upon you, you can empty it out upon another. Love is the glue that will hold things together when the shaking comes. For there will be a shaking in your walk with Me, and you will be tempted to doubt. There will also come a shaking in your relationships in such a way that if there is not true love, that relationship will come to nothing. Love is the greatest.

My love is a power and force stronger than death itself. I am drawing you into it. I'm calling you closer and closer. My affection is a shelter. My love is a wing for you to remain under. My love will drive out the fear that sometimes torments. Can you tell that I am jealous over you?

Again, many are watching you. I have made it to be so. You need to be needed, and you need to need. It's the healthy cycle of living in My kingdom. It's how I have made you. Enter in.

TEARS

The words tears and weep or forms of these words appear over 200 times in the Bible. The original languages describe all sorts of reasons and expressions of these words. Tears can be an indication of pain and grief. In one's own grief, there can be bitter tears, mourning quietly or in a loud voice. There can be weeping because of joy, grief or humiliation.

The first time in the Old Testament we see the word *tears* is in 2 Kings 20:5 (KJV). It says, "*I have heard thy prayer, I have seen thy tears: behold, I will heal thee.*" This is speaking of Hezekiah. He was pleading for his life. He did not want to die. The Lord got word to him through the prophet that He heard Hezekiah's prayers, saw his tears and had come to heal him.

In sickness of body or soul, we should pray. Sometimes we need to cry. We need to beseech the Lord for healing. We ought not just sit back and allow the flood to overtake us without pouring our heart out to God. He gave us the vehicle of tears to help carry us into His throne room of grace.

Tears were given to us as a gift from God. They can come in sorrow or elation. Sometimes, when we are fearful and helpless, tears can come easily. St. Francis of Assisi is said to have gone blind from too much crying. Tears are a language of their own. They are a very appropriate way to talk to God when words fail.

Alex Tan said, "Perhaps our eyes need to be washed by our tears once in a while so that we can see life with a clearer view again." I believe this is true. I heard someone say recently that tears soften the ground. Sometimes our hearts become too hard. Tears have a way of softening and bringing down the wall of defense.

Thou tellest my wanderings: put thou my tears into thy bottle: are they not in thy book?
Psalm 56:8 (KJV)

God has a bottle for my tears. God has a Book that tells about my wanderings. He is dictating my progress upon this earth. He is making notes of when I am sad or bowed low in sorrow and grief. Why would He do this for us? It's beyond comprehension.

He has heard your prayer, and He has seen your tears. He is coming to heal you. He has written about you, taken each tear and collected it in His bottle. How precious is that? When was the last time you have done this for the one that you dearly love? Probably never. God does it every time you wander and can't find your way.

When the tears want to come, let them. God has a purpose for each one and a reason they need to fall. He understands perfectly the language of tears. When words fail but tears don't, turn your heart to

Jesus. He sees your tears and hears your heart's cry. His heart is to heal you. His hand is upon you to bring you into a land flowing with good things for your heart and soul.

Is the ground hard? Maybe you need the gift of tears and repentance. Ask Him. He will give you everything you need to draw close to Him, including tears. Is your heart bleeding? Go be with Him and pour out your tears. He will see them. He will collect them. He will heal you.

I'M BREAKING THE CHILL OFF YOU

I'm coming after the chill that is in and around your heart—the chill of pain—the chill of regret—the chill of sin—the chill of disappointment—the chill of fear.

My beloved, you are always before Me. You are perpetually on My mind. Life has come at you in ways you didn't expect. I am sitting at your side—loving you, watching over you and leading you through this place of bitter cold and indifference.

Where you have become indifferent, I am taking My hand and placing it upon that spot. I am touching you and bringing you to a place of great *caring and passion. When you gave your life to Me, you gave Me permission to touch you and make you what I see when I look at you. I see your end. I see you today. I understand the difficulty you are having of trusting Me. I am in the process of bestowing within you this gift of trust. You will see a day when you will trust Me in a way you never thought you could.*

You and I are on this journey together. I have a way to help and rescue you. It's dark and cold, and your steps are uneven today. I am teaching you trust before you see the answer. I am bringing faith to your heart. I am calling your name over and over. Listen and you will hear the heartbeat of your heavenly Father. It beats for you.

There is no condemnation spoken by Me over your life. My blood covers all your transgressions. I want you to walk upright because you are My child. Sometimes you give in to deep emotions of unworthiness. You are worthy because of My righteousness. My love for you will never be any more or less than it is right now. You can't earn it. You can't do enough good to qualify for it. My love comes to each person in this world the same way. Sinner or saint, My love extends the same.

Do you know what you can do with My love? You can become dripping wet, saturated in it. You can tumble all around in My affection as a child would play with his father. Picture, for Me, a father running through a field of wildflowers with his child, running and jumping and having the time of their lives together. That's you and Me, My dear one. That's how I see us.

Come away from the thought patterns that have kept you bent over. Come away from the voices that lie to you day in and day out. Come away from the temporal circumstances that bog you down. Come away to a secret place that I have prepared for you. It's a place of shelter. It's a place of peace and satisfaction. It's a room of warmth to melt the chill right off you.

In My holy presence, you are free. No, your surroundings may not change, and you need to understand this, dear one. Once you find sweet, intimate fellowship with Me, your quandary will have less of a grip upon your storm-tossed soul. Your circumstances will turn into a vehicle to bring you close to Me.

Come. Taste the new wine of My kingdom, for it will be sweet to your heart and soothing to your soul. No drink compares to My drink. I will take your chilled, indifferent heart and break winter's hold upon you. I will melt the ice and warm your soul as no other can. It's an open invitation. Come.

*T*HE UNDENIABLE SPILLOVER

*For the Eyes of the Lord run to and fro throughout the whole earth to
show Himself strong on behalf of those
whose heart is loyal to Him. 2 Chronicles 16:9 (NKJV)*

Did you know that I was watching you today? I saw when you
let that car go in front of you. I took note when you smiled at that stranger
the other day. They really needed a friendly face, and I used it to lift their
spirits. Do you know that I made a note of it when you asked a friend how
things were going with her family struggles?

My Spirit is pleased to work through your vessel. My personality is eager to be revealed through your personality. People need loving looks and kind gestures. There are many who aren't sure they can make it another day. Be careful to shine your light in and out of your home. It simply takes a willing heart to do the thing that may seem insignificant or unusual.

See their eyes. Note the expression upon their face. They need rescued, even as you did. It's simple to be My witness in the earth—to be My witness means using words and sometimes not. You speak a whole language even without using your mouth. Did you realize that? There are many ways to reach the lost and hurting. Never underestimate the power of an encouragement, a look, a smile, a handshake or a hug.

As you fellowship with Me throughout your day, there will be an undeniable spillover.

Those I bring upon your path will get splashed by My presence with you.

Dear one, I am so near you. I am so in you. I am so into you. Remember Me. Walk with Me. The love feast that you and I share will cause thirst to arise in another. You will feed many out of our union together. You will give drink to numerous ones as you drink of the waters that never shall run dry.

That's all. I just wanted to tell you that I love you and that I'm proud to be your Father. I see all the life that flows from you, even when you're not thinking about it.

Continue on, My child. Continue on.

WHAT? LOVE AN UGLY SOUL?

"Love all men, my dear brothers,
but bestow the greatest part of your love on the ugliest souls." Richard
Wurmbrand, author of Tortured for Christ

Oh my, really? You don't understand—they used me and mistreated me; I was left alone—all alone; I don't believe they deserve my love; you don't know the pain and sorrow that person has caused me; the abuse I received was unmentionable, embarrassing and shameful—I will never, never be able to look them in the eye again.

I'm supposed to what—love them in return?

I—I can't possibly . . .no, I won't do it. I can't do it. I don't know how to love them even if I wanted to.

Dear saint and child of God, this is the mindset of an unredeemed soul. This is the thought pattern of one who has need of a dip in the river of God's love. Even in the face of the greatest violation possible, there is perennial hope to recover and find a love far above the natural realm. Our dear sister Corrie ten Boom is known to have said, "There is no pit that God's love is not deeper still." She endured much torture and abuse in the concentration camps of the Holocaust. To the degree that I can accept the embrace of God's love will be the degree that I will be able to distribute it to another "undeserving" soul. To believe a situation or a person is hopeless is sort of like slapping Jesus in the face while He is in agony on the cross.

To love doesn't equal to trust again. To love doesn't mean there will be automatic friendship. To love doesn't mean I agree with what you did. To love doesn't create amnesia of the evil act that violated me.

To love as God loves means I will forgive and release you from my prison of bitterness and anger. To love means I will cut the ball and chain that has locked us together in a pool of bitterness and torment. To love means to cut the strings of what you owe me for what you did to me.

To love an ugly soul is spiritual warfare in the highest form. To be infused with divine affection means I will let you off the hook and release you into God's care. It equals taking action of courageous proportions that will go against the grain of my sulking flesh that only wants to lash out and make you pay.

The ugly soul will no longer "owe me" when I take an honest, intense look at a holy God that loves this very unholy human being (me).

Oh, my. To demand payment from one who owes me a little compared to the mountain of debt I was forgiven at the cross is unacceptable to Jehovah, who has provided all for me to live debt free before Him.

Christ died for the ugliest of souls. This is the thing: we are all ugly before the blood of Jesus washes over us and makes our sins as white as snow.

Revenge, unforgiveness, bitterness, sinful anger, blame and hate are all weapons of the devil. Those who use these types of weapons are on a collision course with death.

The supreme weapon of holy love will turn a world of evil upside down. The war club of God's love will do more damage to the kingdom of darkness than you could ever imagine. It has the power to bring the haughtiest to their knees and the proudest heart to repentance.

In order to walk in this narrow passage, one must die first. There must be death to what I want and death to what I deserve. All my ambition must be laid at the foot of the cross. The desire to defend must dissolve. Christ will stand in that place. He will defend and protect me. I must die to self and allow Him to define my life.

I have been crucified with Christ; and it is no longer I who live, but Christ lives in me; and the life which I now live in the flesh I live by faith in the Son of God, who loved me and gave Himself up for me. Galatians 2:20 (NASB)

$\mathcal{I}$N MY DARKEST HOUR

by Pam Mitchell (used with permission)

In my darkest hour I knew He was there

I could feel His strength
in my husband's loving embrace I could feel His comfort
in my family's unwavering support I could feel His joy
in my children's sweet laughter I could feel His peace
through the prayers of friends

In my darkest hour
He never failed to light the way steering me down the path
He has laid for me

My dawning realization that I am still here
only for His purpose only by His grace

I have learned faith I have learned hope
I have experienced love that knows no boundaries

Now it is my turn . . .
to offer strength and comfort joy and peace
to encourage faith and hope and to love in His name

NISI DOMINUS FRUSTA

Latin for

Without the Lord, Frustration

My friend, this is the end of this book, yet not the end of what He is doing in your life. Without Him, you will be frustrated. With Him, you will have satisfaction and fulfillment. You were born to co-labor with Him. You were created to advance His kingdom on earth as it is in heaven. Most importantly, you were conceived to walk with Him in true friendship.

Find Him. Worship Him. Love Him. Become one with Him. Walk with Him always.

STUDY/DISCUSSION QUESTIONS ON "LESSONS IN LOVE"

1. In 1 Corinthians 13:13, God says love is greater than faith or hope. Why is this true?

2. What does love look like when someone isn't progressing on their spiritual journey as well as you think they should?

3. When you have a severe disagreement with someone, how can God's love be applied in your heart?

4. Using scripture, what is the enemy of love?

5. Why is offense so dangerous? What should we do when we have been hurt or offended? Explain with scriptures.

6. When should you "let something slide" and when should you confront or "point out" the shortcoming of another? Include scripture with your answer.

7. When do you think that your expression of love and worship to God is the sweetest to Him?

8. Explain the contrast between God's love and the world's love.

$\mathcal{A}$CKNOWLEDGMENTS

$\mathcal{I}$ want to thank $\mathcal{N}$athan, my handsome, loving, faithful friend and husband of thirty-six years. You were the first one to encourage me to get my writings into book form. Thank you for giving me strong shoulders to stand on and for always giving me great feedback and advice. I love you now and always.

To my loving parents, David (who left this earth on September 14, 2016, to his eternal heavenly home) and Barbara Barr, who taught me to love and serve Jesus Christ. Thank you. There is no greater gift a parent could give his child. Your love and support through the years has been a gift.

To Pam Mitchell, thank you for pushing, prodding and telling me to get this project done. Thank you for your initial critiques on the manuscript. Your friendship is priceless to me.

To Tami Hulse, because what He has given us is tried and found true—over 35 years of friendship. Thank you again for helping with some initial editing. You are a pearl of great price. I love to laugh with you. Sharing life with you has been nothing short of a gift.

To Carol McLeod, who has seen what God has put in me and has called it forth so well. Because of you, my tent pegs have expanded and I have been launched into new places of ministry and kingdom influence. Above all, your friendship has spanned over 20 years and I cherish it dearly. Many thanks for introducing me to Athena Dean Holtz!

To Linda Hoeflich, for your editing advice early on. You are a faithful ally to my soul. What would I do without you? Your heart cry that God is faithful is etched upon my heart forever.

To Linda Baker, who has exemplified to me so much of what I have written in this book. You are one of His gems as well as one of my dearest friends. Your life has been a torch for me. Your constant friendship has been a comfort to my soul.

To Becki Devore, the one who holds my feet to the fire and is not afraid to point something out that I might not want to hear. Your "out-of-the-box" faith and journey with God has been sign and a wonder to me that we have no limitations with God. Thank you for your dear friendship.

To Linda Saunders, who is a true comrade in the faith. I am better because of rubbing shoulders with you in the Holy Spirit. I will never forget our meetings with God in the prayer room. We are bound together with cords that cannot be broken. Thank you for believing in me and encouraging the finishing of this project.

To Tammy Stoltzfus, whose friendship has warmed my heart over and over again. Your encouragement to my soul has left an imprint like none other. Thank you for prophesying God's truth for my heart to hear and be reminded of over and over again.

To Trudy Edgerton, for the many prayers I know you have prayed. I want to be like you when I grow up in the faith. Your pilgrimage with Jesus is exemplary to me. I love how God brought us together and used us to advance His kingdom in Fuquay.

To Kristin Hulse, who did some initial professional editing on the manuscript. Thank you for getting me out of the starting block.

To Rebecca Christopher, the precious wife of my son, who graciously volunteered many hours to help me get this book in better editorial condition. Thank you so much for the part you played in helping this project come to life. May the Lord repay you.

To Diane Dove, who volunteered as a labor of love in the editing process. The polishing you have done has brought a shine to this devotional that wouldn't have been there otherwise. I know there is a special reward in store for you. No words will ever fully express what you have done for me.

To Chris Dawson, who always has my back. Thank you for all the details you found that needed fixed. Thank you mostly for your friendship. I love you.

I want to thank Amanda Javens of Amanda Javens Photography LLC, for taking my book cover headshot. Thank you also for helping me format some of the pictures in this book. I appreciate your generous heart so much!

My greatest praise is for Jesus my Savior, for His intimate love for me and for the incredible gift of salvation, for filling me every day with His power to serve and love Him. If there is any praise for this project, I pass it all onto You.

AUTHOR CONTACT INFORMATION

Email: christineachristopher@gmail.com
Facebook: www.facebook.com/untilthedaybreaks
Website: christineachristopher.com

ORDER INFORMATION

REDEMPTION
PRESS

To order additional copies of this book, please visit
www.redemption-press.com.
Also available on Amazon.com and BarnesandNoble.com
Or by calling toll free 1-844-2REDEEM.

CPSIA information can be obtained
at www.ICGtesting.com
Printed in the USA
FFOW02n1650311017
41760FF

9 781683 143801